# A WANDERER IN HOLLAND

# E. V. LUCAS

# PREFACE

It would be useless to pretend that this book is authoritatively informing. It is a series of personal impressions of the Dutch country and the Dutch people, gathered during three visits, together with an accretion of matter, more or less pertinent, drawn from many sources, old and new, to which I hope I have given unity. For trustworthy information upon the more serious side of Dutch life and character I would recommend Mr. Meldrum's Holland and the Hollanders. My thanks are due to my friends, Mr. and Mrs. Emil Lüden, for saving me from many errors by reading this work in MS.

E.V.L.

A WANDERER IN HOLLAND

# CHAPTER I

Rotterdam

To Rotterdam by water--To Rotterdam by rail--Holland's monotony of scenery--Holland in England--Rotterdam's few merits--The life of the river--The Rhine--Walt Whitman--Crowded canals--Barge life--The Dutch high-ways--A perfect holiday--The canal's influence on the national character--The florin and the franc--Lady Mary Wortley Montagu--The old and the poor--Holland's health--Funeral customs--The chemists'

shops--Erasmus of Rotterdam--Latinised names--Peter de Hooch--True aristocracy--The Boymans treasures--Modern Dutch art--Matthew Maris--The Rotterdam Zoo--The herons--The stork's mission—The ourang-outang--An eighteenth-century miser--A successful merchant--The Queen-Mother--Tom Hood in Rotterdam--Gouda.

It was once possible to sail all the way to Rotterdam by either of the two lines of steamships from England--the Great Eastern, viâ Harwich, and the Batavier, direct from London. But that is possible now only by the Batavier, passengers by the better-known Harwich route being landed now and henceforward at the Hook at five A.M. I am sorry for this, because after a rough passage it was very pleasant to glide in the early morning steadily up the Maas and gradually acquire a sense of Dutch quietude and greyness. No longer, however, can this be done, as the Batavier boats reach Rotterdam at night; and one therefore misses the river, with the little villages on its banks, each with a tiny canal-harbour of its own; the groups of trees in the early mist; the gulls and herons; and the increasing traffic as one drew nearer Schiedam and at last reached that forest of masts which is known as Rotterdam.

But now that the only road to Rotterdam by daylight is the road of iron all that is past, and yet there is some compensation, for short as the journey is one may in its progress ground oneself very thoroughly in the characteristic scenery of Holland. No one who looks steadily out of the windows between the Hook and Rotterdam has much to learn thereafter. Only changing skies and atmospheric effects can provide him with novelty, for most of Holland is like that. He has the formula. Nor is it necessarily new to him if he knows England well, North Holland being merely the Norfolk Broads, the Essex marshlands about Burnham-on-Crouch, extended. Only in its peculiarity of light and in its towns has Holland anything that we have not at home.

England has even its canal life too, if one cared to investigate it; the Broads are populous with wherries and barges; cheese is manufactured in England in a score of districts; cows range our meadows as they range the meadows of the Dutch. We go to Holland to see the towns, the pictures and the people. We go also because so many of us are so constituted that we never use our eyes until we are on foreign soil. It is as though a Cook's ticket performed an operation for cataract.

But because one can learn the character of Dutch scenery so quickly--on a single railway journey--I do not wish to suggest that henceforward it becomes monotonous and trite. One may learn the character of a friend very quickly, and yet wish to be in his company continually. Holland is one of the most delightful countries to move about in: everything that happens in it is of interest. I have never quite lost the sense of excitement in crossing a canal in the train and getting a momentary glimpse of its receding straightness, perhaps broken by a brown sail. In a country where, between the towns, so little happens, even the slightest things make a heightened appeal to the observer; while one's eyes are continually kept bright and one's mind stimulated by the ever-present freshness and clearness of the land and its air.

Rotterdam, it should be said at once, is not a pleasant city. It must be approached as a centre of commerce and maritime industry, or not at all; if you do not like sailor men and sailor ways, noisy streets and hurrying people, leave Rotterdam behind, and let the train carry you to The Hague. It is not even particularly Dutch: it is cosmopolitan. The Dutch are quieter than this, and cleaner. And yet Rotterdam is unique--its church of St.

Lawrence has a grey and sombre tower which has no equal in the country; there is a windmill on the Cool Singel which is essentially Holland; the Boymans Museum has a few admirable pictures; there is a curiously fascinating stork in the Zoological Gardens; and the river is a scene of romantic energy by day and night. I think you must go to Rotterdam, though it be only for a few hours.

At Rotterdam we see what the Londoner misses by having a river that is navigable in the larger sense only below his city. To see shipping at home we must make our tortuous way to the Pool; Rotterdam has the Pool in her midst. Great ships pass up and down all day. The Thames, once its bustling mercantile life is cut short by London Bridge, dwindles to a stream of pleasure; the Maas becomes the Rhine.

Walt Whitman is the only writer who has done justice to a great harbour, and he only by that sheer force of enumeration which in this connection rather stands for than is poetry. As a matter of fact it is the reader of such an inventory as we find in "Crossing Brooklyn Ferry" that is the poet: Whitman is only the machinery. Whitman gives the suggestion and the reader's own memory or imagination does the rest. Many of the lines might as easily have been written of Rotterdam as of Brooklyn:--

The sailors at work in the rigging or out astride the spars, The round masts, the swinging motion of the hulls, the slender serpentine pennants, The large and small steamers in motion, the pilots in their pilot-houses, The white wake left by the passage, the quick tremulous whirl of the wheels, The flags of all nations, the falling of them at sunset, The scallop-edged waves in the twilight, the ladled cups, the frolicsome crests and glistening, The stretch afar growing dimmer and dimmer, the grey walls of the granite storehouses by the docks, On the river the shadowy group, the big steam-tug closely flank'd on each side by the barges, the hay-boat, the belated lighter, On the neighbouring shore the fires from the foundry chimneys burning high and glaringly into the night, Casting their flicker of black contrasted with wild red and yellow light over the tops of the houses, and down into the clefts of streets.

There is of course nothing odd in the description of one harbour fitting another, for harbours have no one nationality but all. Whitman was not otherwise very strong upon Holland. He writes in "Salut au Monde" of "the sail and steamships of the world" which in his mind's eye he beholds as they

Wait steam'd up ready to start in the ports of Australia, Wait at Liverpool, Glasgow, Dublin, Marseilles, Lisbon, Naples, Hamburg, Bremen, Bordeaux, The Hague, Copenhagen.

It is not easy for one of the "sail or steamships of the world" to wait steamed up at The Hague; because The Hague has no harbour except for small craft and barges. Shall we assume, with great charity, that Walt feared that the word Rotterdam might impair his rhythm?

4

Not only big shipping: I think one may see barges and canal boats in greater variety at Rotterdam than anywhere else. One curious thing to be noticed as they lie at rest in the canals is the absence of men. A woman is always there; her husband only rarely. The only visible captain is the fussy, shrewish little dog which, suspicious of the whole world, patrols the boat from stem to stern, and warns you that it is against the law even to look at his property. I hope his bite is not equal to his bark.

Every barge has its name. What the popular style was seven years ago, when I was here last, I cannot remember; but to-day it is "Wilhelmina". English suburban villas have not a greater variety of fantastic names than the canal craft of Holland; nor, with all our monopoly of the word "home," does the English suburban villa suggest more compact cosiness than one catches gleams of through their cabin windows or down their companions.

Spring cleaning goes on here, as in the Dutch houses, all the year round, and the domiciliary part of the vessels is spotless. Every bulwark has a washing tray that can be fixed or detached in a moment. "It's a fine day, let us kill something," says the Englishman; "Here's an odd moment, let us wash something," says the Dutch vrouw.

In some of the Rotterdam canals the barges are so packed that they lie touching each other, with their burgees flying all in the same direction, as the vanes of St. Sepulchre's in Holborn cannot do. How they ever get disentangled again and proceed on their free way to their distant homes is a mystery. But in the shipping world incredible things can happen at night.

One does not, perhaps, in Rotterdam realise all at once that every drop of water in these city-bound canals is related to every other drop of water in the other canals of Holland, however distant. From any one canal you can reach in time every other. The canal is really much more the high road of the country than the road itself. The barge is the Pickford van of Holland. Here we see some of the secret of the Dutch deliberateness. A country which must wait for its goods until a barge brings them has every opportunity of acquiring philosophic phlegm.

After a while one gets accustomed to the ever-present canal and the odd spectacle (to us) of masts in the streets and sails in the fields. All the Dutch towns are amphibious, but some are more watery than others.

The Dutch do not use their wealth of water as we should. They do not swim in it, they do not race on it, they do not row for pleasure at all. Water is their servant, never a light-hearted companion.

I can think of no more reposeful holiday than to step on board one of these barges wedged together in a Rotterdam canal, and never lifting a finger to alter the natural course of events--to accelerate or divert--be earned by it to, say, Harlingen, in Friesland: between the meadows; under the noses of the great black and white cows; past herons fishing in the rushes; through little villages with dazzling milk-cans being scoured on the banks, and the

good-wives washing, and saturnine smokers in black velvet slippers passing the time of day; through big towns, by rows of sombre houses seen through a delicate screen of leaves; under low bridges crowded with children; through narrow locks; ever moving, moving, slowly and surely, sometimes sailing, sometimes quanting, sometimes being towed, with the wide Dutch sky overhead, and the plovers crying in it, and the clean west wind driving the windmills, and everything just as it was in Rembrandt's day and just as it will be five hundred years hence.

Holland when all is said is a country of canals. It may have cities and pictures, windmills and cows, quaint buildings, and quainter costumes, but it is a country of canals before all. The canals set the tune. The canals keep it deliberate and wise.

One can be in Rotterdam, or in whatever town one's travels really begin, but a very short time without discovering that the Dutch unit--the florin--is a very unsatisfactory servant. The dearness of Holland strikes one continually, but it does so with peculiar force if one has crossed the frontier from Belgium, where the unit is a franc. It is too much to say that a sovereign in Holland is worth only twelve shillings: the case is not quite so extreme as that; but a sovereign in Belgium is, for all practical purposes, worth twenty-five shillings, and the contrast after reaching Dutch soil is very striking. One has to recollect that the spidery letter "f," which in those friendly little restaurants in the Rue Hareng at Brussels had stood for a franc, now symbolises that far more serious item the florin; and f. 1.50, which used to be a trifle of one and threepence, is now half a crown.

Even in our own country, where we know something about the cost of things, we are continually conscious of the fallacy embodied in the statement that a sovereign is equal to twenty shillings. We know that in theory that is so; but we know also that it is so only as long as the sovereign remains unchanged. Change it and it is worth next to nothing--half a sovereign and a little loose silver. But in Holland the disparity is even more pathetic. To change a sovereign there strikes one as the most ridiculous business transaction of one's life.

Certain things in Holland are dear beyond all understanding. At The Hague, for example, we drank Eau d'Evian, a very popular bottled water for which in any French restaurant one expects to pay a few pence; and when the bill arrived this simple fluid cut such a dashing figure in it that at first I could not recognise it at all. When I put the matter to the landlord, he explained that the duty made it impossible for him to charge less than f. 1.50 (or half a crown) a bottle; but I am told that his excuse was too fanciful. None the less, half a crown was the charge, and apparently no one objects to pay it.

The Dutch, on pleasure or eating bent, are prepared to pay anything. One would expect to get a reasonable claret for such a figure; but not in Holland. Wine is good there, but it is not cheap. Only in one hotel--and that in the unspoiled north, at Groningen--did I see wine placed automatically upon the table, as in France.

Rotterdam must have changed for the worse under modern conditions; for it is no longer as it was in Lady Mary Wortley Montagu's day. From Rotterdam in 1716 she sent the Countess of Mar a pretty account of the city: "All the streets are paved with broad stones, and before the meanest artificers' doors seats of various coloured marbles, and so neatly kept that, I will assure you, I walked all over the town yesterday, incognita, in my slippers, without receiving one spot of dirt; and you may see the Dutch maids washing the pavement of the street with more application than ours do our bed-chambers. The town seems so full of people, with such busy faces, all in motion, that I can hardly fancy that it is not some celebrated fair; but I see it is every day the same.

"The shops and warehouses are of a surprising neatness and magnificence, filled with an incredible quantity of fine merchandise, and so much cheaper than what we see in England, I have much ado to persuade myself I am still so near it. Here is neither dirt nor beggary to be seen. One is not shocked with those loathsome cripples, so common in London, nor teased with the importunities of idle fellows and wenches, that choose to be nasty and lazy. The common servants and the little shopwomen here are more nicely clean than most of our ladies; and the great variety of neat dresses (every woman dressing her head after her own fashion) is an additional pleasure in seeing the town."

The claims of business have now thrust aside many of the little refinements described by Lady Mary, her description of which has but to be transferred to some of the smaller Dutch towns to be however in the main still accurate. But what she says of the Dutch servants is true everywhere to this minute. There are none more fresh and capable; none who carry their lot with more quiet dignity. Not the least part of the very warm hospitality which is offered in Dutch houses is played by the friendliness of the servants. Every one in Holland seems to have enough; no one too much. Great wealth there may be among the merchants, but it is not ostentatious. Holland still seems to have no poor in the extreme sense of the word, no rags. Doubtless the labourers that one sees are working at a low rate, but they are probably living comfortably at a lower, and are not to be pitied except by those who still cherish the illusion that riches mean happiness. The dirt and poverty that exist in every English town and village are very uncommon. Nor does one see maimed, infirm or very old people, except now and then--so rarely as at once to be reminded of their rarity.

One is struck, even in Rotterdam, which is a peculiarly strenuous town, by the ruddy health of the people in the streets. In England, as one walks about, one sees too often the shadow of Death on this face and that; but in Holland it is difficult to believe in his power, the people have so prosperous, so permanent, an air.

That the Dutch die there is no doubt, for a funeral is an almost daily object, and the aanspreker is continually hurrying by; but where are the dead? The cemeteries are minute, and the churches have no churchyards. Of Death, however, when he comes the nation is very proud. The mourning customs are severe and enduring. No expense is spared in spreading the interesting tidings. It is for this purpose that the aanspreker flourishes in his importance and pomp. Draped heavily in black, from house to house he moves, wherever the slightest ties of personal or business acquaintanceship exist, and announces his news. A lady of Hilversum tells me that she was once formally the recipient of the message, "Please, ma'am, the baker's compliments, and he's dead," the time and place of the interment following. I said draped in black, but the aanspreker is not so monotonous an official as that. He has his subtleties, his nuances. If the deceased is a child, he adds a white rosette; if a bachelor or a maid, he intimates the fact by degrees of trimming.

The aanspreker was once occasionally assisted by the huilebalk, but I am afraid his day is over. The huilebalk accompanied the aansprekers from house to house and wept on the completion of their sad message. He wore a wide-awake hat with a very large brim and a long-tailed coat. If properly paid, says my informant, real tears coursed down his cheeks; in any case his presence was a luxury possible only to the rich.

The aanspreker is called in also at the other end of life. Assuming a more jocund air, he trips from house to house announcing little strangers.

That the Dutch are a healthy people one might gather also from the character of their druggists. In this country, even in very remote towns, one may reveal one's symptoms to a chemist or his assistant feeling certain that he will know more or less what to prescribe. But in Holland the chemists are often young women, who preside over shops in which one cannot repose any confidence. One likes a chemist's shop at least to look as if it contained reasonable remedies. These do not. Either our shops contain too many drugs or these too few. The chemist's sign, a large comic head with its mouth wide open (known as the gaper), is also subversive of confidence. A chemist's shop is no place for jokes. In Holland one must in short do as the Dutch do, and remain well.

Rotterdam's first claim to consideration, apart from its commercial importance, is that it gave birth to Erasmus, a bronze statue of whom stands in the Groote Market, looking down on the stalls of fruit. Erasmus of Rotterdam--it sounds like a contradiction in terms. Gherardt Gherardts of Rotterdam is a not dishonourable cacophany--and that was the reformer's true name; but the fashion of the time led scholars to adopt a Hellenised, or Latinised, style. Erasmus Desiderius, his new name, means Beloved and long desired. Grotius, Barlaeus, Vossius, Arminius, all sacrificed local colour to smooth syllables. We should be very grateful that the fashion did not spread also to the painters. What a loss it would be had the magnificent rugged name of Rembrandt van Rhyn been exchanged for a smooth emasculated Latinism.

Rotterdam had another illustrious son whose work as little suggests his birthplace--the exquisite painter Peter de Hooch. According to the authorities he modelled his style upon Rembrandt and Fabritius, but the influence of Rembrandt is concealed from the superficial observer. De Hooch, whose pictures are very scarce, worked chiefly at Delft and Haarlem, and it was at Haarlem that he died in 1681. If one were put to it to find a new standard of aristocracy superior to accidents of blood or rank one might do worse than demand as the ultimate test the possession of either a Vermeer of Delft or a Peter de Hooch.

One only of Peter de Hooch's pictures is reproduced in this book--"The Store Cupboard". This is partly because there are, I think, better paintings of his in London than at Amsterdam. At least it seems to me that his picture in our National Gallery of the waiting maid is finer than anything by De Hooch in Holland. But in no other work of his that I know is his simple charm so apparent as in "The Store Cupboard". This is surely the Christmas supplement carried out to its highest power--and by its inventor. The thousands of domestic scenes which have proceeded from this one canvas make the memory reel; and yet nothing has staled the prototype. It remains a sweet and genuine and radiant thing. De Hooch had two fetishes--a rich crimson dress or jacket and an open door. His compatriot Vermeer, whom he sometimes resembles, was similarly addicted to a note of blue.

No one has managed direct sunlight so well as De Hooch. The light in his rooms is the light of day. One can almost understand how Rembrandt and Gerard Dou got their concentrated effects of illumination; but how this omnipresent radiance streamed from De Hooch's palette is one of the mysteries. It is as though he did not paint light but found light on his canvas and painted everything else in its midst.

Rotterdam has some excellent pictures in its Boymans Museum; but they are, I fancy, overlooked by many visitors. It seems no city in which to see pictures. It is a city for anything rather than art--a mercantile centre, a hive of bees, a shipping port of intense activity. And yet perhaps the quietest little Albert Cuyp in Holland is here, "De Oude Oostpoort te Rotterdam," a small evening scene, without cattle, suffused in a golden glow. But all the Cuyps, and there are six, are good--all inhabited by their own light.

Among the other Boymans treasures which I find I have marked (not necessarily because they are good--for I am no judge--but because I liked them) are Ferdinand Bols fine free portrait of Dirck van der Waeijen, a boy in a yellow coat; Erckhart's "Boaz and Ruth," a small sombre canvas with a suggestion of Velasquez in it; Hobbema's "Boomrijk Landschap," one of the few paintings of this artist that Holland possesses. The English, I might remark, always appreciative judges of Dutch art, have been particularly assiduous in the pursuit of Hobbema, with the result that his best work is in our country. Holland has nothing of his to compare with the "Avenue at Middelharnis," one of the gems of our National Gallery. And his feathery trees may be studied at the Wallace Collection in great comfort.

Other fine landscapes in the Boymans Museum are three by Johan van Kessel, who was a pupil of Hobbema, one by Jan van der Meer, one by Koninck, and, by Jacob van Ruisdael, a corafield in the sun and an Amsterdam canal with white sails upon it. The most notable head is that by Karel Fabritius; Hendrick Pot's "Het Lokstertje" is interesting for its large free manner and signs of the influence of Hals; and Emmanuel de Witte's Amsterdam fishmarket is curiously modern. But the figure picture which most attracted me was "Portret van een jongeling," by Jan van Scorel, of whom we shall learn more at Utrecht. This little portrait, which I reproduce on the opposite page, is wholly charming and vivid.

The Boymans Museum contains also modern Dutch paintings. Wherever modern Dutch paintings are to be seen, I look first for the delicate art of Matthew Maris, and next for Anton Mauve. Here there is no Matthew Maris, and but one James Maris. There is one Mauve. The modern Dutch painter for the most part paints the same picture so often. But Matthew Maris is full of surprises. If a new picture by any of his contemporaries stood with its face to the wall one would know what to expect. From Israels, a fisherman's wife; from Mesdag, a grey stretch of sea; from Bosboom, a superb church interior; from Mauve, a peasant with sheep or a peasant with a cow; from Weissenbruch, a stream and a willow; from Breitner, an Amsterdam street; from James Maris a masterly scene of boats and wet sky. Usually one would have guessed aright. But with Matthew Maris is no certainty. It may be a little dainty girl lying on her side and watching butterflies; it may be a sombre hillside at Montmartre; it may be a girl cooking; it may be scaffolding in Amsterdam, or a mere at evening, or a baby's head, or a village street. He has many moods, and he is always distinguished and subtle.

Rotterdam has a zoological garden which, although inferior to ours, is far better than that at Amsterdam, while it converts The Hague's Zoo into a travesty. Last spring the lions were in splendid condition. They are well housed, but fewer distractions are provided for them than in Regent's Park. I found myself fascinated by the herons, who were continually soaring out over the neighbouring houses and returning like darkening clouds. In England, although the heron is a native, we rarely seem to see him; while to study him is extremely difficult. In Holland he is ubiquitous: both wild and tame.

More interesting still was the stork, whose nest is set high on a pinnacle of the buffalo house. He was building in the leisurely style of the British working man. He would negligently descend from the heavens with a stick. This he would lay on the fabric and then carefully perform his toilet, looking round and down all the time to see that every one else was busy.

Whenever his eye lighted upon a toddling child or a perambulator it visibly brightened. "My true work!" he seemed to say; "this nest building is a mere by-path of industry." After prinking and overlooking, and congratulating himself thus, for a few minutes, he would stroll off, over the housetops, for another stick. He was the unquestionable King of the Garden.

Why are there no heronries in the English public parks? And why is there no stork? The Dutch have a proverb, "Where the stork abides no mother dies in childbed". Still more, why are there no storks in France? The author of Fécondité should have imported them.

No Zoo, however well managed, can keep an ourang-outang long, and therefore one should always study that uncomfortably human creature whenever the opportunity occurs. I had great fortune at Rotterdam, for I chanced to be in the ourang-outang's house when his keeper came in.

Entering the enclosure, he romped with him in a score of diverting ways. They embraced each other, fed each other, teased each other. The humanness of the creature was frightful. Perhaps our likeness to ourang-outangs (except for our ridiculously short arms, inadequate lower jaws and lack of hair) made him similarly uneasy.

Rotterdam, I have read somewhere, was famous at the end of the eighteenth century for a miser, the richest man in the city. He always did his own marketing, and once changed his butcher because he weighed the paper with the meat He bought his milk in farthingsworths, half of which had to be delivered at his front door and half at the back, "to gain the little advantage of extra measure". Different travellers note different things, and William Chambers, the publisher, in his Tour in Holland in 1839, selected for special notice another type of Rotterdam resident: "One of the most remarkable men of this [the merchant] class is Mr. Van Hoboken of Rhoon and Pendrecht, who lives on one of the havens. This individual began life as a merchant's porter, and has in process of time attained the highest rank among the Dutch mercantile aristocracy. He is at present the principal owner of twenty large ships in the East India trade, each, I was informed, worth about fourteen thousand pounds, besides a large landed estate, and much floating wealth of different descriptions. His establishment is of vast extent, and contains departments for the building of ships and manufacture of all their necessary equipments. This gentleman, until lately, was in the habit of giving a splendid fête once a year to his family and friends, at which was exhibited with modest pride the porter's truck which he drew at the outset of his career. One seldom hears of British merchants thus keeping alive the remembrance of early meanness of circumstances."

At one of Rotterdam's stations I saw the Queen-Mother, a smiling, maternal lady in a lavender silk dress, carrying a large bouquet, and saying pretty things to a deputation drawn up on the platform. Rotterdam had put out its best bunting, and laid six inches of sand on its roads, to do honour to this kindly royalty. The band played the tender national anthem, which is always so unlike what one expects it to be, as her train steamed away, and then all the grave bearded gentlemen in uniforms and frock coats who had attended her drove in their open carriages back to the town. Not even the presence of the mounted guard made it more formal than a family party.

Everybody seemed on the best of friendly terms of equality with everybody else. Tom Hood, who had it in him to be so good a poet, but living in a country where art and literature do not count, was permitted to coarsen his delicate genius in the hunt for bread, wrote one of his comic poems on Rotterdam. In it are many happy touches of description:--

Before me lie dark waters In broad canals and deep, Whereon the silver moonbeams Sleep, restless in their sleep; A sort of vulgar Venice Reminds me where I am; Yes, yes, you are in England, And I'm at Rotterdam.

Tall houses with quaint gables, Where frequent windows shine, And quays that lead to bridges, And trees in formal line, And masts of spicy vessels From western Surinam, All tell me you're in England, But I'm in Rotterdam.

With headquarters at Rotterdam one may make certain small journeys into the neighbourhood--to Dordrecht by river, to Delft by canal, to Gouda by canal; or one may take longer voyages, even to Cologne if one wishes. But I do not recommend it as a city to linger in. Better than Rotterdam's large hotels are, I think, the smaller, humbler and more Dutch inns of the less commercial towns. This indeed is the case all over Holland: the plain Dutch inn of the neighbouring small town is pleasanter than the large hotels of the city; and, as I have remarked in the chapter on Amsterdam, the distances are so short, and the trains so numerous, that one suffers no inconvenience from staying in the smaller places.

Gouda (pronounced Howda) it is well to visit from Rotterdam, for it has not enough to repay a sojourn in its midst. It has a Groote Kerk and a pretty isolated white stadhuis. But Gouda's fame rests on its stained glass--gigantic representations of myth, history and scripture, chiefly by the brothers Crabeth. The windows are interesting rather than beautiful. They lack the richness and mystery which one likes to find in old stained glass, and the church itself is bare and cold and unfriendly. Hemmed in by all this coloured glass, so able and so direct, one sighs for a momentary glimpse of the rose window at Chartres, or even of the too heavily kaleidoscopic patterns of Brussels Cathedral. No matter, the Gouda windows in their way are very fine, and in the sixth, depicting the story of Judith and Holofernes, there is a very fascinating little Düreresque tower on a rock under siege.

If one is taking Gouda on the way from Rotterdam to Amsterdam, the surrounding country should not be neglected from the carriage windows. Holland is rarely so luxuriant as here, and so peacefully beautiful.

# CHAPTER II

The Dutch in English Literature

Hard things against the Dutch--Andrew Marvell's satire--The iniquity of living below sea-level--Historic sarcasms--"Invent a shovel and be a magistrate"--Heterogeneity--Foot warmers--A champion of the Hollow Land--The Dutch Drawn to the Life--Dutch suspicion--Sir William Temple's opinion--and Sir Thomas Overbury's--Dr. Johnson's project--Dutch courtesy--Dutch discourtesy--National manners--A few phrases--The origin of "Dutch News"--A vindication of Dutch courage.

To say hard things of the Dutch was once a recognised literary pastime. At the time of our war with Holland no poet of any pretensions refrained from writing at least one anti-Batavian satire, the classical example of which is Andrew Marvell's "Character of Holland" (following Samuel Butler's), a pasquinade that contains enough wit and fancy and contempt to stock a score of the nation's ordinary assailants. It begins perfectly:--

HOLLAND, that scarce deserves the name of land, As but th' off-scouring of the British sand, And so much earth as was contributed By English pilots when they heav'd the lead, Or what by the ocean's slow alluvion fell Of shipwrackt cockle and the muscle-shell: This indigested vomit of the sea Fell to the Dutch by just propriety. Glad then, as miners who have found the ore They, with mad labour, fish'd the land to shoar And div'd as desperately for each piece Of earth, as if't had been of ambergreece; Collecting anxiously small loads of clay, Less than what building swallows bear away; Or than those pills which sordid beetles roul, Transfusing into them their dunghil soul. How did they rivet, with gigantick piles, Thorough the center their new-catchèd miles; And to the stake a struggling country bound, Where barking waves still bait the forcèd ground; Building their wat'ry Babel far more high To reach the sea, than those to scale the sky!

Yet still his claim the injur'd ocean laid, And oft at leap-frog ore their steeples plaid: As if on purpose it on land had come To show them what's their mare liberum. A daily deluge over them does boyl; The earth and water play at level-coyl. The fish oft times the burger dispossest, And sat, not as a meat, but as a guest, And oft the Tritons and the sea-nymphs saw Whole sholes of Dutch serv'd up for Cabillau; Or, as they over the new level rang'd For pickled herring, pickled heeren chang'd. Nature, it seem'd, asham'd of her mistake, Would throw their land away at duck and drake.

The poor Dutch were never forgiven for living below the sea-level and gaining their security by magnificent feats of engineering and persistence. Why the notion of a reclaimed land should have seemed so comic I cannot understand, but Marvell certainly justified the joke.

Later, Napoleon, who liked to sum up a nation in a phrase, accused Holland of being nothing but a deposit of German mud, thrown there by the Rhine: while the Duke of Alva remarked genially that the Dutch were of all peoples those that lived nighest to hell; but Marvell's sarcasms are the best. Indeed I doubt if the literature of droll exaggeration has anything to compare with "The Character of Holland".

The satirist, now thoroughly warmed to his congenial task, continues:--

Therefore Necessity, that first made kings, Something like government among them brings; For, as with pygmees, who best kills the crane, Among the hungry, he that treasures grain, Among the blind, the one-ey'd blinkard reigns, So rules among the drowned he that draines: Not who first sees the rising sun, commands, But who could first discern the rising lands; Who best could know to pump an earth so leak, Him they their Lord, and Country's Father, speak; To make a bank, was a great plot of State, Invent a shov'l, and be a magistrate.

So much for the conquest of Neptune, which in another nation were a laudable enough enterprise. Marvell then passes on to the national religion and the heterogeneity of Amsterdam:--

'Tis probable Religion, after this, Came next in order, which they could not miss, How could the Dutch but be converted, when Th' Apostles were so many fishermen? Besides, the waters of themselves did rise, And, as their land, so them did re-baptize. Though Herring for their God few voices mist, And Poor-John to have been th' Evangelist, Faith, that could never twins conceive before, Never so fertile, spawn'd upon this shore More pregnant than their Marg'ret, that laid down For Hans-in-Kelder of a whole

Hans-Town. Sure when Religion did itself imbark, And from the East would Westward steer its ark, It struck, and splitting on this unknown ground, Each one thence pillag'd the first piece he found: Hence Amsterdam, Turk-Christian-Pagan-Jew, Staple of sects, and mint of schisme grew; That bank of conscience, where not one so strange Opinion but finds credit, and exchange. In vain for Catholicks ourselves we bear; The universal Church is only there. Nor can civility there want for tillage, Where wisely for their Court, they chose a village: How fit a title clothes their governours, Themselves the hogs, as all their subject bores! Let it suffice to give their country fame, That it had one Civilis call'd by name, Some fifteen hundred and more years ago, But surely never any that was so.

There is something rather splendid in the attitude of a man who can take a whole nation as his butt and bend every circumstance to his purpose of ridicule and attack. Our satirists to-day are contented to pillory individuals or possibly a sect or clique. Marvell's enjoyment in his own exuberance and ingenuity is so apparent and infectious that it matters nothing to us whether he was fair or unfair.

The end is inconclusive, being a happy recollection that he had omitted any reference to stoofjes, the footstools filled with burning peat which are used to keep the feet warm in church. Such a custom was of course not less reprehensible than the building of dykes to keep out the sea. Hence these eight lines, which, however, would have come better earlier in the poem:--

See but their mermaids, with their tails of fish, Reeking at church over the chafing-dish! A vestal turf, enshrin'd in earthen ware, Fumes through the loopholes of a wooden square; Each to the temple with these altars tend, But still does place it at her western end; While the fat steam of female sacrifice Fills the priest's nostrils, and puts out his eyes. Not all the poets, however, abused the Dutch. John Hagthorpe, in his England's Exchequer in 1625 (written before the war: hence, perhaps, his kindness) thus addressed the "hollow land":--

Fair Holland, had'st thou England's chalky rocks, To gird thy watery waist; her healthful mounts, With tender grass to feed thy nibbling flocks: Her pleasant groves, and crystalline clear founts, Most happy should'st thou be by just accounts, That in thine age so fresh a youth do'st feel Though flesh of oak, and ribs of brass and steel.

13

But what hath prudent mother Nature held From thee--that she might equal shares impart Unto her other sons--that's not compell'd To be the guèrdons of thy wit and art? And industry, that brings from every part Of every thing the fairest and the best, Like the Arabian bird to build thy nest?

Like the Arabian bird thy nest to build, With nimble wings thou flyest for Indian sweets, And incense which the Sabáan forests yield, And in thy nest the goods of each pole meets,-- Which thy foes hope, shall serve thy funeral rites-- But thou more wise, secur'd by thy deep skill, Dost build on waves, from fires more safe than hill.

To return to the severer critics--in 1664 was published a little book called The Dutch Drawn to the Life, a hostile work not improbably written with the intention of exciting English animosity to the point of war. A great deal was made of the success of the Dutch fisheries and the mismanagement of our own. The nation was criticised in all its aspects--"well nigh three millions of men, well-proportioned, great lovers of our English beer". The following passage on the drinking capacity of the Dutch would have to be modified to-day:--

By their Excise, which riseth with their charge, the more money they pay, the more they receive again, in that insensible but profitable way: what is exhaled up in clouds, falls back again in showers: what the souldier receives in pay, he payes in Drink: their very enemies, though they hate the State, yet love their liquor, and pay excise: the most idle, slothful, and most improvident, that selleth his blood for drink, and his flesh for bread, serves at his own charge, for every pay day he payeth his sutler, and he the common purse.

Here are other strokes assisting to the protraiture "to the life" of this people: "Their habitations are kept handsomer than their bodies, and their bodies than their soules".--"The Dutch man's building is not large, but neat; handsome on the outside, on the inside hung with pictures and tapestry. He that hath not bread to eat hath a picture."--"They are seldom deceived, for they will trust nobody. They may always deceive, for you must trust them, as for instance, if you travel, to ask a bill of Particulars is to purre in a wasp's nest, you must pay what they ask as sure as if it were the assessment of a Subsidy."

But the wittiest and shrewdest of the prose critics of Holland was Owen Feltham, from whom I quote later. His little book on the Low Countries is as packed with pointed phrase as a satire by Pope: the first half of it whimsically destructive, the second half eulogistic. It is he who charges the Dutch convivial spirits with drinking down the Evening Starre and drinking up the Morning Starre.

The old literature tells us also that the Dutch were not always clean. Indeed, their own painters prove this: Ostade pre-eminently. There are many allusions in Elizabethan and early Stuart literature to their dirt and rags. In Earle's Microcosmography, for example, a younger brother's last refuge is said to be the Low Countries, "where rags and linen are no scandal". But better testimony comes perhaps from The English Schole-Master, a seventeenth-century Dutch-English manual, from which I quote at some length later in this book. Here is a specimen scrap of dialogue:--

S. May it please you to give me leave to go out? M. Whither? S. Home. M. How is it that you goe so often home? S. My mother commanded that I and my brother should come to her this day. M. For what cause? S. That our mayd may beat out our clothes. M. What is that to say? Are you louzie? S. Yea, very louzie. Sir William Temple, the patron of Swift, the husband of

Dorothy Osborne, and our ambassador at The Hague--where he talked horticulture, cured his gout by the remedy known as Moxa, and collected materials for the leisurely essays and memoirs that were to be written at Moor Park--knew the Dutch well and wrote of them with much particularity. In his Observations upon the United Provinces he says this: "Holland is a country, where the earth is better than the air, and profit more in request than honour; where there is more sense than wit; more good nature than good humour, and more wealth than pleasure: where a man would chuse rather to travel than to live; shall find more things to observe than desire; and more persons to esteem than to love. But the same qualities and dispositions do not value a private man and a state, nor make a conversation agreeable, and a government great: nor is it unlikely, that some very great King might make but a very ordinary private gentleman, and some very extraordinary gentleman might be capable of making but a very mean Prince."

Among other travellers who have summed up the Dutch in a few phrases is Sir Thomas Overbury, the author of some witty characters, including that very charming one of a Happy Milk Maid. In 1609 he thus generalised upon the Netherlander: "Concerning the people: they are neither much devout, nor much wicked; given all to drink, and eminently to no other vice; hard in bargaining, but just; surly and respectless, as in all democracies; thirsty, industrious, and cleanly; disheartened upon the least ill-success, and insolent upon good; inventive in manufactures, and cunning in traffick: and generally, for matter of action, that natural slowness of theirs, suits better (by reason of the advisedness and perseverance it brings with it) than the rashness and changeableness of the French and Florentine wits; and the equality of spirits, which is among them and Switzers, renders them so fit for a democracy: which kind of government, nations of more stable wits, being once come to a consistent greatness, have seldom long endured."

Many Englishmen have travelled in Holland and have set down the record of their experiences, from Thomas Coryate downwards. But the country has not been inspiring, and Dutch travels are poor reading. Had Dr. Johnson lived to accompany Boswell on a projected journey we should be the richer, but I doubt if any very interesting narrative would have resulted. One of Johnson's contemporaries, Samuel Ireland, the engraver, and the father of the fraudulent author of Vortigern, wrote A Picturesque Tour through Holland, Brabant, and part of France, in 1789, while a few years later one of Charles Lamb's early "drunken companions," Fell, wrote A Tour through the Batavian Republic, 1801; and both of these books yield a few experiences not without interest. Fell's is the duller. I quote from them now and again throughout this volume, but I might mention here a few of their more general observations.

Fell, for example, was embarrassed by the very formal politeness of the nation. "The custom of bowing in Holland," he writes, "is extremely troublesome. It is not sufficient, as in England, that a person slightly moves his hat, but he must take it off his head, and continue uncovered till the man is past him to whom he pays the compliment. The ceremony of bowing is more strictly observed at Leyden and Haarlem, than at Rotterdam or The Hague. In either of the former cities, a stranger of decent appearance can scarcely walk in the streets without being obliged every minute to pull off his hat, to answer some civility of the same kind which he receives; and these compliments are paid him not only by opulent people, but by mechanics and labourers, who bow with all the gravity and politeness of their superiors."

Such civilities to strangers have become obsolete. So far from courtesy being the rule of the street, it is now, as I have hinted in the next chapter, impossible for an English-woman whose clothes chance to differ in any particular from those of the Dutch to escape embarrassing notice. Staring is carried to a point where it becomes almost a blow, and laughter and humorous sallies resound. I am told that the Boer war to a large extent broke down old habits of politeness to the English stranger.

When one thinks of it, the Dutch habit of staring at the visitor until he almost wishes the sea would roll in and submerge him, argues a want of confidence in their country, tantamount to a confession of failure. Had they a little more trust in the attractive qualities of their land, a little more imagination to realise that in other eyes its flatness and quaintness might be even alluring, they would accept and acknowledge the compliment by doing as little as possible to make their country's admirers uncomfortable.

"Dutch courage," to which I refer below, is not our only use of Dutch as a contemptuous adjective. We say "Dutch Gold" for pinchbeck, "Dutch Myrtle" for a weed. "I shall talk to you like a Dutch uncle" is another saying, not in this case contemptuous but rather complimentary-- signifying "I'll dress you down to some purpose". One piece of slang we share with Holland: the reference to the pawnbroker as an uncle. In Holland the kindly friend at the three brass balls (which it may not be generally known are the ancient arms of Lombardy, the Lombards being the first money lenders,) is called Oom Jan or Uncle John.

There is still another phrase, "Dutch news," which might be explained. The term is given by printers to very difficult copy--Dean Stanley's manuscript, for example, was probably known as Dutch news, so terrible was his hand,--and also to "pie". The origin is to be found in the following paragraph from Notes and Queries. (The Sir Richard Phillips concerned was the vegetarian publisher so finely touched off by Borrow in Lavengro.)

In his youth Sir Richard Phillips edited and published a paper at Leicester, called the Herald. One day an article appeared in it headed 'Dutch Mail,' and added to it was an announcement that it had arrived too late for translation, and so had been cut up and printed in the original. This wondrous article drove half of England crazy, and for years the best Dutch scholars squabbled and pored over it without being able to arrive at any idea of what it meant. This famous 'Dutch Mail' was, in reality, merely a column of pie. The story Sir Richard tells of this particular pie he had a whole hand in is this:--

"One evening, before one of our publications, my men and a boy overturned two or three columns of the paper in type. We had to get ready in some way for the coaches, which, at four o'clock in the morning, required four or five hundred papers. After every exertion we were short nearly a column; but there stood on the galleys a tempting column of pie. It suddenly struck me that this might be thought Dutch. I made up the column, overcame the scruples of the foreman, and so away the country edition went with its philological puzzle, to worry the honest agricultural reader's head. There was plenty of time to set up a column of plain English for the local edition." Sir Richard tells of one man whom he met in Nottingham who for thirty-four years preserved a copy of the Leicester Herald, hoping that some day the matter would be explained.

I doubt if any one nation is braver than any other; and the fact that from Holland we get the contemptuous term "Dutch courage," meaning the courage which is dependent upon spirits (originally as supplied to malefactors about to mount the scaffold), is no indication that the Dutch lack bravery. To one who inquired as to the derivation of the phrase a poet unknown to me thus replied, somewhen in the reign of William IV. The retort, I think, was sound:--

Do you ask what is Dutch courage? Ask the Thames, and ask the fleet, That, in London's fire and plague years, With De Ruyter yards could mete: Ask Prince Robert and d'Estrées, Ask your Solebay and the Boyne, Ask the Duke, whose iron valour With our chivalry did join, Ask your Wellington, oh ask him, Of our Prince of Orange bold, And a tale of nobler spirit Will to wond'ring ears be told; And if ever foul invaders Threaten your King William's throne, If dark Papacy be running, Or if Chartists want your own, Or whatever may betide you, That needs rid of foreign will, Only ask of your Dutch neighbours, And you'll see Dutch courage still.

# CHAPTER III

Dordrecht and Utrecht

By water to Dordrecht--Her four rivers--The milkmaid and the coat of arms--The Staple of Dort--Overhanging houses--Albert Cuyp--Nicolas Maes--Ferdinand Bol--Ary Scheffer--G.H. Breitner--A Dort carver--The Synod of Dort--"The exquisite rancour of theologians"--La Tulipe

Noire--Bernard Mandeville--The exclusive Englishman--The Castle of Loevenstein--The escape of Grotius--Gorcum's taste outraged--By rail to Utrecht--A free church--The great storm of 1674--Utrecht Cathedral--Jan van Scorel--Paul Moreelse--A too hospitable museum.

Dordrecht must be approached by water, because then one sees her as she was seen so often, and painted so often, by her great son Albert Cuyp, and by countless artists since.

I steamed from Rotterdam to Dordrecht on a grey windy morning, on a passenger boat bound ultimately for Nymwegen. We carried a very mixed cargo. In a cage at the bows was a Friesland mare, while the whole of the deck at the stern was piled high with motor spirit. Between came myriad barrels of beer and other merchandise.

The course to Dordrecht (which it is simpler to call Dort) is up the Maas for some miles; past shipbuilding yards, at Sylverdyk (where is a great heronry) and Kinderdyk; past fishermen dropping their nets for salmon, which they may take only on certain days, to give their German brethren, higher up the river, a chance; past meadows golden with marsh marigolds; past every kind of craft, most attractive of all being the tjalcks with their brown or black sails and green-lined hulls, not unlike those from Rochester which swim so steadily in the reaches of the Thames about Greenwich. The journey takes an hour and a half, the last half-hour being spent in a canal leading south from the Maas and ultimately joining Dort's confluence of waters. It is these rivers that give Dort her peculiar charm. There is a little café on the quay facing the sunset where one may sit and lose oneself in the eternally interesting movement of the shipping. I found the town distracting under the incessant clanging of the tram bell (yet grass grows among the paving-stones between the rails); but there is no distraction opposite the sunset. On the evening that I am remembering the sun left a sky of fiery orange barred by clouds of essential blackness.

Dort's rivers are the Maas and the Waal, the Linge and the Merwede; and when in 1549 Philip of Spain visited the city, she flourished this motto before him:--

Me Mosa, me Vahalis, me Linga Morvaque cingunt Biternam Batavæ virginis ecce fidens.

The fidelity, at least to Philip and Spain, disappeared; but the four rivers still as of old surround Dort with a cincture.

I must give, in the words of the old writer who tells it, the pretty legend which explains the origin of the Dort coat of arms: "There is an admirable history concerning that beautiful and maiden city of Holland called Dort. The Spaniards had intended an onslaught against it, and so they had laid thousands of old soldiers in ambush. Not far from it there did live a rich farmer who did keep many cows in his ground, to furnish Dort with butter and milk. The milkmaid coming to milk saw all under the hedges soldiers lying; seemed to take no notice, but went singing to her cows; and having milked, went as merrily away. Coming to her master's house, she told what she had seen. The master wondering at it, took the maid with him and presently came to Dort, told it to the Burgomaster, who sent a spy immediately, found it true, and prepared for their safety; sent to the States, who presently sent soldiers into the city, and gave order that the river should be let in at such a sluice, to lay the country under water. It was done, and many Spaniards were drowned and utterly disappointed of their design, and the town saved. The States, in the memory of the merry milkmaid's good service to the country, ordered the farmer a large revenue for ever, to recompense his loss of house, land, and cattle; caused the coin of the city to have the milkmaid under her cow to be engraven, which is to be seen upon the Dort dollar, stivers, and doights to this day; and so she is set upon the water gate of Dort; and she had, during her life, and her's for ever, an allowance of fifty pounds per annum. A noble requital for a virtuous action."

Dort's great day of prosperity is over; but once she was the richest town in Holland--a result due to the privilege of the Staple. In other words, she obtained the right to act as intermediary between the rest of Holland and the outer world in connection with all the wine, corn, timber and whatever else might be imported by way of the Rhine. At Dort the cargoes were unloaded. For some centuries she enjoyed this privilege, and then in 1618 Rotterdam began to resent it so acutely as to take to arms, and the financial prosperity of the town, which would be tenable only by the maintenance of a fleet, steadily crumbled. To-day she is contented enough, but the cellars of Wyn Straat, once stored with the juices of Rhenish vineyards, are empty. The Staple is no more.

Dort is perhaps the most painted of all Dutch towns, and with reason; for certainly no other town sits with more calm dignity among the waters, nor has any other town so quaintly medieval a canal as that which extends from end to end, far below the level of the streets, crossed by a series of little bridges. Seen from these bridges it is the nearest thing to Venice in all Holland--nearer than anything in Amsterdam. One may see it not only from the bridges, but also from little flights of steps off the main street, and everywhere it is beautiful: the walls rising from its surface reflected in its depths, green paint splashed about with perfect effect, bright window boxes, here and there a woman washing clothes, odd gables above and bridges in the distance.

Dordrecht's converging facades, which incline towards each other like deaf people, are, I am told, the result not of age and sinking foundations, but of design. When they were built, very many years ago, the city had a law directing that its roofs should so far project beyond the perpendicular as to shed their water into the gutter, thus enabling the passers-by on the pavement to walk unharmed. I cannot give chapter or verse for this comfortable theory; which of course preceded the ingenious Jonas Hanway's invention of the umbrella. In a small and very imperfect degree the enactment anticipates the covered city of Mr. H.G. Wells's vision. A Dutch friend to whom I put the point tells me that more probably the preservation of bricks and mural carvings was intended, the dryness of the wayfarer being quite secondary or unforeseen.

Dort's greatest artist was Albert Cuyp, born in 1605. His body lies in the church of the Augustines in the same city, where he died in 1691--true to the Dutch painters' quiet gift of living and dying in their birthplaces. Cuyp has been called the Dutch Claude, but it is not a good description. He was more human, more simple, than Claude. The symbol for him is a scene of cows; but he had great versatility, and painted horses to perfection. I have also seen good portraits from his busy brush. Faithful to his native town, he painted many pictures of Dort. We have two in the National Gallery. I have reproduced opposite page 30 his beautiful quiet view of the town in the Ryks Museum. Dort has changed but little since then; the schooner would now be a steamer--that is almost all. The reproduction can give no adequate suggestion of Cuyp's gift of diffusing golden light, his most precious possession.

Another Dort painter, below Albert Cuyp in fame, but often above him, I think, in interest and power, is Nicolas Maes, born in 1632--a great year in Dutch art, for it saw the birth also of Vermeer of Delft and Peter de Hooch. Maes, who studied in Rembrandt's studio, was perhaps the greatest of all that master's pupils. England, as has been so often the case, appreciated Maes more wisely than Holland, with the result that some of his best pictures are here.

But one must go to the Ryks Museum in Amsterdam to see his finest work of all--"The Endless Prayer," No. 1501, reproduced on the opposite page. We have at the National Gallery or the Wallace Collection no Maes equal to this. His "Card players," however, at the National Gallery, a free bold canvas, more in the manner of Velasquez than of his immediate master, is in its way almost as interesting. To "The Endless Prayer" one feels that Maes's master, Rembrandt, could have added nothing. It is even conceivable that he might have injured it by some touch of asperity. From this picture all Newlyn seems to have sprung.

According to Pilkington, Maes gave up his better and more Rembrandtesque manner on account of the objection of his sitters to be thus painted. Such are sitters!

Dordrecht claims also Ferdinand Bol, the pupil and friend of Rembrandt, and the painter of the Four Regents of the Leprosy Hospital in the Amsterdam stadhuis. He was born in 1611. For a while his pictures were considered by connoisseurs to be finer than those of his master. We are wiser to-day; yet Bol had a fine free way that is occasionally superb, often united, as in the portrait of Dirck van der Waeijen at Rotterdam, to a delicate charm for which Rembrandt cared little. His portrait of an astronomer in our National Gallery is a great work, and at the Ryks Museum at Amsterdam his "Roelof Meulenaer," No. 543, should not be missed. Bol's favourite sitter seems to have been Admiral de Ruyter--if one may judge by the number of his portraits of that sea ravener which Holland possesses.

By a perversity of judgment Dort seems to be more proud of Ary Scheffer than of any of her really great sons. It is Ary Scheffer's statue--not Albert Cuyp's or Nicolas Maes's--which rises in the centre of the town; and Ary Scheffer's sentimental and saccharine inventions fill three rooms in the museum. It is amusing in the midst of this riot of meek romanticism to remember that Scheffer painted Carlyle. Dort has no right to be so intoxicated with the excitement of having given birth to Scheffer, for his father was a German, a mere sojourner in the Dutch town.

The old museum of Dort has just been moved to a new building in the Lindengracht, and in honour of the event a loan exhibition of modern paintings and drawings was opened last summer. The exhibition gave peculiar opportunity for studying the work of G. H. Breitner, the painter of Amsterdam canals. The master of a fine sombre impressionism, Breitner has made such scenes his own. But he can do also more tender and subtle things. In this collection was a little oil sketch of a mere which would not have suffered had it been hung between a Corot and a Daubigny; and a water-colour drawing of a few cottages and a river that could not have been strengthened by any hand.

Another artist of Dort was Jan Terween Aertz, born in 1511, whose carvings in the choir of the Groote Kerk are among its chief glories. It is amazing that such spirit and movement can be suggested in wood. That the very semblance of life can be captured by a painter is wonderful enough; but there seems to me something more extraordinary in the successful conquest of the difficulties which confront an artist of such ambition as this Dort carver. His triumph is even more striking than that of the sculptor in marble. The sacristan of Dort's Groote Kerk seems more eager to show a brass screen and a gold christening bowl than these astounding choir stalls; but tastes always differ.

By the irony of fate it was Dort--the possessor of Terween's carving of the Triumph of Charles V. (a pendant to the Triumph of the Church and the Eucharist)--that, in 1572, only a few years after the carving was made, held the Congress which virtually decided the fate of Spain in the Netherlands. Brill had begun the revolution (as we shall see in our last chapter), Flushing was the first to follow suit, Enkhuisen then caught the fever; but these were individual efforts: it was the Congress of Dort that authorised and systematised the revolt.

The scheme of this book precludes a consecutive account of the great struggle between Holland and Spain--a struggle equal almost to that between Holland and her other implacable foe, the sea. I assume in the reader a sufficient knowledge of history to be able to follow the course of the contest as it moves backwards and forwards in these pages--the progress of the narrative being dictated by the sequence of towns in the itinerary rather than by the sequence of events in time. The death of William the Silent, for example, has to be set forth in the chapter on Delft, where the tragedy occurred, and where he lies buried, long before we reach the description of the siege of Haarlem and the capture of De Bossu off Hoorn, while for the insurrection of Brill, which was the first tangible token of Dutch independence, we have to wait until the last chapter of all. The reader who is endowed with sufficient history to reconcile these divagations should, I think, by the time the book is finished, have (with Motley's assistance) a vivid idea of this great war, so magnificently waged by Holland, which lowers in the background of almost every Dutch town.

A later congress at Dort was the famous Synod in 1618-19, in which a packed house of Gomarians or Contra-Remonstrants, pledged to carry out the wishes of Maurice, Prince of Orange, the Stadtholder, affected to subject the doctrines of the Arminians or Remonstrants to conscientious examination. These doctrines as contained in the five articles of the Arminians were as follows, in the words of Davies, the historian of Holland: "First, that God had resolved from the beginning to elect into eternal life those who through his grace believed in Jesus Christ, and continued stedfast in the faith; and, on the contrary, had resolved to leave the obstinate and unbelieving to eternal damnation; secondly, that Christ had died for the whole world, and obtained for all remission of sins and reconciliation with God, of which, nevertheless, the faithful only are made partakers; thirdly, that man cannot have a saving faith by his own free will, since while in a state of sin he cannot think or do good, but it is necessary that the grace of God, through Christ, should regenerate and renew the understanding and affections; fourthly, that this grace is the beginning, continuance, and end of salvation, and that all good works proceed from it, but that it is not irresistible; fifthly, that although the faithful receive by grace sufficient strength to resist Satan, sin, the world, and the flesh, yet man can by his own act fall away from this state of grace."

After seven months wrangling and bitterness, at a cost of a million guelders, the Synod came to no conclusion more Christian than that no punishment was too bad for the holder of such opinions, which were dangerous to the State and subversive of true religion. The result was that Holland's Calvinism was intensified; Barneveldt (who had been in prison all the time) was, as we shall see, beheaded; Grotius and Hoogenbeets were sentenced to imprisonment for life; and Episcopius, the Remonstrant leader at the Synod, was, together with many others, banished.

Episcopius heard his sentence with composure, merely remarking, "God will require of you an account of your conduct at the great day of His judgment. There you and the whole Synod will appear. May you never meet with a judge such as the Synod has been to us."

Davies has a story of Episcopius which is too good to be omitted. On banishment he was given his expenses by the States. Among the dollars given to Episcopius was one, coined apparently in the Duchy of Brunswick, bearing on the one side the figure of Truth, with the motto, "Truth overcomes all things"; and on the reverse, "In well-doing fear no one".

Episcopius was so struck with the coincidence that he had the coin set in gold and carefully preserved.

It is impossible for any one who has read La Tulipe Noire not to think of that story when wandering about Dort; but it is a mistake to read it in the town itself, for the Great Alexandre's fidelity to fact will not bear the strain. Dumas never wore his historical, botanical, geographical and ethnographical knowledge more like a flower than in this brave but breathless story. In Boxtel's envy we may perhaps believe; in Gryphon's savagery; and in the craft and duplicity of the Stadtholder; but if ever a French philosopher and a French grisette masqueraded as a Dutch horticulturist and a Frisian waiting-maid they are Cornelius van Baerle and his Rosa; and if ever a tulip grew by magic rather than by the laws of nature it was the tulipe noire. No matter; there is but one Dumas. According to Flotow the composer, William III. of Holland told Dumas the story of the black tulip at his coronation in 1849, remarking that it was time that the novelist turned his attention to Holland; but two arguments are urged against this origin, one being that Paul Lacroix--the "Bibliophile Jacob"--is said, on better authority, to have supplied the germ of the romance, and the other (which is even better evidence), that had the stimulus come from a monarch Dumas would hardly have refrained from saying so (and more) in the preface of the book.

Cornelius de Witt, whose tragedy is at the threshold of the romance, was apprehended at Dort, on his bed of sickness, and carried thence to the Hague, to be imprisoned in the Gevangenpoort, which we shall visit, and torn to pieces by the populace close by. Another literary association. From Dort came the English cynical writer Bernard Mandeville, born in 1670, author of The Fable of the Bees, that very shrewd and advanced commentary upon national hypocrisies--so advanced, indeed, that several of the more revolutionary of the thinkers of the present day, whose ideas are thought peculiarly modern, have not really got beyond it. After leaving Leyden as a doctor of medicine, Mandeville settled in England, somewhen at the end of the seventeenth century, and became well known in the Coffee Houses as a wit and good fellow.

We are a curious people when we travel. At Dort I heard a young Englishman inquiring of the landlord how best to spend his Sunday. "One can hardly go on one of the river excursions," he remarked; "they are so mixed." And the landlord, with a lunch at two florins, fifty, in his mind, which it was desirable that as many persons as possible should eat and pay for, heartily agreed with him. None the less it seemed well to join the excursion to Gorinchem; and thence we steamed on a fine cloudy Sunday, the river whipped grey by a strong cross wind, and the little ships that beat up and passed us, all aslant. At Gorinchem (pronounced Gorcum) we changed at once into another steamer, a sorry tub, as wide as it was short, and steamed to Woudrichem (called Worcum) hoping to explore the fortress of Loevenstein. But Loevenstein is enisled and beyond the reach of the casual visitor, and we had therefore to sit in the upper room of the Bellevue inn, overlooking the river, and await the tub's deliberate return, while the tugs and the barges trailed past. Save for modifications brought about by steam, the scene can be now little different from that in the days when Hugo Grotius was imprisoned in the castle.

The philosopher's escape is one of the best things in the history of wives. Two ameliorations were permitted him by Maurice--the presence of the Vrouw Grotius and the solace of books. As it happened, this lenience could not have been less fortunately (or, for Grotius, more fortunately) framed.

Books came continually to the prisoner, which, when read, were returned in the same chest that conveyed his linen to the Gorcum wash. At first the guard carefully examined each departing load; but after a while the form was omitted. Grotius's wife, a woman of no common order (when asked why she did not sue for her husband's pardon, she had replied, "I will not do it: if he have deserved it let them strike off his head"), was quick to notice the negligence of the guard, and giving out that her husband was bedridden, she concealed him in the chest, and he was dumped on a tjalck and earned over to Gorcum. While on his journey he had the shuddering experience of hearing some one remark that the box was heavy enough to have a man in it; but it was his only danger. A Gorcum friend extricated him; and, disguised as a carpenter armed with a footrule, he set forth on his travels to Antwerp. Once certain that Grotius was safe, his wife informed the guard, and the hue and cry was raised. But it was raised in vain. At first there was a suggestion that the lady should be retained in his stead, but all Holland applauded her deed and she was permitted to go free.

The river, as I have said, must be still much the same as in Grotius's day; while the two towns Gorcum and Worcum cluster about their noble church towers as of old. Worcum is hardly altered; but Gorcum's railway and factories have enlarged her borders. She has now twelve thousand inhabitants, some eleven thousand of whom were in the streets when, the tub having at length crawled back with us, we walked through them to the station.

Odd how one nation's prettiness is another's grotesque. My companion was wearing one of those comely straw hats trimmed with roses which we call Early Victorian, and which the hot summer of 1904 brought into fashion again on account of their peculiar suitability to keep off the sun. In England we think them becoming; upon certain heads they are charming. But no head must wear such a hat at Gorcum unless it would court disaster. The town is gay and spruce, bright as a new pin; the people are outrageous. I suppose that the hat turned down at the precise point at which, according to Gorcum's canons of taste, it should have turned up. Whatever it did was unpardonable, and we had to be informed of the solecism. We were informed in various ways; the men whistled, the women sniggered, the girls laughed, the children shouted and ran beside us. The same hat had been disregarded by the sweet-mannered friendly Middelburgians; it had raised no smile at Breda. At Dordrecht, it is true, eyes had been opened wide; at Bergen-op-Zoom mouths had opened too; but such attention was nothing compared with Gorcum's pains to make two strangers uncomfortable. As it happened, we had philosophy, and the discomfort was very slight. Indeed, after a while, as we ran the gauntlet to the station, annoyance gave way to interest. We found ourselves looking ahead for distant wayfarers who had not yet tasted the rare joy which rippled like a ship's wake behind us. We waited for the ecstatic moment when their faces should light with the joke. Sometimes a mother standing at the door would see us and call to her family to come--and come quickly, if they would not be disappointed! Women, lurking behind Holland's blue gauze blinds, would be seen to break away with a hasty summoning movement. Children down side streets who had just realised their exceptional fortune would be heard shouting the glad tidings to their friends. The porter who wheeled our luggage was stopped again and again to answer questions concerning his fantastic employers.

In course of time--it is a long way to the station--we grew to feel a shade of pique if any one passed us and took no notice. To bulk so hugely in the public eye became a new pleasure. I had not known before what Britannia must feel like on the summit of the largest of the cars in a circus procession.

I am convinced that such costly and equivocal success as the British arms achieved over the Boers had nothing to do with Gorcum's feelings. The town's æsthetic ideals were honestly outraged, and it took the simplest means of making its protest.

We did not mean to wait at the station; having left our luggage there, we had intended to explore the town. But there is a limit even to the passion for notoriety, and we had reached it, passed it. We read and wrote letters in that waiting-room for nearly three hours.

At Gorcum was born, in 1637, Jan van der Heyden, a very attractive painter of street scenes, combining exactitude of detail with rich colour, who used to get Andreas van der Velde to put in the figures. He has a view of Cologne in the National Gallery which is exceedingly pleasing, and a second version in the Wallace Collection. I shall never forget his birthplace. We came into Utrecht in the evening. At Culemberg the country begins to grow very green and rich: smooth meadows and vast woods as far as one can see: plovers all the way. The light transfiguring this scene was exactly the golden light which one sees in Albert Cuyp's most peaceful landscapes.

When I was last on this journey the time was spring, and the sliding, pointed roofs of the ricks were at their lowest, with their four poles high and naked above them, like scaffolding. But now, in August, they were all resting on the top pegs, a solid square tower of hay beneath each; looking in the evening light for all the world as if every farmer had his private Norman church.

The note of Utrecht is superior satisfaction. It has discreet verdant parks, a wonderful campanile, a University, large comfortable houses, carriages and pairs. Its cathedral is the only church in Holland (with the exception of the desecrated fane at Veere) for the privilege of entering which I was not asked to pay. I have an uneasy feeling that it was an oversight, and that if by any chance this statement meets an authoritative eye some one may be removed to one of the penal establishments and steps be taken to collect my debt. But so it was. And yet it is possible that the free right of entrance is intentional; since to charge for a building so unpardonably disfigured would be a hardy action. The Gothic arches have great beauty, but it is impossible from any point to get more than a broken view on account of the high painted wooden walls with which the pews have been enclosed.

The cathedral is only a fragment; the nave fell in, isolating the bell tower, during a tempest in 1674, and by that time all interest in churches as beautiful and sacred buildings having died out of Holland, never to return, no effort was made to restore it. But it must, before the storm, have been superb, and of a vastness superior to any in the country.

I find a very pleasant passage upon Holland's great churches, and indeed upon its best architecture in general, in an essay on Utrecht Cathedral by Mr. L.A. Corbeille. "Gothic churches on a grand scale are as abundant in the Netherlands as they are at home, but to find one of them drawn or described in any of the otherwise comprehensive architectural works, which appear from time to time, is the rarest of experiences. The Hollanders are accused of mere apishness in employing the Gothic style, and of downright dulness in apprehending its import and beauty. Yet a man who has found that bit of Rotterdam which beats Venice; who has seen, from under Delft's lindens on a summer evening, the image of the Oude Kerk's leaning tower in the still canal, and has gone to bed, perchance to awake in the moonlight while the Nieuwe Kerk's many bells are rippling a silver tune over the old roofs and gables; who has drunk his beer full opposite the stadhuis at Leyden, and seen Haarlem's huge church across magnificent miles of gaudy tulips, and watched from a brown-sailed boat on the Zuider Zee a buoy on the horizon grow into the water-gate of Hoorn; who knows his Gouda and Bois-le-duc and Alkmaar and Kampen and Utrecht: this man does not fret over wasted days."

Mr. Corbeille continues, later: "Looking down a side street of Rotterdam at the enormous flank of St. Lawrence's, and again at St. Peter's in Leyden, it seems as if all the bricks in the world have been built up in one place. Apart from their smaller size, bricks appear far more numerous in a wall than do blocks of stone, because they make a stronger contrast with the mortar. In the laborious articulation of these millions of clay blocks one first finds Egypt; then quickly remembers how indigenous it all is, and how characteristic of the untiring Hollander, who rules the waves even more proudly than the Briton, and has cheated them of the very ground beneath his feet. And if sermons may be found in bricks as well as stones, one has a thought while looking at them about Christianity itself. Certainly there is often pitiful littleness and short-comings in the individual believer, just as each separate brick of these millions is stained or worn or fractured; and yet the Christian Church, august and significant, still towers before men; even as these old blocks of clay compile vastly and undeniably in an overpowering whole."

Among a huddle of bad and indifferent pictures in the Kunstliefde Museum is a series of four long paintings by Jan van Scorel (whom we met at Rotterdam), representing a band of pilgrims who travelled from Utrecht to Jerusalem in the sixteenth century. Two of these pictures are reproduced on the opposite page, the principal figure in the lower one--in the middle, in white--being Jan van Scorel himself. The faces are all such as one can believe in; just so, we feel, did the pilgrims look, and what a thousand pities there was no Jan van Scorel to accompany Chaucer! These are the best pictures in Utrecht, which cannot have any great interest in art or it would not allow that tramway through its bell tower. In the reproduction the faces necessarily become very small, but they are still full of character, and one may see the sympathetic hand of a master in all.

Jan van Scorel was only a settler in Utrecht; the most illustrious citizen to whom it gave birth was Paulus Moreelse, but the city has, I think, only one of his pictures, and that not his best. He was born in 1571, and he died at Utrecht in 1638. His portraits are very rich: either he had interesting sitters or he imparted interest to them. Opposite page 40 I have reproduced his portrait of a lady in the Ryks Museum at Amsterdam, which amongst so many fine pictures one may perhaps at the outset treat with too little ceremony, but which undoubtedly will assert itself. It is a picture that, as we say, grows on one: the Unknown Lady becomes more and more mischievous, more and more necessary.

The little Archiepiscopal Museum at Utrecht is as small--or as large--as a museum should be: one can see it comfortably. It has many treasures, all ecclesiastical, and seventy different kinds of lace; but to me it is memorable for the panel portrait of a woman by Jan van Scorel, a very sweet sedate face, beautifully painted, which one would like to coax into a less religious mood.

Utrecht is very proud of a wide avenue of lime trees--a triple avenue, as one often sees in Holland--called the Maliebaan; but more beautiful are the semi-circular Oude and Nieuwe Grachts, with their moat-like canals laving the walls of serene dignified houses, each gained by its own bridge.

At the north end of the Maliebaan is the Hoogeland Park, with a fringe of spacious villas that might be in Kensington; and here is the Antiquarian Museum, notable among its very miscellaneous riches, which resemble the bankrupt stock of a curiosity dealer, for the most elaborate dolls' house in Holland--perhaps in the world. Its date is 1680, and it represents accurately the home of a wealthy aristocratic doll of that day. Nothing was forgotten by the designer of this miniature palace; special paintings, very nude, were made for its salon, and the humblest kitchen utensils are not missing. I thought the most interesting rooms the office where the Major Domo sits at his intricate labours, and the store closet. The museum has many very valuable treasures, but so many poor pictures and articles--all presents or legacies--that one feels that it must be the rule to accept whatever is offered, without any scrutiny of the horse's teeth.

# CHAPTER IV

Delft

To Delft by canal--House-cleaning by immersion--The New Church--William the Silent's tomb--His assassin--The story of the

crime--The tomb of Grotius--Dutch justice--The Old Church--Admiral Tromp--The mission of the broom--The sexton's pipe--Vermeer of

Delft--Lost masterpieces--The wooden petticoat--Modern Delft pottery and old breweries.

I travelled to Delft from Rotterdam in a little steam passenger barge, very long and narrow to fit it for navigating the locks; which, as it is, it scrapes. We should have started exactly at the hour were it not that a very small boy on the bank interrupted one of the crew who was unmooring the boat by asking for a light for his cigar, and the transaction delayed us a minute.

It rained dismally, and I sat in the stuffy cabin, either peering at the country through the window or talking with a young Dutchman, the only other traveller. At one village a boy was engaged in house-cleaning by immersing the furniture, piece by piece, bodily in the canal. Now and then we met a barge in full sail on its way to Rotterdam, or overtook one being towed towards Delft, the man at the rope bent double under what looked like an impossible task.

Little guides to the tombs in both the Old and the New Church of Delft have been prepared for the convenience of visitors by Dr. G. Morre, and translations in English have been made by D. Goslings, both gentlemen, I presume, being local savants. The New Church contains the more honoured dust, for there repose not only William the Silent, who was perhaps the greatest of modern patriots and rulers, but also Grotius.

The tomb of William the Silent is an elaborate erection, of stone and marble, statuary and ornamentation. Justice and Liberty, Religion and Valour, represented by female figures, guard the tomb. It seems to me to lack impressiveness: the man beneath was too fine to need all this display and talent. More imposing is the simplicity of the monument to the great scholar near by. Yet remembering the struggle of William the Silent against Spain and Rome, it is impossible to stand unmoved before the marble figure of the Prince, lying there for all time with his dog at his feet--the dog who, after the noble habit of the finest of such animals, refused food and drink when his master died, and so faded away rather than owe allegiance and affection to a lesser man.

There is an eloquent Latin epitaph in gold letters on the tomb; but a better epitaph is to be found in the last sentence of Motley's great history, perhaps the most perfect last sentence that any book ever had: "As long as he lived, he was the guiding-star of a whole brave nation, and when he died the little children cried in the streets".

Opposite the Old Church is the Gymnasium Publicum. Crossing the court-yard and entering the confronting doorway, one is instantly on the very spot where William the Silent, whose tomb we have just seen, met his death on July 10th, 1584.

The Prince had been living at Delft for a while, in this house, his purpose partly being to be in the city for the christening of his son Frederick Henry. To him on July 8th came a special messenger from the French Court with news of the death of the Duke of Anjou; the messenger, a protégé of the Prince's, according to his own story being Francis Guion, a mild and pious Protestant, whose father had been martyred as a Calvinist. How far removed was the truth Motley shall tell: "Francis Guion, the Calvinist, son of the martyred Calvinist, was in reality Balthazar Gérard, a fanatical Catholic, whose father and mother were still living at Villefans in Burgundy. Before reaching man's estate, he had formed the design of murdering the Prince of Orange, 'who, so long as he lived, seemed like to remain a rebel against the Catholic King, and to make every effort to disturb the repose of the Roman Catholic Apostolic religion'. When but twenty years of age, he had struck his dagger with all his might into a door, exclaiming, as he did so, 'Would that the blow had been in the heart of Orange!'" In 1582, however, the news had gone out that Jaureguy had killed the Prince at Antwerp, and Gérard felt that his mission was at an end. But when the Prince recovered, his murderous enthusiasm redoubled, and he offered himself formally and with matter-of-fact precision to the Prince of Parma as heaven's minister of vengeance. The Prince, who had long been seeking such an emissary, at first declined the alliance: he had become too much the prey of soldiers of fortune who represented themselves to be expert murders but in whom he could put no trust. In Motley's words: "Many unsatisfactory assassins had presented themselves from time to time, and Alexander had paid money in hand to various individuals--Italians, Spaniards, Lorrainers, Scotchmen, Englishmen, who had generally spent the sums received without attempting the job. Others were supposed to be still engaged in the enterprise, and at that moment there were four persons--each unknown to the others, and of different nations--in the city of Delft, seeking to compass the death of William the Silent. Shag-eared, military, hirsute ruffians, ex-captains of free companies and such marauders, were daily offering their services; there was no lack of them, and they had done but little. How should Parma, seeing this obscure, undersized, thin-bearded, runaway clerk before him, expect pith and energy from him? He thought him quite unfit for an enterprise of moment, and declared as much to his secret councillors and to the King."

Gérard, however, had supporters, and in time the Prince of Parma came to take a more favourable view of his qualifications and sincerity, but his confidence was insufficient to warrant him in advancing any money for the purpose. The result was that Gérard, whose dominating idea amounted to mania, proceeded in his own way. His first step was to ingratiate himself with the Prince of Orange. This he did by a series of misrepresentations and fraud, and was recommended by the Prince to the Signeur of Schoneval, who on leaving Delft on a mission to the Duke of Anjou, added him to his suite.

The death of the Duke gave Gérard his chance, and he obtained permission to carry despatches to the Prince of Orange, as we have seen. The Prince received him in his bedroom, after his wont. Motley now relates the tragedy: "Here was an opportunity such as he (Gérard) had never dared to hope for. The arch-enemy to the Church and to the human race, whose death would confer upon his destroyer wealth and nobility in this world, besides a crown of glory in the next, lay unarmed, alone, in bed, before the man who had thirsted seven long years for his blood.

"Balthazar could scarcely control his emotions sufficiently to answer the questions which the Prince addressed to him concerning the death of Anjou, but Orange, deeply engaged with the despatches, and with the reflections which their deeply important contents suggested, did not observe the countenance of the humble Calvinistic exile, who had been recently recommended to his patronage by Villiers. Gérard had, moreover, made no preparation for an interview so entirely unexpected, had come unarmed, and had formed no plan for escape. He was obliged to forego his prey most when within his reach, and after communicating all the information which the Prince required, he was dismissed from the chamber.

"It was Sunday morning, and the bells were tolling for church. Upon leaving the house he loitered about the courtyard, furtively examining the premises, so that a sergeant of halberdiers asked him why he was waiting there. Balthazar meekly replied that he was desirous of attending divine worship in the church opposite, but added, pointing to his shabby and travel-stained attire, that, without at least a new pair of shoes and stockings, he was unfit to join the congregation. Insignificant as ever, the small, pious, dusty stranger excited no suspicion in the mind of the good-natured sergeant. He forthwith spoke of the want of Gérard to an officer, by whom they were communicated to Orange himself, and the Prince instantly ordered a sum of money to be given him. Thus Balthazar obtained from William's charity what Parma's thrift had denied--a fund for carrying out his purpose!

"Next morning, with the money thus procured he purchased a pair of pistols, or small carabines, from a soldier, chaffering long about the price because the vendor could not supply a particular kind of chopped bullets or slugs which he desired. Before the sunset of the following day that soldier had stabbed himself to the heart, and died despairing, on hearing for what purpose the pistols had been bought. "On Tuesday, the 10th of July, 1584, at about half-past twelve, the Prince, with his wife on his arm, and followed by the ladies and gentlemen of his family, was going to the dining-room. William the Silent was dressed upon that day, according to his usual custom, in very plain fashion. He wore a wide-leaved, loosely shaped hat of dark felt, with a silken cord round the crown,--such as had been worn by the Beggars in the early days of the revolt. A high ruff encircled his neck, from which also depended one of the Beggars' medals, with the motto, 'Fidèles au roy jusqu'à la besace,' while a loose surcoat of gray frieze cloth, over a tawny leather doublet, with wide slashed underclothes completed his costume. [1]

"Gérard presented himself at the doorway, and demanded a passport. The Princess, struck with the pale and agitated countenance of the man, anxiously questioned her husband concerning the stranger. The Prince carelessly observed, that 'it was merely a person who came for a passport,' ordering, at the same time, a secretary forthwith to prepare one. The Princess, still not relieved, observed in an undertone that 'she had never seen so villanous a countenance'. Orange, however, not at all impressed with the appearance of Gérard, conducted himself at table with his usual cheerfulness, conversing much with the burgomaster of Leeuwarden, the only guest present at the family dinner, concerning the political and religious aspects of Friesland. At two o'clock the company rose from table. The Prince led the way, intending to pass to his private apartments above. The dining-room, which was on the ground-floor, opened into a little square vestibule which communicated, through an arched passage-way, with the main entrance into the court-yard. This vestibule was also directly at the foot of the wooden staircase leading to the next floor, and was scarcely six feet in width. [2]

"Upon its left side, as one approached the stairway, was an obscure arch, sunk deep in the wall, and completely in the shadow of the door. Behind this arch a portal opened to the narrow lane at the side of the house. The stairs themselves were completely lighted by a large window, half-way up the flight. The Prince came from the dining-room, and began leisurely to ascend. He had only reached the second stair, when a man emerged from the sunken arch, and, standing within a foot or two of him, discharged a pistol full at his heart."

When Jaureguy had fired at the Prince two years earlier, the ball passing through his jaw, the Prince, at he faltered under the shock, cried, "Do not kill him--I forgive him my death!" But he had no time to express any such plea for his assailant after Gérard's cruel shots. "Three balls," says Motley, "entered his body, one of which, passing quite through him, struck with violence against the wall beyond. The Prince exclaimed in French, as he felt the wound, 'O my God, have mercy upon my soul! O my God, have mercy upon this poor people!'

"These were the last words he ever spoke, save that when his sister, Catherine of Schwartzburgh, immediately afterwards asked him if he commended his soul to Jesus Christ, he faintly answered, 'Yes'."

Never has the pistol done worse work. The Prince was only fifty-one; he was full of vigour; his character had never been stronger, his wisdom never more mature. Had he lived a few years longer the country would have been saved years of war and misery.

One may stand to-day exactly where the Prince stood when he was shot. The mark of a bullet in the wall is still shown. The dining-room, from which he had come, now contains a collection of relics of his great career.

Let us return to the New Church, past the statue of Grotius in the great square, in order to look again at that philosopher's memorial. Grotius, who was born at Delft, was extraordinarily precocious. He went to Leyden University and studied under Scaliger when he was eleven; at sixteen he was practising as a lawyer at The Hague. This is D. Goslings' translation of the inscription on his tomb:--

Sacred to Hugo Grotius

The Wonder of Europe, the sole astonishment of the learned world, the splendid work of nature surpassing itself, the summit of genius, the image of virtue, the ornament raised above mankind, to whom the defended honour of true religion gave cedars from the top of Lebanon, whom Mars adorned with laurels and Pallas with olive branches, when he had published the right of war and peace: whom the Thames and the Seine regarded as the wonder of the Dutch, and whom the court of Sweden took in its service: Here lies Grotius. Shun this tomb, ye who do not burn with love of the Muses and your country.

Grotius can hardly have burned with love of the sense of justice of his own country, for reasons with which we are familiar. His sentence of life-long imprisonment, passed by Prince Maurice of Orange, who lies hard by in the same church, was passed in 1618. His escape in the chest (like General Monk in Twenty Years After) was his last deed on Dutch soil.

Thenceforward he lived in Paris and Sweden, England and Germany, writing his De Jure Belli et Pacis and other works. He died in 1645, when Holland claimed him again, as Oxford has claimed Shelley.

The principal tomb in the Old Church of Delft is that of Admiral Tromp, the Dutch Nelson. While quite a child he was at sea with his father off the coast of Guinea when an English cruiser captured the vessel and made him a cabin boy. Tromp, if he felt any resentment, certainly lived to pay it back, for he was our victor in thirty-three naval engagements, the last being the final struggle in the English-Dutch war, when he defeated Monk off Texel in the summer of 1653, and was killed by a bullet in his heart. The battle is depicted in bas-relief on the tomb, but the eye searches the marble in vain for any reminder of the broom which the admiral is said to have lashed to his masthead as a sign to the English that it was his habit to sweep their seas. The story may be a myth, but the Dutch sculptor who omitted to remember it and believe in it is no friend of mine.

This is D. Goslings' translation of Tromp's epitaph:--

For an Eternal Memorial

You, who love the Dutch, virtue and true labour, read and mourn. The ornament of the Dutch people, the formidable in battle, lies low, he who never lay down in his life, and taught by his example that a commander should die standing, he, the love of his fellow-citizens, the terror of his enemies, the wonder of the ocean.

Maarten Harpertszoon Tromp, a name comprehending more praise than this stone can contain, a stone truly too narrow for him, for whom East and West were a school, the sea the occasion of triumph, the whole world the scene of his glory, he, a certain ruin to pirates, the successful protector of commerce; useful through his familiarity, not low; after having ruled the sailors and the soldiers, a rough sort of people, in a fatherly and efficaciously benignant manner; after fifty battles in which he was commander or in which he played a great part; after incredible victories, after the highest honours though below his merits, he at last in the war against the English, nearly victor but certainly not beaten, on the 10th of August, 1653, of the Christian era, at the age of fifty-six years, has ceased to live and to conquer.

The fathers of the United Netherlands have erected this memorial in honour of this highly meritorious hero.

There lie in Delft's Old Church also Pieter Pieterzoon Hein, Lieut.-Admiral of Holland; and Elizabeth van Marnix, wife of the governor of

Bergen-op-Zoom, whose epitaph runs thus:--

Here am I lying, I Elizabeth, born of an illustrious and ancient family, wife to Morgan, I, daughter of Marnix, a name not unknown in the world, which, in spite of time, will always remain. There is virtue enough in having pleased one husband, which his so precious love testifies.

The tomb of Antony van Leeuwenhoek, the inventor of the microscope, is also to be seen in the church. "As everybody, O Wanderer," the epitaph concludes, "has respect for old age and wonderful parts, tread this spot with respect; here grey science lies buried with Leeuwenhoek." Each of the little guide-books, which are given to every purchaser of a ticket to enter the churches, is prefaced by four "Remarks," of which I quote the third and fourth:--

3. Visitors are requested not to bestow gifts on the sexton or his assistants, as the former would lose his situation, if he accepted; he is responsible for his assistants.

4. The sexton or his assistants will treat the visitors with the greatest politeness.

I am not certain about the truth of either of these clauses, particularly the last. Let me explain.

The sexton of the Old Church hurried me past these tombs with some impatience. I should naturally have taken my time, but his attitude of haste made it imperative to do so. Sextons must not be in a hurry. After a while I found out why he chafed: he wanted to smoke. He fumbled his pipe and scraped his boots upon the stones. I studied the monuments with a scrutiny that grew more and more minute and elaborate; and soon his matches were in his hand. I wanted to tell him that if I were the only obstacle he might smoke to his heart's content, but it seemed to be more amusing to watch and wait. My return to the tomb of the ingenious constructor of the microscope settled the question. Probably no one had ever spent more than half a minute on poor Leeuwenhoek before; and when I turned round again the pipe was alight. The sexton also was a changed man: before, he had been taciturn, contemptuous; now he was communicative, gay. He told me that the organist was blind--but none the less a fine player; he led me briskly to the carved pulpit and pointed out, with some exaltation, the figure of Satan with his legs bound. The cincture seemed to give him a sense of security.

In several ways he made it impossible for me to avoid disregarding Clause 3 in the little guide-books; but I feel quite sure that he has not in consequence lost his situation. Delft's greatest painter was Johannes Vermeer, known as Vermeer of Delft, of whom I shall have much to say both at the Hague and Amsterdam. He was born at Delft in 1632, he died there in 1675; and of him but little more is known. It has been said that he studied under Karel Fabritius (also of Delft), but if this is so the term of pupil-age must have been very brief, for Fabritius did not reach Delft (from Rembrandt's studio) until 1652, when Vermeer was twenty, and he was killed in an explosion in 1654. One sees the influence of Fabritius, if at all, most strongly in the beautiful early picture at The Hague, in the grave, grand manner, of Diana? but the influence of Italy is even more noticeable. Fabritius's "Siskin" is hung beneath the new Girl's Head by Vermeer (opposite page 2 of this book), but they have nothing in common. To see how Vermeer derived from Rembrandt viâ Fabritius one must look at the fine head by Fabritius in the Boymans Museum at Rotterdam, so long attributed to Rembrandt, but possessing a certain radiance foreign to him.

How many pictures Vermeer painted between 1653, when he was admitted to the Delft Guild as a master, and 1675, when he died, cannot now be said; but it is reasonable to allot to each of those twenty-three years at least five works. As the known pictures of Vermeer are very few--fewer than forty, I believe--some great discoveries may be in store for the diligent, or, more probably, the lucky.

I have read somewhere--but cannot find the reference again--of a ship that left Holland for Russia in the seventeenth century, carrying a number of paintings by the best artists of that day--particularly, if I remember, Gerard Dou. The vessel foundered and all were lost. It is possible that Vermeer may have been largely represented.

Only comparatively lately has fame come to him, his first prophet being the French critic Thoré (who wrote as "W. Burger"), and his second Mr. Henri Havard, the author of very pleasant books on Holland from which I shall occasionally quote. Both these enthusiasts wrote before the picture opposite page 2 was exhibited, or their ecstasies might have been even more intense. In the Senate House at Delft in 1641 John Evelyn the diarist saw "a mighty vessel of wood, not unlike a butter-churn, which the adventurous woman that hath two husbands at one time is to wear on her shoulders, her head peeping out at the top only, and so led about the town, as a penance". I did not see this; but the punishment was not peculiar to Delft. At Nymwegen these wooden petticoats were famous too.

Nor did I visit the porcelain factory, having very little interest in its modern products. But the old Delft ware no one can admire more than I do. A history of Delft written by Dirk van Bleyswijck and published in 1667, tells us that the rise of the porcelain industry followed the decline of brewing.

The author gives with tears a list of scores of breweries that ceased to exist between 1600 and 1640. All had signs, among them being:--

The Popinjay. The Great Bell. The White Lily. The Three Herrings. The Double Battle-axe. The Three Acorns. The Black Unicorn. The Three Lilies. The Curry-Comb. The Three Hammers. The Double Halberd.

I would rather have explored any of those breweries than the modern Delft factory.

Ireland, by the way, mentions a whimsical sign-board which he saw somewhere in Holland, but which I regret to say I did not find. "It was a tree bearing fruit, and the branches filled with little, naked urchins, seemingly just ripened into life, and crying for succour: beneath, a woman holds up her apron, looking wistfully at the children, as if intreating them to jump into her lap. On inquiry, I found it to be the house of a sworn midwife, with this Dutch inscription prefixed to her name:--

'Vang my, ik zal zoet zyn,' that is, 'Catch me, I'll be a sweet boy'. This new mode of procreation, so truly whimsical, pleased me," Ireland adds, "not a little."

Let me close this chapter by quoting from an essay by my friend, Mr. Belloc, a lyrical description of the Old Church's wonderful wealth of bells: "Thirdly, the very structure of the thing is bells. Here the bells are more even than the soul of a Christian spire; they are its body, too, its whole self. An army of them fills up all the space between the delicate supports and framework of the upper parts. For I know not how many feet, in order, diminishing in actual size and in the perspective also of that triumphant elevation, stand ranks on ranks of bells from the solemn to the wild, from the large to the small, a hundred, or two hundred or a thousand. There is here the prodigality of Brabant and Hainaut and the Batavian blood, a generosity and a productivity in bells without stint, the man who designed it saying: 'Since we are to have bells, let us have bells; not measured out, calculated, expensive, and prudent bells, but careless bells, self-answering multitudinous bells; bells without fear, bells excessive and bells innumerable; bells worthy of the ecstacies that are best thrown out and published in the clashing of bells. For bells are single, like real pleasures, and we will combine such a great number that they may be like the happy and complex life of a man. In a word, let us be noble and scatter our bells and reap a harvest till our town is famous in its bells,' So now all the spire is more than clothed with them; they are more than stuff or ornament: they are an outer and yet sensitive armour, all of bells.

"Nor is the wealth of these bells in their number only, but also in their use--for they are not reserved in any way, out ring tunes and add harmonies at every half and a quarter and at all the hours both by night and by day.

Nor must you imagine that there is any obsession of noise through this; they are far too high and melodious, and (what is more) too thoroughly a part of all the spirit of Delft to be more than a perpetual and half-forgotten impression of continual music; they render its air sacred and fill it with something so akin to an uplifted silence as to leave one--when one has passed from their influence--asking what balm that was which soothed all the harshness of sound about one."

# CHAPTER V

The Hague

Dutch precision--Shaping hands--Nature under control--Willow v. Neptune--The lost star--S'Gravenhage--The Mauritshuis--Rembrandt--The "School of Anatomy"--Jan Vermeer of Delft--The frontispiece--Other pictures--The Municipal Museum--Baron Steengracht's collection--The Mesdag treasures--French romantics at The Hague--The Binnenhof--John van Olden Barneveldt--Man's cruelty to man--The churches--The fish market and first taste of Scheveningen--A crowded street--Holland's reading--The Bosch--The club--The House in the Wood--Mr. "Secretary" Prior--Old marvels--Howell the receptive and Coryate the credulous.

Although often akin to the English, the Dutch character differs from it very noticeably in the matter of precision. The Englishman has little precision; the Dutchman has too much. He bends everything to it. He has at its dictates divided his whole country into parellelograms. Even the rushes in his swamps are governed by the same law. The carelessness of nature is offensive to him; he moulds and trains on every hand, as one may see on the railway journey to The Hague. Trees he endures only so long as they are obedient and equidistant: he likes them in avenues or straight lines; if they grow otherwise they must be pollarded. It is true that he has not touched the Bosch, at The Hague; but since his hands perforce have been kept off its trees, he has run scores of formal straight well-gravelled paths beneath their branches.

This passion for interference grew perhaps from exultation upon successful dealings with the sea. A man who by his own efforts can live in security below sea-level, and graze cattle luxuriantly where sand and pebbles and salt once made a desert, has perhaps the right to feel that everything in nature would be the better for a little manipulation. Eyes accustomed to the careless profusion that one may see even on a short railway journey in England are shocked to find nature so tractable both in land and water. The Dutchman's pruning, however, is not done solely for the satisfaction of exerting control. These millions of pollarded willows which one sees from the line have a deeper significance than might ever be guessed at: it is they that are keeping out Holland's ancient enemy, the sea. In other words, a great part of the basis of the strength of the dykes is imparted by interwoven willow boughs, which are constantly being renewed under the vigilant eyes of the dyke inspectors. For the rest, the inveterate trimming of trees must be a comparatively modern custom, for many of the old landscapes depict careless foliage--Koninck's particularly. And look, for instance, at that wonderful picture--perhaps the finest landscape in Dutch art--Rembrandt's etching "The Three Trees". There is nothing in North Holland to-day as unstudied as that. I doubt if you could now find three trees of such individuality and courage.

When I was first at The Hague, seven years ago, I stayed not, as on my last visit, at the Oude Doelen, which is the most comfortable hotel in Holland, but at a more retired hostelry. It was spacious and antiquated, with large empty rooms, and cool passages, and an air of decay over all. Servants one never saw, nor any waiter proper; one's every need was carried out by a very small and very enthusiastic boy. "Is the hroom good, sare?" he asked, as he flung open the door of the bedroom with a superb flourish. "Is the sham good, sare?" he asked as he laid a pot of preserve on the table. He was the landlady's son or grandson, and a better boy never lived, but his part, for all his spirit and good humour, was a tragic one. For the greatest misfortune that can come upon an hotel-keeper had crushed this house: Bædeker had excised their star!

The landlady moved in the background, a disconsolate figure with a grievance. She waylaid us as we went out and as we came in. Was it not a good hotel? Was not the management excellent? Had we any complaints? And yet--see--once she had a star and now it was gone. Could we not help to regain it? Here was the secret of the grandson's splendid zeal. The little fellow was fighting to hitch the old hotel to a star once more, as Emerson had bidden. Alas, it was in vain; for that was seven years ago, and I see that Bædeker still withholds the distinction. What a variety of misfortune this little world holds! While some of us are indulging our right to be unhappy over a thousand trivial matters, such as illness and disillusion, there are inn-keepers on the Continent who are staggering and struggling under real blows.

I wondered if it were better to have had a star and lost it, than never to have had a star at all. But I did not ask. The old lady's grief was too poignant, her mind too practical, for such questions.

S'Gravenhage or Den Haag, or The Hague as we call it, being the seat of the court, is at once the most civilised and most expensive of the Dutch cities. But it is not conspicuously Dutch, and is interesting rather for its pictures and for its score of historic buildings about the Vyver than for itself. Take away the Vyver and its surrounding treasures and a not very noteworthy European town would remain.

And yet to say so hardly does justice to this city, for it has a character of its own that renders it unique: cosmopolitan and elegant; catholic in its tastes; indulgent to strangers; aristocratic; well-spaced and well built; above all things, bland.

And the Vyver is a jewel set in its midst, beautiful by day and beautiful by night, with fascinating reflections in it at both times, and a special gift for the transmission of bells in a country where bells are really honoured. On its north side is the Vyverberg with pleasant trees and a row of spacious and perfectly self-composed white houses, one of which, at the corner, has in its windows the most exquisite long lace curtains in this country of exquisite long lace curtains.

On the south side are the Binnenhof and the Mauritshuis--in the Mauritshuis being the finest works of the two greatest Dutch painters, Rembrandt of the Rhine and Vermeer of Delft. It is largely by these possessions that The Hague holds her place as a city of distinction. Rembrandt's "School of Anatomy" and Paul Potter's "Bull" are the two pictures by which every one knows the Mauritshuis collection; and it is the bull which maintains the steadier and larger crowd. But it is not a work that interests me. My pictures in the Mauritshuis are above all the "School of Anatomy," Vermeer's "View of Delft," his head of a young girl, and the Jan Steens. We have magnificent Rembrandts in London; but we have nothing quite on the same plane of interest or mastery as the "School of Anatomy ". Holland has not always retained her artists' best, but in the case of Rembrandt and Hals, Jan Steen and Vermeer, she has made no mistakes.

Rembrandt's "School of Anatomy," his "Night Watch," and his portrait of Elizabeth Bas are all in Holland. I can remember no landscape in Holland in the manner of that in our National Gallery in which, in conformity with the taste of certain picture buyers, he dropped in an inessential Tobias and Angel; but for the finest examples of his distinction and power as a painter of men one must go to The Hague and Amsterdam. In the Mauritshuis are sixteen Rembrandts, including the portrait of himself in a steel casque, and (one of my favourites) the head of the demure nun-like and yet merry-hearted Dutch maiden reproduced opposite the next page, which it is impossible to forget and yet difficult, when not looking at it, to recall with any distinctness--as is so often the case with one's friends in real life.

If any large number of visitors to Holland taken at random were asked to name the best of Rembrandt's pictures they would probably say the "Night Watch". But I fancy that a finer quality went to the making of the "School of Anatomy". I fancy that the "School of Anatomy" is the greatest work of art produced by northern Europe.

To Jan Steen and his work we come later, in the chapter on Leyden, but of Vermeer, whom we saw at Delft, this is one place to speak. Of the "View of Delft" there is a reproduction opposite page 58, yet it can convey but little suggestion of its beauty. In the case of the picture opposite page 2 there is only a loss of colour: a great part of its beauty is retained; but the "View of Delft" must be seen in the original before one can speak of it at all. Its appeal is more intimate than any other old Dutch landscape that I know. I say old, because modern painters have a few scenes which soothe one hardly less--two or three of Matthew Maris's, and Mauve's again and again. But before Maris and Mauve came the Barbizon influence; whereas Vermeer had no predecessors, he had to find his delicate path for himself. To explain the charm of the "View of Delft" is beyond my power; but there it is. Before Rembrandt one stands awed, in the presence of an ancient giant; before Vermeer one rejoices, as in the presence of a friend and contemporary.

The head of a young girl, from the same brush, which was left to the nation as recently as 1903, is reproduced opposite page 2. To me it is one of the most beautiful things in Holland. It is, however, in no sense Dutch: the girl is not Dutch, the painting is Dutch only because it is the work of a Dutchman. No other Dutch painter could compass such liquid clarity, such cool surfaces. Indeed, none of the others seem to have tried: a different ideal was theirs. Apart, however, from the question of technique, upon which I am not entitled to speak, the picture has to me human interest beyond description. There is a winning charm in this simple Eastern face that no words of mine can express. All that is hard in the Dutch nature dissolves beneath her reluctant smile. She symbolises the fairest and sweetest things in the Eleven Provinces. She makes Holland sacred ground.

Vermeer, although always a superb craftsman, was not always inspired. In the next room to the "View of Delft" and the girl's head is his "New Testament Allegory," a picture which I think I dislike more than any other, so false seems to me its sentiment and so unattractive its character. Yet the sheer painting of it is little short of miraculous.

Among other Dutch pictures in the Mauritshuis which I should like to mention for their particular charm are Gerard Dou's "Young Housekeeper," to which we come in the chapter on Leyden's painters; Ostade's "Proposal," one of the pleasantest pictures which he ever signed; Ruisdael's "View of Haarlem" and Terburg's portraits. I single these out. But when I think of the marvels of painting that remain, of which I have said not a word, I am only too conscious of the uselessness of such a list. Were this a guide-book I should say more, mentioning also the work of the other schools, not Dutch, notably a head of Jane Seymour by Holbein, a Velasquez, and so forth. But I must not. After the Mauritshuis, the Municipal Museum, which also overlooks the Vyver's placid surface, is a dull place except for the antiquary. In its old views of the city, which are among its most interesting possessions, the evolution of the neighbouring Doelen hotel may be studied by the

curious--from its earliest days, when it was a shooting gallery, to its present state of spaciousness and repute, basking in its prosperity and cherishing the proud knowledge that Peter the Great has slept under its hospitable roof, and that it was there that the Russian delegate resided when, in 1900, the Czar convoked at The Hague the Peace Conference which he was the first to break.

In one room of the Municipal Museum are the palette and easel of Johannes Bosboom, Holland's great painter of churches. His last unfinished sketch rests on the easel. No collection of modern Dutch art is complete without a sombre study of Gothic arches by this great artist. All his work is good, but I saw nothing better than the water-colour drawing in the Boymans Museum at Rotterdam, which is reproduced opposite page 132.

At The Hague one may also see, whenever the family is not in residence, the collection of Baron Steengracht in one of the ample white mansions on the Vyverberg. Most interesting of the pictures to me are Jan Steen's family group, which, however, for all its wonderful drawing, is not in his most interesting manner; a very deft Metsu, "The Sick Child"; a horse by Albert Cuyp; a characteristic group of convivial artists by Adrian Brouwer, including Hals, Ostade, Jan Steen and the painter himself; and--best of all--Terburg's wholly charming "Toilette," an old woman combing the head of a child.

Quite recently the Mesdag Museum has been added to the public exhibitions of The Hague. This is the house of Hendriks Willem Mesdag, the artist, which, with all its Barbizon treasures, with noble generosity he has made over to the nation in his lifetime. Mesdag, who is himself one of the first of living Dutch painters, has been acquiring pictures for many years, and his collection, by representing in every example the taste of a single connoisseur, has thus the additional interest of unity. Mesdag's own paintings are mostly of the sea--a grey sea with a few fishing boats, very true, very quiet and simple. How many times he and James Maris painted Scheveningen's shore probably no one could compute. His best-known work is probably the poster advertising the Harwich and Hook-of-Holland route, in which the two ports are joined by a chain crossing a grey sea--best known, because every one has seen this picture: it is at all the stations; although few, I imagine, have connected with it the name and fame of the Dutch artist and patron of the arts.

In the description of the Ryks collection at Amsterdam I shall say something about the pleasure of choosing one's own particular picture from a gallery. It was amusing to indulge the same humour in the Mesdag Museum: perhaps even more so than at the Ryks, for one is certain that by no means could Vermeer's little picture of "The Reader,"--the woman in the blue jacket--for example, be abstracted from those well-guarded walls, whereas it is just conceivable that one could select from these crowded little Mesdag rooms something that might not be missed. I hesitated long between a delicate Matthew Maris, the very essence of quietude, in which a girl stands by a stove, cooking; Delacroix's wonderful study of dead horses in the desert; a perfect Diaz (No. 114), an old woman in a red shawl by a pool in a wood, with its miracle of lighting; a tender little Daumier, that rare master; a Segantini drenched in sincerity and pity; and a bridge at evening (No. 127) by Jules Dupré. All these are small and could be slipped under the overcoat with the greatest ease!

Having made up my mind I returned to each and lost all my decision. I decided again, and again uncertainty conquered. And then I made a final examination, and chose No. 64--a totally new choice--a little lovely Corot, depicting a stream, two women, much essential greenness, and that liquid light of which Corot had the secret.

But I am not sure that the Diaz (who began by being an old master) is not the more exquisite picture.

For the rest, there are other Corots, among them one of his black night pieces; a little village scene by Troyon; some apples by Courbet, in the grandest manner surely in which apples ever were painted; a Monticelli; a scene of hills by Georges Michel which makes one wish he had painted the Sussex Downs; a beautiful chalk drawing by Millet; some vast silent Daubignys; a few Mauves; a very interesting early James Maris in the manner of Peter de Hooch, and a superb later James Maris--wet sand and a windy sky.

The flower of the French romantic school is represented here, brought together by a collector with a sure eye. No visitor to The Hague who cares anything for painting should miss it; and indeed no visitor who cares nothing for painting should miss it, for it may lure him to wiser ways.

The Binnenhof is a mass of medieval and later buildings extending along the south side of the Vyver, which was indeed once a part of its moat. The most attractive view of it is from the north side of the Vyver, with the long broken line of roof and gable and turret reflected in the water. The nucleus of the Binnenhof was the castle or palace of William II., Count of Holland in the thirteenth century--also Emperor of Germany and father of Florence V., who built the great hall of the knights (into which, however, one may penetrate only on Thursdays), and whose tomb we shall see in Alkmaar church. The Stadtholders made the Binnenhof their headquarters; but the present Royal Palace is half a mile north-west of it. Other buildings have been added from time to time, and the trams are now allowed to rush through with their bells jangling the while. The desecration is not so glaring as at Utrecht, but it seems thoroughly wrong--as though we were to permit a line to traverse Dean's Yard at Westminster. A more appropriate sanction is that extended to one or two dealers in old books and prints who have their stalls in the Binnenhof's cloisters.

It was in the Binnenhof that the scaffold stood on which John van Barneveldt was beheaded in 1619, the almost inevitable result of his long period of differences with the Stadtholder Maurice, son of William the Silent. His arrest, as we have seen, followed the Synod of Dort, Grotius being also removed by force. Barneveldt's imprisonment, trial and execution resemble Spanish methods of injustice more closely than one likes to think. I quote Davies' fine account of the old statesman's last moments: "Leaning on his staff, and with his servant on the other side to support his steps, grown feeble with age, Barneveldt walked composedly to the place of execution, prepared before the great saloon of the court-house. If, as it is not improbable, at the approach of death in the midst of life and health, when the intellect is in full vigour, and every nerve, sense and fibre is strung to the highest pitch of tension, a foretaste of that which is to come is sometimes given to man, and his over-wrought mind is enabled to grasp at one single effort the events of his whole past life--if, at this moment and on this spot, where Barneveldt was now to suffer a felon's death,--where he had first held out his fostering hand to the infant republic, and infused into it strength and vigour to conquer the giant of Europe,-- where he had been humbly sued for peace by the oppressor of his country,--where the ambassadors of the most powerful sovereigns had vied with each other in soliciting his favour and support,--where the wise, the eloquent, and the learned, had bowed in deference to his master-spirit;--if, at this moment, the memory of all his long and glorious career on earth flashed upon his mind in fearful contrast to the present reality, with how deep feeling must he have uttered the exclamation as he ascended the scaffold, 'Oh God! what then is man?'

"Here he was compelled to suffer the last petty indignity that man could heap upon him. Aged and infirm as he was, neither stool nor cushion had been provided to mitigate the sense of bodily weakness as he performed the last duties of mortal life; and kneeling down on the bare boards, he was supported by his servant, while the minister, John Lamotius, delivered a prayer. When prepared for the block, he turned to the spectators and said, with a loud and firm voice, 'My friends, believe not that I am a traitor. I have lived a good patriot, and such I die.' He then, with his own hands, drew his cap over his eyes, and bidding the executioner 'be quick,' bowed his venerable head to the stroke.

"The populace, from various feelings, some inspired by hatred, some by affection, dipped their handkerchiefs in his blood, or carried away morsels of the blood-stained wood and sand; a few were even found to sell these as relics. The body and head were laid in a coffin and buried decently, but with little ceremony, at the court church of the Hague. "The States of Holland rendered to his memory that justice which he had been denied while living, by the words in which they recorded his death. After stating the time and manner of it, and his long period of service to his country, the resolution concludes, 'a man of great activity, diligence, memory, and conduct; yea, remarkable in every respect. Let him that thinketh he standeth take heed lest he fall; and may God be merciful to his soul.'"

A very beautiful story is told of Barneveldt's widow. Her son plotting to avenge his father and crush the Stadtholder was discovered and imprisoned.

His mother visited Maurice to ask his pardon. "Why," said he, "how is this--you value your son more than your husband! You did not ask pardon for him." "No," said Barneveldt's widow; "I did not ask pardon for my husband, because he was innocent; I ask pardon for my son, because he is guilty."

Prince Maurice never recovered from the error--to put for the moment no worse epithet to it--of the death of Barneveldt. He had killed his best counsellor; thenceforward his power diminished; and with every rebuff he who had abandoned his first adviser complained that God had abandoned him. Davies sums up the case thus: "The escutcheon of Maurice is bright with the record of many a deed of glory; the fabric of his country's greatness raised by his father, strengthened and beautified by himself; her armies created the masters of military science to the civilized world; her States the centre and mainspring of its negotiations; her proud foe reduced to sue humbly at her feet. But there is one dark, deep stain on which the eye of posterity, unheeding the surrounding radiance, is constantly fixed: it is the blood of Barneveldt."

The Binnenhof leads to the Buitenhof, a large open space, the old gateway to which is the Gevangenpoort prison--scene of another shameful deed in the history of Holland, the death of John and Cornelius de Witt. The massacre occurred two hundred and thirty-three years ago-- in 1672.

Cornelius de Witt was wrongfully accused of an attempt to procure the assassination of the Stadtholder, William III. To him, in his cell in the Gevangenpoort, came, on 22nd August, John de Witt, late Grand Pensionary, brought hither by a bogus message.

I quote from Davies, who elsewhere makes it clear that (as Dumas says) William III was privy to the crime: "His friends, fearful of some treachery, besought him to pause and inquire into the truth of the summons before he obeyed it; and his only daughter threw herself at his feet, and implored him with floods of tears not to risk unnecessarily a life so precious. But his anxiety for his brother, with whom he had ever lived on terms of the tenderest affection, proved stronger than their remonstrances; and setting out on foot, attended by his servant and two secretaries, he hastened to the prison. On seeing him, Cornelius de Witt exclaimed in astonishment, 'My brother, what do you here?' 'Did you not then send for me?' he asked; and receiving an answer in the negative, 'Then,' rejoined he, 'we are lost'.

"During this time one of the judges sent for Tichelaar, and suggested to him that he should incite the people not to suffer a villain who had intended to murder the Prince to go unpunished. True to his instructions, the miscreant spread among the crowd collected before the prison doors the report, that the torture inflicted on Cornelius de Witt was a mere pretence, and that he had only escaped the death he deserved because the judges favoured his crime. Then, entering the gaol, he presented himself at the window, and exclaimed to the crowd below, 'The dog and his brother are going out of prison! Now is your time; revenge yourselves on these two knaves, and then on thirty more, their accomplices.'

"The populace received his address with shouts and cries of 'To arms, to arms! Treason, treason!' and pressed in a still denser crowd towards the prison door. The States of Holland, immediately on information of the tumult, sent three troops of cavalry, in garrison at the Hague, for the protection of the gaol, and called out to arms six companies of burgher guards. But in the latter they only added fresh hosts to the enemies of the unfortunate captives. One company in especial, called the 'Company of the Blue Flag,' was animated with a spirit of deadly vengeance against them; its leader, Verhoef, having that morning loaded his musket with a determination either to kill the De Witts or perish in the attempt. They pressed forward towards the prison, but were driven back by the determined appearance of the cavalry, commanded by the Count de Tilly.

"So long as these troops remained, it was evident that the fell purpose of the rioters was impracticable. Accordingly, a report was raised that a band of peasants and sailors was coming to plunder The Hague; and two captains of the burgher guards took occasion from thence to demand of the Council of State, that the soldiers should be drawn off from their station, in order to protect the houses from pillage. First a verbal order, and on Tilly's refusing obedience to such, a written one, was sent, commanding him to divide his troops into four detachments, and post them upon the bridges leading into the town. 'I shall obey,' said he, as he perused the mandate; 'but it is the death-warrant of the brothers.'

"His anticipations were too soon realized. No sooner had he departed than the rioters were supplied by some of those mysterious agents who were actively employed throughout the whole of these transactions, with wine, brandy, and other incitements to inflame their already maddening fury. Led on by Verhoef and one Van Bankhem, a sheriff of The Hague, they assailed the prison door with axes and sledge-hammers, threatening to kill all the inmates if it were not instantly opened. Terrified, or corrupted, the gaoler obeyed their behests. On gaining admittance they rushed to an upper room, where they found their victims, who had throughout the whole of the tumult maintained the greatest composure. The bailiff, reduced to a state of extreme debility by the torture, was reclining on his bed; his brother was seated near him, reading the Bible. They forced them to rise and follow them 'to the place,' as they said, 'where criminals were executed'.

"Having taken a tender leave of each other, they began to descend the stairs, Cornelius de Witt leaning on his brother for support. They had not advanced above two or three paces when a heavy blow on the head from behind precipitated the former to the bottom. He was then dragged a short distance towards the street, trampled under foot, and beaten to death.

Meanwhile, John de Witt, after receiving a severe wound on the head with the butt-end of a musket, was brought by Verhoef, bleeding and bare-headed, before the furious multitude. One Van Soenen immediately thrust a pike into his face, while another of the miscreants shot him in the neck, exclaiming as he fell, 'There goes down the Perpetual Edict'. Raising himself on his knees, the sufferer lifted up his hands and eyes to heaven in deep and earnest prayer. At that moment, one Verhagen struck him with his musket. Hundreds followed his example, and the cruel massacre was completed.

"Barbarities too dreadful for utterance or contemplation, all that phrenzied passion or brutal ferocity could suggest, were perpetrated on the bodies of these noble and virtuous citizens; nor was it till night put an end to the butchery, that their friends were permitted to convey their mangled remains to a secret and obscure tomb."

In the Nieuwe Kerk at The Hague the tomb of the De Witts may be seen and honoured.

The Gevangenpoort is well worth a visit. One passes tortuously from cell to cell--most of them associated with some famous breaker of the laws of God or man, principally of man. Here you may see a stone hollowed by the drops of water that plashed from the prisoner's head, on which they were timed to fall at intervals of a few seconds--a form of torture imported, I believe, from China, and after some hours ending inevitably in madness and death. Beside such a refinement the rack is a mere trifle and the Gevangenpoort's branding irons and thumb screws become only toys. A block, retaining the cuts made by the axe after it had crashed through the offending neck, is also shown; and the names of prisoners written in their blood on the walls may be traced. The building is a monument in stone of what man can do to man in the name of justice.

I referred just now to the Nieuwe Kerk, the resting-place of the De Witts. There lies also their contemporary, Spinoza, whose home at Rynsburg we shall pass on our way to Katwyk from Leyden. His house at The Hague still stands--near his statue. The Groote Kerk is older; but neither church is particularly interesting. From the Groote Kerk's tower one may, however, see a vast deal of country around The Hague--a landscape containing much greenery--and in the west the architectural monsters of Scheveningen only too visible. We shall reach Scheveningen in the next chapter, but while at The Hague it is amusing to visit the fish market in order to have sight of the good women of that town clustered about the stalls in their peculiar costume. They are Scheveningen's best. The adjoining stadhuis is a very interesting example of Dutch architecture.

The Hague has excellent shops, and one street--the Lange Pooten--more crowded in the evening, particularly on Sunday evening, than any I know. Every Dutch town has certain crowded streets in the evening, because to walk up and down after dinner is the national form of recreation. There are in the large cities a few theatres and music halls, and in the smaller, concerts in the summer; but for the most part the streets and the cafés are the great attraction. Each town has one street above all others which is frequented in this way. At The Hague it is the Lange Pooten, running into Spui Straat; at Amsterdam it is Kalverstraat.

Dutch shops are not very interesting, and the book-shops in particular are a disappointment. This is because it is not a reading people. The newspapers are sound and

41

practical before all things: business before pleasure is their motto; and native literature is not fostered. Publishers who bring out new Dutch books usually do so on the old subscription plan. But the book-shops testify to the popularity of translations from other nations and also of foreign books in the original. The latest French and German fiction is always obtainable. Among translations from the English in 1904 I noticed a considerable number of copies of the Sherlock Holmes tales and also of two or three of Miss Corelli's works. These for adults; for boys the reading par excellence was a serial romance, in weekly or monthly parts, entitled "De Wilsons en de Ring des Doods of het Spoor van pen Diamenten". The Wilsons, I gather, have been having a great run in Holland. A lurid scene in Maiden Lane was on the cover. Another story which seemed to be popular had the engaging title "Beleaguered by Jaguars".

The Hague is very proud of the Bosch--the great wood to the east of the city, with a few deer and many tall and unpollarded trees, where one may walk and ride or drive very pleasantly. The Bosch has no restaurant within its boundaries. I mention this in order to save the reader the mortification of being conducted by a polite but firm waiter back to the gates of the pavilion in which he may reasonably have supposed he was as much entitled to order tea as any of the groups enjoying that beverage at the little tables within the enclosure, whose happiness had indeed led him to enter it. They are, however, members of a club, to which he has no more right of entry than any Dutch stranger would have to the Athenæum.

The Huis ten Bosch, or House in the Wood, which all good travellers must explore, is at the extreme eastern end of the Bosch, with pleasure grounds of its own, including a lake where royal skating parties are held. This very charming royal residence, now only occasionally occupied, is well worth seeing for its Chinese and Japanese decorations alone--apart from historical associations and mural paintings. For mural paintings unless they are very quiet I must confess to caring nothing, nor does a bed on which a temporal prince breathed his last, or his first, move me to any degree of interest; but on the walls of one room of the House in the Wood is some of the most charming Chinese embroidery I ever saw, while another is decorated in blue and white of exquisite delicacy. With these gracious schemes of upholstery I shall always associate the Huis ten Bosch.

At Leyden we shall find traces of Oliver Goldsmith: here at The Hague one may think of Mat. Prior, who was secretary to our Ambassador for some years and even wrote a copy of spritely verses on the subject.

THE SECRETARY.

Written at The Hague, 1696.

With labour assiduous due pleasure I mix, And in one day atone for the bus'ness of six. In a little Dutch chaise, on a Saturday night, On my left hand my Horace, a nymph on my right: No memoirs to compose, and no post-boy to move, That on Sunday may hinder the softness of love; For her, neither visits, nor parties at tea, Nor the long-winded cant of a dull refugee: This night and the next shall be hers, shall be mine To good or ill-fortune the third we resign. Thus scorning the world, and superior to Fate, I drive in my car in professional state; So with Phia thro' Athens Pisistratus rode, Men thought her Minerva, and him a new god. But why should I stories of Athens rehearse, Where people knew love, and were partial to verse, Since none can with justice my pleasures oppose In Holland half-drownèd in int'rest and prose? By Greece and past ages what need I be tried When The Hague and the present are both on my side? And is it enough for the joys of the day To think what Anacreon or Sappho would say, When good

Vandergoes and his provident Vrow, As they gaze on my triumph, do freely allow, That, search all the province, you'll find no man dar is So blest as the Englishen Heer Secretár is?

Let me close this rambling account of The Hague with a passage from James Howell, in one of his conspicuously elaborate Familiar Letters, written in 1622, describing some of the odd things to be seen at that day in or about the Dutch city: "We went afterwards to the Hague, where there are hard by, though in several places, two wonderful things to be seen, the one of Art, the other of Nature; that of Art is a Waggon or Ship, or a monster mixt of both like the Hippocentaure who was half man and half horse; this Engin hath wheels and sails that will hold above twenty people, and goes with the wind, being drawn or mov'd by nothing else, and will run, the wind being good, and the sails hois'd up, above fifteen miles an hour upon the even hard sands: they say this Invention was found out to entertain Spinola when he came thither to treat of the last Truce." Upon this wonder, which I did not see, civilisation has now improved, the wind being but a captious and untrustworthy servant compared with petrol or steam. None the less there is still a very rapid wheeled ship at Zandvoort.

But the record of Howell's other wonder is visible still. He continues: "That wonder of Nature is a Church-monument, where an Earl and a Lady are engraven with 365 children about them, which were all delivered at one birth; they were half male, half female; the two Basons in which they were Christened hang still in the Church, and the Bishop's Name who did it; and the story of this Miracle, with the year and the day of the month mentioned, which is not yet 200 years ago; and the story is this: That the Countess walking about her door after dinner, there came a Begger-woman with two Children upon her back to beg alms, the Countess asking whether those children were her own, she answer'd, she had them both at one birth, and by one Father, who was her husband. The Countess would not only not give her any alms, but reviled her bitterly, saying, it was impossible for one man to get two children at once. The Begger-woman being thus provok'd with ill words, and without alms, fell to imprecations, that it should please God to show His judgment upon her, and that she might bear at one birth as many children as there be days in the year, which she did before the same year's end, having never born child before."

The legend was naturally popular in a land of large families, and it was certainly credited without any reservation for many years. In England the rabbit-breeding woman of Dorking had her adherents too. What the beggar really wished for the Dutch lady was as many children at one birth as there were days in the year in which the conversation occurred--namely three, for the encounter was on January 3rd. Or so I have somewhere read. But it is more amusing to believe in the greater number, especially as a Dutch author has put it on record that he saw the children with his own eyes. They were of the size of shrimps, and were baptised either singly or collectively by Guy, Bishop of Utrecht. All the boys were named John and all the girls Elizabeth, They died the same day.

Thomas Coryate of the Crudities, who also tells the tale, believed it implicitly. "This strange history," he says, "will seem incredible (I suppose) to all readers. But it is so absolutely and undoubtedly true as nothing in the world more."

And here, hand in hand with Veritas, we leave The Hague.

# CHAPTER VI

Scheveningen and Katwyk

The Dutch heaven--Huyghens' road--Sorgh Vliet's builder--Jacob Cats--Homely wisdom--President Kruger--A monstrous resort--Giant snails--The black-headed mannikins--The etiquette of petticoats--Katwyk--The old Rhine--Noordwyk--Noordwyk-Binnen.

Good Dutchmen when they die go to Scheveningen; but my heaven is elsewhere. To go thither is, however, no calamity, so long as one chooses the old road. It is being there that so lowers the spirits. The Oude Scheveningen Weg is perhaps the pleasantest, and certainly the shadiest, road in Holland: not one avenue but many, straight as a line in Euclid. On either side is a spreading wood, among the trees of which, on the left hand, as one leaves The Hague, is Sorgh Vliet, once the retreat of old Jacob Cats, lately one of the residences of a royal Duke, and now sold to a building company. The road dates from 1666, its projector being Constantin Huyghens, poet and statesman, whose statue may be seen at the half-way halting-place. By the time this is reached the charm of the road is nearly over: thenceforward it is all villas and Scheveningen.

But we must pause for a little while at Sorgh Vliet (which has the same meaning as Sans Souci), where two hundred years ago lived in genial retirement the writer who best represents the shrewd sagacity of the Dutch character--Jacob Cats, or Vader Cats as he was affectionately called, the author of the Dutch "Household Bible," a huge miscellaneous collection of wise saws and modern instances, humour and satire, upon all the businesses of life.

Mr. Austin Dobson, who leaves grains of gold on all he touches, has described in his Side-Walk Studies the huge, illustrated edition of Cats' Works (Amsterdam, 1655) which is held sacred in all rightly constituted old-fashioned Dutch households. I have seen it at the British Museum, and it seems to me to be one of the best picture-books in the world. As Mr. Dobson says, the life of old Holland is reproduced in it. "What would one not give for such an illustrated copy of Shakespeare! In these pages of Jacob Cats we have the authentic Holland of the seventeenth century:--its vanes and spires and steep-roofed houses; its gardens with their geometric tulip-beds, their formally-clipped alleys and arches, their shining parallelograms of water. Here are its old-fashioned interiors, with the deep fire-places and queer andirons, the huge four-posters, the prim portraits on the wall, the great brass-clamped coffers and carved armories for the ruffs and starched collars and stiff farthingales of the women. In one picture you may see the careful housewife mournfully inspecting a moth-eaten garment which she has just taken from a chest that Wardour Street might envy; in another she is energetically cuffing the 'foolish fat scullion,' who has let the spotted Dalmatian coach-dog overturn the cauldron at the fire. Here an old crone, with her spectacles on, is cautiously probing the contents of the said cauldron with a fork; here the mistress of the house is peeling pears; here the plump and soft-hearted cheese-wife is entertaining an admirer--outside there are pictures as vivid. Here are the clumsy leather-topped coach with its masked occupant and stumbling horses; the towed trekschuit, with its merry freight, sliding swiftly through the low-lying landscape; the windy mole, stretching seaward, with its blown and flaring beacon-fire. Here again in the street is the toy-shop with its open front and store of mimic drums and halberds for the martial little burghers; here are the fruiteress with her stall of grapes and melons, the rat-catcher with his string of trophies, the fowler and his clap-net, the furrier with his stock of skins."

44

In 1860 a number of Van der Venne's best pictures were redrawn by John Leighton to accompany translations of the fables by Richard Pigot. As a taste of Cats' quality I quote two of the pieces. Why the pictures should have been redrawn when they might have been reproduced exactly is beyond my understanding. This is one poem:--

LIKE MELONS, FRIENDS ARE TO BE FOUND IN PLENTY OF WHICH NOT EVEN ONE IS GOOD IN TWENTY. In choosing Friends, it's requisite to use The self-same care as when we Melons choose: No one in haste a Melon ever buys, Nor makes his choice till three or four he tries; And oft indeed when purchasing this fruit, Before the buyer can find one to suit, He's e'en obliged t' examine half a score, And p'rhaps not find one when his search is o'er. Be cautious how you choose a friend; For Friendships that are lightly made, Have seldom any other end Than grief to see one's trust betray'd!

And here is another:--

SMOKE IS THE FOOD OF LOVERS.

When Cupid open'd Shop, the Trade he chose Was just the very one you might suppose. Love keep a shop?--his trade, Oh! quickly name! A Dealer in tobacco--Fie for shame! No less than true, and set aside all joke, From oldest time he ever dealt in Smoke; Than Smoke, no other thing he sold, or made; Smoke all the substance of his stock in trade; His Capital all Smoke, Smoke all his store, 'Twas nothing else; but Lovers ask no more-- And thousands enter daily at his door! Hence it was ever, and it e'er will be The trade most suited to his faculty:-- Fed by the vapours of their heart's desire, No other food his Votaries require; For, that they seek--The Favour of the Fair, Is unsubstantial as the Smoke and air.

From these rhymes, with their home-spun philosophy, one might assume Cats to have been merely a witty peasant. But he was a man of the highest culture, a great jurist, twice ambassador to England, where Charles I. laid his sword on his shoulder and bade him rise Sir Jacob, a traveller and the friend of the best intellects. From an interesting article on Dutch poetry in an old Foreign Quarterly Review I take an account of the aphorist: "Vondel had for his contemporary a man, of whose popularity we can hardly give an idea, unless we say that to speak Dutch and to have learnt Cats by heart, are almost the same thing. Old Father Jacob Cats--(we beg to apologize for his unhappy name--and know not why, like the rest of his countrymen, he did not euphonize it into some well-sounding epithet, taken from Greece or Rome--Elouros, for example, or Felisius; Catsius was ventured upon by his contemporaries, but the honest grey-beard stuck to his paternities)--was a man of practical wisdom--great experience--much travel--considerable learning--and wonderful fluency. He had occupied high offices of state, and retired a patriarch amidst children and children's children, to that agreeable retreat which we mentioned as not far from The Hague, where we have often dreamed his sober and serious--but withal cheerful and happy, spirit, might still preside. His moralities are sometimes prolix, and sometimes rather dull. He often sweeps the bloom away from the imaginative anticipations of youth--and in that does little service. He will have everything substantial, useful, permanent. He has no other notion of love than that it is meant to make good husbands and wives, and to produce painstaking and obedient children.

"His poetry is rhymed counsel--kind, wise, and good. He calculates all results, and has no mercy for thoughts, or feelings, or actions, which leave behind them weariness, regret or misery. His volumes are a storehouse of prudence and worldly wisdom. For every state of life he has fit lessons, so nicely dovetailed into rhyme, that the morality seems made expressly for the language, or the language for the morality. His thoughts--all running about among the duties of life--voluntarily move in harmonious numbers, as if to think and to rhyme were one solitary attribute. For the nurse who wants a song for her babe--the boy who is tormented by the dread of the birch--the youth whose beard begins to grow--the lover who desires a posey for his lady's ring--for the husband--father--grandsire--for all there is a store--to encourage--to console--and to be grateful for. The titles of his works are indices to their contents. Among them are De Ouderdom, Old Age; Buyten Leven, Out-of-Doors Life; Hofgedachten, Garden Thoughts; Gedachten op Slapelooze Nachten, Thoughts of Sleepless Nights; Trouwring, Marriage Ring; Zelfstrijt, Self-struggle, etc. Never was a poet so essentially the poet of the people. He is always intelligible--always sensible--and, as was well said of him by Kruijff,

Smiling he teaches truth, and sporting wins to virtue."

When President Kruger died last year the memoirs of him agreed in fixing upon the Bible as his only reading. But I am certain he knew Vader Cats by heart too. If ever a master had a faithful pupil, Vader Cats had one in Oom Paul. The vivid yet homely metaphors and allegories in which Oom Paul conveyed so many of his thoughts were drawn from the same source as the emblems of Vader Cats. Both had the Æsopian gift.

We have no one English writer with whom to compare Cats; but a syndicate formed of Fuller and Burton, Cobbett and Quarles might produce something akin.

Scheveningen is half squalid town, half monstrous pleasure resort. Upon its sea ramparts are a series of gigantic buildings, greatest of which is the Curhaus, where the best music in Holland is to be heard. Its pier and its promenade are not at the first glimpse unlike Brighton's; but the vast buildings have no counterpart with us, except perhaps at Blackpool. What is, however, peculiar to Scheveningen is its expanse of sand covered with sentry-box wicker chairs. To stand on the pier on a fine day in the season and look down on these thousands of chairs and people is to receive an impression of insect-like activity that I think cannot be equalled.

Immovable as they are, the chairs seem to add to the restlessness of the seething mass. What a visitor from Mars would make of it is a mystery; but he could hardly fail to connect chair and occupant. Here, he would say, is surely the abode of giant snails!

On a windy day the chairs must be of great use; but in heat they seem to me too vertical and too hard. One must, however, either sit in them or lie upon sand. There is not a pebble on the whole coast: indeed there is not a pebble in Holland. Life after lying upon sand can become to some of us a burden almost too difficult to bear; but the Dutch holiday-maker does not seem to find it so. As for the children, they are truly in Paradise. There can be no sand better to dig in than that of Scheveningen; and they dig in it all day. A favourite game seems to be to surround the parental sentry-boxes with a fosse. Every family has its castle, and every castle its moat.

I have been twice to Scheveningen, and on each occasion I acquired beneath its glittering magnitude a sense of depression. That leaven of tenderness which every collection of human beings must have was harder to find at Scheveningen than anywhere in Holland--everything was so ordered, so organised, for pleasure, pleasure at any price, pleasure almost at the point of the bayonet.

But on the second occasion one little incident saved the day--an encounter with a strolling bird-fancier who dealt in Black-Headed Mannikins. Two of these tiny brisk birds, in

46

their Quaker black and brown, sat upon his cane to attract purchasers. They fluttered to his finger, perched on his hat, simulated death in the palm of his hand, and went through other evolutions with the speed of thought and the bright spontaneous alacrity possible only to a small loyal bird. These, however, were not for sale: these were decoys; the saleable birds lay, packed far too close, in little wooden boxes in the man's bag. And Scheveningen to me means no longer a mile of palaces, no longer a "hot huddle of humanity" on the sand among myriad sentry-boxes: its symbol is just two Black-Headed Mannikins.

From the Curhaus it is better to return to the Hague by electric tram along the new road. Save for passing a field where the fishwives of Scheveningen in their blue shawls spread and mend their nets, this road is dull and suburban; but from it, when the light is failing, a view of Scheveningen's domes and spires may be gained which, softened and made mysterious by the gloaming, translates the chief watering-place of Holland into an Eastern city of romance.

The fishwives of Scheveningen, I am told, carry the art of petticoat wearing to a higher point than any of their sisters. The appearance of the homing fleet in the offing is a signal for as many as thirty of these garments to be put on as a mark of welcome to a returning husband.

Probably no shore anywhere in the world has been so often painted as that of Scheveningen--ever since the painting of landscape seemed a worthy pursuit. James Maris' pictures of Scheveningen's wet sand, grey sea, and huge flat-bottomed ships must run into scores; Mesdag's too. Perhaps it was the artists that prevailed on the fishermen to wear crimson knickerbockers--the note of warm colour that the scene demands. Here, although it is separated from Scheveningen by some miles of sand, I should like to say something of Katwyk--which is Leyden's marine resort. A steam-tram carries people thither many times a day. The rail, when first I travelled upon it, in April, ran through tulips; in August, when I was there again, the patches of scarlet and orange had given way to acres of massive purple-green cabbages which, in the evening light, were vastly more beautiful.

At Rynsburg, one of the villages on the way, dwelt in 1650-51 Benedict Spinoza, the philosopher, and there he wrote his abridgement of the Meditations of Descartes, his master in philosophy, who had for a while lived close by at Endegeest. Spinoza, who was born at Amsterdam in 1632, died in 1677. His house at Rynsburg, which he shared with a Colleginat (one of a sect of Remonstrants who had their headquarters there) is now a Spinoza museum; his statue is at The Hague.

Katwyk-aan-Zee is a compact little pleasure resort with the usual fantastic childish villas. Its most interesting possession is the mouth of the Old Rhine, now restricted by a canal and controlled by locks. There is perhaps no better example of the Dutch power over water than the contrast between the present narrow canal through which the river must disembogue and the unprofitable marsh which once spread here. The locks, which are nearly a hundred years old, were among the works of the engineer Conrad, whose monument is in Haarlem church.

From the Old Rhine's mouth to Noordwyk is a lonely but very bracing walk of three miles along the sand, with the dunes on one's right hand and the sea on one's left. One may meet perhaps a few shell gatherers, but no one else. We drove before us all the way a white company consisting of a score of gulls, twice as many tern, two oyster catchers and one curlew. They rose and settled, rose and settled, always some thirty yards away, until Noordwyk was reached, when we left them behind. Never was a Japanese screen so realised as by these birds against the pearl grey sea and yellow sand. Katwyk is more cheery than Noordwyk; but Noordwyk has a prettier street--indeed, in its old part there is no prettier street in Holland in the light of sunset. As Hastings is to Eastbourne, so is Katwyk to Noordwyk; Scheveningen is Brighton, Yarmouth, and Blackpool in one. A very pretty lace cap is worn at Noordwyk by villagers and visitors alike, to hold the hair against the west wind.

From Noordwyk we walked to Noordwyk-Binnen, the real town, parent of the seaside resort; and there, at a table at the side of the main street, by an avenue so leafy as to exclude even glints of the sky, we sipped something Dutch whose name I could not assimilate, and waited for the tram for Leyden. It was the greenest tunnel I ever saw.

# CHAPTER VII

Leyden

Steam-trams--Holland for the people--Quiet Leyden--The Meermansburg--Leyden's museums--The call of the open--Oliver Goldsmith--A view of the Dutch--"Polite Learning"--"The Traveller"--James Howell--John Evelyn and the Burgundian

Jew--Colloquia Peripatetica--St. Peter's and St. Pancras's--The

Kermis--Drinking in Holland--Poffertjes and Wafelen--America's master.

We travelled to Leyden from The Hague by the steam-tram, through cheerful domestic surroundings, past little Englishy cottages and gardens. It was Sunday morning, and the villagers of Voorburg and Voorschoten and the other little places en route were idle and gay.

In England light railways are a rarity; Holland is covered with a net-work of them. The little trains rush along the roads all over the country, while the roadside willows rock in their eddying wake. To stand on the steam-tram footboard is one very good way to see Holland. In England of course we can never have such conveniences, England being a free country in which individual rights come first. But Holland exists for the State, and such an idea as the depreciation or ruin of property by running a tram line over it has never suggested itself. It is true that when the new electric tramway between Amsterdam and Haarlem was projected, the comic papers came to the defence of outraged Nature; but they did not really mean it, as the æsthetic minority in England would have meant it.

The steam-tram journeys are always interesting; and my advice to a traveller in Holland is to make as much use of them as he can. This is quite simple as their time-tables are included in the official Reisgids. I like them at all times; but best perhaps when one has to wait in the heart of some quiet village for the other tram to come up. There is something very soothing and attractive in these sudden cessations of noise and movement in the midst of a totally strange community. Leyden is a paradise of clean, quiet streets--a city of professors, students and soldiers. It has, I think, the prettiest red roofs in any considerable Dutch town: not prettier than Veere's, but Veere is now only a village.

Philosophers surely live here: book-worms to whom yesterday, to-day and to-morrow are one. The sense of commercial enterprise dies away: whatever they are at Amsterdam, the Dutch at Leyden cease to be a nation of shopkeepers.

It was holiday time when I was there last, and the town was comparatively empty. No songs floated through the windows of the clubs. In talk with a stranger at one of the cafés, I learned that the Dutch student works harder in the holidays than in term. In term he is a social and imbibing creature; but when the vacation comes and he returns to a home to which most of the allurements which an English boy would value are wanting, he applies himself to his books. I give the statement as I heard it.

One of the pleasantest buildings in Leyden is the Meermansburg--a spreading almshouse in the Oude Vest, surrounding a square garden with a massive pump in the midst. A few pictures are shown in the Governors' room over the entrance, but greater interest attaches to the little domiciles for the pensioners of the Meerman trust. A friendly concierge with a wooden leg showed us one of these compact houses--a sitting-room with a bed-cupboard in one wall, and below it a little larder, like the cabin of a ship. At the back a tiny range, and above, a garret. One could be very comfortable in such quarters.

Leyden has other hofjes, as these homes of rest are called, into one of which, gay with geraniums, I peeped--a little court of clean cottages seen through the doorway like a Peter de Hooch.

I did not, I fear, do my duty by Leyden's many museums. The sun shone; the boats swam continually down the Old Rhine and the New; and the sea at Katwyk and Noordwyk sent a call across the intervening meadows.

Some day perhaps I shall find myself at Leyden again, when the sky is grey and the thirst for information is more strongly upon me. Ethnography, comparative anatomy, physiology-- there is nothing that may not be learned in the Leyden museums; but such learning is not peculiarly Dutch, nor are the treasures of these museums peculiarly Dutch, and I felt that I might with a clear conscience leave them to others. Have we not Bloomsbury?

I did, however, climb the Burg, which is a circular fortress on a mound between the two rivers, so cleverly hidden away among houses that it was long ere I could find it. It is gained through an ancient courtyard full of horses and carriages--like a scene in Dumas. From the Burg one ought to have a fine view, but Leyden's roofs are too near. And in the Natural History Museum I walked through miles of birds stuffed, and birds articulated, until I felt that I could give a year's income to be on terms again with a living blackbird--even one of those that eat our Kentish strawberries at sunrise.

I did not penetrate to the interior of the University, having none to guide me, but I was pleased to remember that Oliver Goldsmith had been a student there not so very long ago. Indeed, as I walked about the town, I thought much of Goldsmith as he was in 1755, aged twenty-seven, with all his books to write, wandering through the same streets, looking upon the same houses and canals, in the interval of acquiring his mysterious medical degree (ultimately conferred at Louwain). His ingenious project, it will be remembered--by those whose memories (like my own) cling to that order of information, to the exclusion of everything useful and

improving--Goldsmith's delightful plan for subsistence in Holland was to teach the English language to the Dutch, and in return receive enough money to keep him at the University of Leyden and enable him to hear the great Professor Albinus. It was not until he reached Holland that those adorable Irish brains of his realised that he who teaches English to a Dutchman must first know Dutch.

Goldsmith, who spent his life in doing characteristic things--few men have done more- -when once he had determined to go to Holland, took a passage in a vessel bound for Bordeaux. At Newcastle-on-Tyne, however, on going ashore to be merry, he was arrested as a Jacobite and thrown into prison for a fortnight. The result was that the ship sailed without him. It was just as well for him and for us, for it sank at the mouth of the Garonne. In 1755, however, he was in Leyden, although by what route, circuitous or direct, he reached that city we do not know.

He lost little time in giving his Uncle Contarine an account of his impressions of Holland and its people. Here is a portion of a long letter: "The modern Dutchman is quite a different creature from him of former times: he in everything imitates a Frenchman, but in his easy disengaged air, which is the result of keeping polite company. The Dutchman is vastly ceremonious, and is perhaps exactly what a Frenchman might have been in the reign of Louis XIV. Such are the better bred. But the downright Hollander is one of the oddest figures in nature: upon a head of lank hair he wears a half-cocked narrow hat laced with black ribbon; no coat, but seven waistcoats, and nine pairs of breeches; so that his hips reach almost up to his arm-pits. This well-clothed vegetable is now fit to see company, or make love. But what a pleasing creature is the object of his appetite! Why she wears a large fur cap with a deal of Flanders lace: and for every pair of breeches he carries, she puts on two petticoats.

"A Dutch lady burns nothing about her phlegmatic admirer but his tobacco. You must know, sir, every women carries in her hand a stove with coals in it, which, when she sits, she snugs under her petticoats; and at this chimney dozing Strephon lights his pipe. I take it that this continual smoking is what gives the man the ruddy healthful complexion he generally wears, by draining his superfluous moisture, while the woman, deprived of this amusement, overflows with such viscidities as tint the complexion, and give that paleness of visage which low fenny grounds and moist air conspire to cause. A Dutch woman and Scotch will bear an opposition. The one is pale and fat, the other lean and ruddy: the one walks as if she were straddling after a go-cart, and the other takes too masculine a stride. I shall not endeavour to deprive either country of its share of beauty; but must say, that of all objects on this earth, an English farmer's daughter is most charming. Every woman there is a complete beauty, while the higher class of women want many of the requisites to make them even tolerable.

"Their pleasures here are very dull though very various. You may smoke, you may doze, you may go to the Italian comedy, as good an amusement as either of the former. This entertainment always brings in Harlequin, who is generally a magician, and in consequence of his diabolical art performs a thousand tricks on the rest of the persons of the drama, who are all fools. I have seen the pit in a roar of laughter at this humour, when with his sword he touches the glass from which another was drinking. 'Twas not his face they laughed at, for that was masked. They must have seen something vastly queer in the wooden sword, that neither I, nor you, sir, were you there, could see.

"In winter, when their canals are frozen, every house is forsaken, and all people are on the ice; sleds drawn by horses, and skating, are at that time the reigning amusements. They have boats here that slide on the ice, and are driven by the winds. When they spread all their sails they go more than a mile and a half a minute, and their motion is so rapid the eye can scarcely accompany them. Their ordinary manner of travelling is very cheap and very convenient: they sail in covered boats drawn by horses; and in these you are sure to meet people of all nations. Here the Dutch slumber, the French chatter, and the English play at cards. Any man who likes company may have them to his taste. For my part I generally detached myself from all society, and was wholly taken up in observing the face of the country.

Nothing can equal its beauty; wherever I turn my eye, fine houses, elegant gardens, statues, grottos, vistas, presented themselves; but when you enter their towns you are charmed beyond description. No misery is to be seen here; every one is usefully employed.

"Scotland and this country bear the highest contrast. There hills and rocks intercept every prospect: here 'tis all a continued plain. There you might see a well-dressed duchess issuing from a dirty close; and here a dirty Dutchman inhabiting a palace. The Scotch may be compared to a tulip planted in dung; but I never see a Dutchman in his own house but I think of a magnificent Egyptian temple dedicated to an ox. Physic is by no means here taught so well as in Edinburgh: and in all Leyden there are but four British students, owing to all necessaries being so extremely dear and the professors so very lazy (the chemical professor excepted) that we don't much care to come hither." When the time came to make the "Inquiry into the State of Polite Learning" Leyden had to suffer. Goldsmith laid about him with no gentle hand. "Holland, at first view, appears to have some pretensions to polite learning. It may be regarded as the great emporium, not less of literature than of every other commodity. Here, though destitute of what may be properly called a language of their own, all the languages are understood, cultivated and spoken. All useful inventions in arts, and new discoveries in science, are published here almost as soon as at the places which first produced them. Its individuals have the same faults, however, with the Germans, of making more use of their memory than their judgment. The chief employment of their literati is to criticise, or answer, the new performances which appear elsewhere.

"A dearth of wit in France or England naturally produces a scarcity in Holland. What Ovid says of Echo may be applied here, ----'nec reticere loquenti, Nec prior ipsa loqui didicit'---- they wait till something new comes out from others; examine its merits and reject it, or make it reverberate through the rest of Europe.

"After all, I know not whether they should be allowed any national character for polite learning. All their taste is derived to them from neighbouring nations, and that in a language not their own. They somewhat resemble their brokers, who trade for immense sums without having any capital."

Goldsmith did not finish there. His observations on the Continent served him, with a frugality that he did not otherwise practise, at least thrice. He used them in the "Inquiry into Polite Learning," he used them in the story of the Philosophic Vagabond in the Vicar of Wakefield, and still again in "The Traveller". This is the summary of Holland in that poem:--

To men of other minds my fancy flies, Embosom'd in the deep where Holland lies. Methinks her patient sons before me stand, Where the broad ocean leans against the land, And, sedulous to stop the coming tide, Lift the tall rampire's artificial pride. Onward, methinks, and diligently slow, The firm connected bulwark seems to grow; Spreads its long arms amidst the watery roar, Scoops out an empire, and usurps the shore. While the pent ocean, rising o'er the pile, Sees an amphibious world beneath him smile; The slow canal, the yellow-blossom'd vale, The willow-tufted bank, the gliding sail, The crowded mart, the cultivated plain, A new creation rescued from his reign.

Thus, while around the wave-subjected soil Impels the native to repeated toil, Industrious habits in each bosom reign, And industry begets a love of gain. Hence all the good from opulence that springs, With all those ills superfluous treasure brings, Are here display'd. Their much-lov'd wealth imparts Convenience, plenty, elegance, and arts: But view them closer, craft and fraud appear, Even liberty itself is barter'd here. At gold's superior charms all freedom flies, The needy sell it, and the rich man buys; A land of tyrants, and a den of slaves, Here wretches seek dishonourable graves, And calmly bent, to servitude conform, Dull as their lakes that slumber in the storm.

It was with his good Uncle Contarine's money that Goldsmith travelled to Leyden. The time came to leave, and Oliver was again without resources. He borrowed a sufficient sum from

Dr. Ellis, a fellow-countryman living there, and prepared for his departure. But on his way from the doctor's he had to pass a florist's, in whose window there chanced to be exhibited the very variety of flower which Uncle Contarine had so often praised and expressed a desire to possess. Given the man and the moment, what can you expect? Goldsmith, chief among those blessed natures who never interrupt a generous impulse, plunged into the florist's house and despatched a costly bundle of bulbs to Ireland. The next day he left Leyden with a guinea in his pocket, no clothes but those he stood in, and a flute in his hand. For the rest you must see the story of the Philosophic Vagabond.

Evelyn records an amusing experience at Leyden in August, 1641: "I was brought acquainted with a Burgundian Jew, who had married an apostate Kentish woman. I asked him divers questions; he told me, amongst other things, that the World should never end, that our souls transmigrated, and that even those of the most holy persons did penance in the bodies of brutes after death, and so he interpreted the banishment and savage life of Nebuchadnezzar; that all the Jews should rise again, and be led to Jerusalem; that the Romans only were the occasion of our Saviour's death, whom he affirmed (as the Turks do) to be a great prophet, but not the Messiah. He showed me several books of their devotion, which he had translated into English for the instruction of his wife; he told me that when the Messiah came, all the ships, barks, and vessels of Holland should, by the power of certain strange whirlwinds, be loosed from their anchors, and transported in a moment to all the desolate ports and havens throughout the world, wherever the dispersion was, to convey their brethren and tribes to the Holy City; with other such-like stuff. He was a merry drunken fellow, but would by no means handle any money (for something I purchased of him), it being Saturday; but desired me to leave it in the window, meaning to receive it on Sunday morning."

In an old book-shop at Leyden I bought from an odd lot of English books, chiefly minor fiction for travellers, the Colloquia Peripatetica of John Duncan, LL.D., Professor of Hebrew in the New College, Edinburgh. "I'm first a Christian, next a Catholic, then a Calvinist, fourth a Pædo-baptist, and fifth a Presbyterian. I cannot reverse the order," is one of his emphatic utterances. Here are others, not unconnected with the country we are travelling in: "Poor Erasmus truckled all his life for a hat. If he could only have been made a cardinal! You see the longing for it in his very features, and can't help regarding him with mingled respect and pity." Of Thomas à Kempis, the recluse of Deventer: "A fine fellow, but hazy, and weak betimes. He and his school tend (as some one has well said) to make humility and humiliation change places." Finally, of the Bible: "The three best translations of the Bible, in my opinion, are, in order of merit, the English, the Dutch, and Diodati's Italian version. As to Luther, he is admirable in rendering the prophets. He says either just what the prophets did say, or that which you see at once they might have said."

Leyden has two vast churches, St. Peter's and St. Pancras's. Both are immense and unadorned, I think that St. Pancras's is the lightest church I was ever in. St. Peter's ought to be filled with memorials of the town's illustrious sons, but it has few. As I have said elsewhere, I asked in vain for the grave of Jan Steen, who was buried here.

It was at Leyden that I saw my first Kermis, or fair, seven years ago, and ate my first poffertjes and wafelen. Writing as a foreigner, in no way concerned with the matter, I may express regret that the Kermis is not what it was in Holland. Possibly were one living in Holland, one would at once join the anti-Kermis party; but I hope not. In Amsterdam the anti-Kermis party has succeeded, and though one may still in that city at certain seasons eat wafelen and poffertjes, the old glories have departed, just as they have departed from so many English towns which once broke loose for a few nights every year. Even Barnet Fair is not what it was.

Noise seems to be the principal objection. Personally, I never saw any drunkenness; and there is so little real revelry that one turns one's back on the naphtha lamps in this town and that, in Leyden and the Hoorn, Apeldoorn and Middelburg, with the sad conviction that the times are out of joint, and that Teniers and Ostade and Brouwer, were they reborn to-day, would probably either have to take to painting Christmas supplements or earn their living at a reputable trade. It is not that the Dutch no longer drink, but that they now do it with more privacy.

The travelling temples reserved for the honour of poffertjes and wafelen are the most noticeable features of any Kermis. They are divided, quite like restaurants, into little cubicles for separate parties. Flowers and ferns make them gay; the waiters may even wear evening dress, but this is a refinement which would have annoyed Jan Steen; on the tables is white American cloth; and curtains of coloured material and muslin, with bright ribbons, add to the vivacity of the occasion. To eat poffertjes and wafelen is no light matter: one must regard it as a ritual.

Poffertjes come first--these are little round pancakey blobs, twisted and covered with butter and sugar. Then the wafelen, which are oblong wafers stamped in a mould and also buttered and sugared. You eat twenty-four poffertjes and two wafelen: that is, at the first onset. Afterwards, as many more as you wish. Lager beer is drunk with them. Some prefer Frambozen lemonade.

To eat them is a duty; to see them cooked is a joy. I have watched the cooks almost for hours. The poffertjes are made by hundreds at once, in a tray indented with little hollows over a fire. The cook is continually busy in twisting the little dabs of paste into the hollows and removing those that are ready. The wafelen are baked in iron moulds (there is one in Jan Steen's "Oyster Feast") laid on a rack in the fire. The cook has eight moulds in working order at once. When the eighth is filled from the pail of batter at his side, the first is done; and so on, ceaselessly, all day and half the night, like a natural law.

A woman stands by to spread butter and sugar, and the plate is whisked away in a moment. The Americans boast of their quick lunches; but I am convinced that they borrowed celerity in cooking and serving from some Knickerbocker deviser of poffertjes and wafelen in the early days of New York. I wonder that Washington Irving omitted to say so.

# CHAPTER VIII

Leyden's Painters, a Fanatic and a Hero

Rembrandt of the Rhine--His early life at Leyden--Jan Steen--Jan van Goyen--Brewer and painter--Pictures for beer--Jan Steen's grave--His delicacy and charm--His native refinement--A painter of hands--Jan Steen and Morland--Jan Steen and Hogarth--The Red Sea--The Flood--Jan of Leyden--The siege of Münster--Gigantic madness--Gerard Dou--Godfrey Schalcken--Frans van Mieris--William van Mieris--Gabriel

Metsu--Beckford's satire--Leyden's poor pictures--The siege of Leyden--Adrian van der Werf.

Leyden was the mother of some precious human clay. Among her sons was the greatest of Dutch painters, Rembrandt van Rijn; the most lovable of them, Jan Steen; and the most patient of them, Gerard Dou.

Of Rembrandt's genius it is late in the day to write, nor have I the power. We have seen certain of his pictures at The Hague; we shall see others at Amsterdam. I can add nothing to what is said in those places, but here, in Leyden (which has ten thousand stuffed birds, and not a single picture by her greatest son), one may dwell upon his early days and think of him wandering as a boy in the surrounding country unconsciously absorbing effects of light and shade.

Rembrandt Harmenszoon van Rijn was born on July 15, 1606, probably in a house at the corner of the Weddesteg, near the Witteport, on the bank of the Rhine. It was the same year that gave England Macbeth and King Lear. His father was a miller, his mother the daughter of a Leyden baker: it was destined that the son of these simple folk should be the greatest painter that the north of Europe has produced.

They did not foresee such a fate, but they seem sufficiently to have realised that their son had unusual aptitude for him to be sent to study law at the University. But he meant from the first to paint, and when he should have been studying text-books he was studying nature. The old miller, having a wise head, gave way, and Rembrandt was allowed to enter the studio of Jacob van Swanenburgh. That was probably in 1622, when he was sixteen; in 1624 he knew so much more than Swanenburgh had ever dreamed of that he passed on to Amsterdam, to see what could be learned from Peter Lastman. But Lastman was of little use, and Rembrandt soon returned to Leyden.

There he set up his own studio, painting, however, at his father's house--possibly even in the mill itself--as much as he could; and for seven years he taught younger men at Leyden his secrets. He remained at Leyden until 1631, moving then again to Amsterdam and beginning the greatest period of his life. At Leyden he had painted much and etched much; perhaps the portrait of himself in a steel gorget, at The Hague, is his finest Leyden picture. It was not until 1632, the year in which he married his Saskia, that the first of his most famous works, "The School of Anatomy," was painted. Yet Leyden may consider that it was she that showed the way; she may well be proud.

Rembrandt's later life belongs to Amsterdam; but Leyden had other illustrious sons who were faithful to her to the end. Chief of these was Jan Steen.

Harmens the miller, as we have seen, became the father of a boy named Rembrandt in 1606; it was twenty years later that Steen the brewer rejoiced over the birth of a son called Jan.

Of Jan's childhood we know nothing, but as a young man he was sent by his father to Utrecht to study under Nicholas Knupfer. Then he passed on to Adrian van Ostade and probably to Adrian Brouwer, with both of whom and Frans Hals we saw him carousing, after his wont, in a picture by Brouwer in Baron Steengracht's house at The Hague. Finally he became the pupil of Jan van Goyen, painter of the beautiful "Valkhof at Nymwegen," No. 991 in the Ryks Museum, a picture which always makes me think of Andrew Marvell's poem on the Bermudas. Like many another art pupil, Jan Steen married his master's daughter. Jan van Goyen, I might add, was another of Leyden's sons. He was born in 1596 and he died at The Hague in 1666, while London was suffering under the Plague.

Jan Steen seems to have intended to make brewing his staff and painting merely his cane; but good nature and a terrible thirst were too much for him. From brewing he descended to keeping a tavern, "in which occupation," to quote Ireland, "he was himself his best customer". After a while, having exhausted his cellar, he took seriously to painting in order to renew it, paying for his liquor with his brush. Thus "for a long time his works were to be found only in the hands of dealers in wine". Who, after this, shall have the hardihood to speak evil of the grape?

Jan is not supposed to have lived at Leyden after his marriage to Margaretta van Goyen, in 1649, until 1669, when his father died. In 1672 he is known to have taken a tavern at Leyden at the Lange Brug.

Of the intervening years little is known. He was probably at Haarlem part of the time and at The Hague part of the time, In 1667 he paid his rent--only twenty-nine florins--with three pictures "painted well as he was able". Margaretta died in 1669--a merry large woman we must suppose her from her appearance in Jan's pictures, and the mother of four or five children who may often be seen in the same scenes. Jan married again in 1673 and died in 1697.

He was buried in St. Peter's Church, Leyden, leaving more than five hundred pictures to his name. The youth who, in the absence of the koster, accompanied me through St. Peter's Church, so far from knowing where Jan Steen was buried, had never even heard his name. (And at the Western Church in Amsterdam, where Rembrandt is said to have been buried, his resting-place cannot be pointed out. But never a Dutch admiral's grave is in doubt.)

For all his roystering and recklessness, for all his drinking and excess, Jan Steen's work is essentially delicate. He painted the sublimated essence of comedy. Teniers, Ostade, Brouwer are coarse and boorish beside him; Metsu and Mieris genteel. Even when he is painting low life Jan Steen is distinguished, a gentleman. And now and then he touches the springs of tears, so exquisite in his sympathetic understanding. He remains the most lovable painter in Holland, and the tenderest--in a country where tenderness is not easily found.

Look, for example, at the two pictures at The Hague which are reproduced opposite pages 74 and 80. The first represents the Steen family. The jolly Jan himself is smoking at the table; the old brewer and the elder Mrs. Steen are in the foreground. I doubt if any picture exists in which the sense of innocent festivity is better expressed. It is all perhaps rather a muddle: Mrs.

56

Steen has some hard work before her if the house is to be restored to a Dutch pitch of cleanliness and order; but how jolly every one is! Jan himself looks just as we should expect.

The triumph of the "Oyster Feast," on the opposite page, seems to me to be the girl kneeling in the corner. Here is drawing indeed. The charge brought by the mysterious painter in Balzac's story against Pourbus, that one was unable to walk behind the figure in his picture, could never hold with Jan Steen. His every figure stands out surrounded by atmosphere, and never more so than in the "Oyster Feast". Again, in the "Cat's Dancing Lesson" (opposite page 158), what drawing there is in the girl playing the pipe, and what life in the whole scene!

It is odd that Jan Steen in Holland, and George Morland in England, both topers, should have had this secret of simple charm so highly developed: one of nature's curious ironies, very confusing to the moralist. In the second Hague picture (opposite page 80) Leyden's genial tosspot has achieved a farther triumph--he has painted one of the most radiantly delicate figures in all art. One must go to Italy and seek among the early Madonnas to find anything to set beside the sweet Wordsworthian character of this little Dutch girl who feeds the animals.

It was Jan Steen's way to scamp much of every picture; but in every picture you will find one figure that could not be excelled. Nothing probably could be more slovenly, more hideously unpainted, than, for example, the bed and the guitar-case in the "Sick Woman"--No. 2246 at the Ryks

Museum--opposite page 22. But I doubt if human skill has ever transcended the painting of the woman's face, or the sheer drawing of her. Look at her arm and hand--Jan Steen never went wrong with arms and hands. Look at the hands of the boy playing the pipe in the picture opposite page 74; look at the woman filling a pipe at the table. To-day we are accustomed to pictures containing children: they are as necessary as sunsets to picture buyers: all our figure-painters lavish their talents upon them; but who had ever troubled to paint a real peasant child before Jan Steen? It was this rough toper that showed the way, and no one since has ever excelled him.

Parallels have been drawn between Jan Steen and Hogarth, and there are critics who would make Jan a moralist too. But I do not see how we can compare them. Steen did what Hogarth could not, Hogarth did what Steen would not. Hogarth is rarely charming, Steen is rarely otherwise. It is not Hogarth with whom I should associate Jan, but Burns. He is the Dutch Burns--in colour.

I wish we had more facts concerning him, for he must have been a great man and humorist. The story is told of Hogarth that on being commissioned to paint a scriptural picture of the Red Sea for a too parsimonious patron who had beaten him down and down, he rebuked him for his meanness by producing a canvas entirely covered with red paint. "But what is this?" the patron asked. "The Red Sea--surely." "Where then are the Israelites?" "They have all crossed over." "And Pharaoh's hosts?" "They are all drowned." The story is perhaps an invention; but a somewhat similar joke is credited to Jan Steen. His commission was the Flood, and his picture when finished consisted of a sheet of water with a Dutch cheese in the midst bearing the arms of Leyden. The cheese and the arms, he pointed out, proved that people had been on the earth; as for Noah and the ark, they were out of the picture.

Jan Steen's picture of "A Quaker's Funeral" I have not seen, but according to Pilkington it is impossible to behold it and refrain from laughter. The subject does not strike one as being in itself mirthful. A century earlier Leyden had produced another Jan, separated from Jan Steen by a difference wide asunder as the poles. Yet a very wonderful man in his brief season, standing high among the world's great madmen. I mean Jan Bockelson, the Anabaptist, known as Jan of Leyden, who, beginning as pure enthusiast, succumbed, as so many a leader of women has done, to the intoxication of authority, and became the slave of grandiose ambition and excesses. Every country has had its mock Messiahs: they rise periodically in England, not less at the present day than in the darker ages (hysteria being more powerful than light); yet the history of none of these spiritual monarchs can compare with that of the tailor's son of Leyden.

The story is told in many places, but nowhere with such dramatic picturesqueness as by Professor Karl Pearson in his Ethic of Freethought. "As the illegitimate son of a tailor in Leyden," says Professor

Pearson--Jan's mother was the maid of his father's wife--"his early life was probably a harsh and bitter one. Very young he wandered from home, impressed with the miseries of his class and with a general feeling of much injustice in the world. Four years he spent in England seeing the poor driven off the land by the sheep; then we find him in Flanders, married, but still in vague search of the Eldorado; again roaming, he visits Lisbon and Lübeck as a sailor, ever seeking and inquiring. Suddenly a new light bursts upon him in the teaching of Melchior Hofmann [the Anabaptist]; he fills himself with dreams of a glorious kingdom on earth, the rule of justice and of love. Still a little while and the prophet Mathys crosses his path, and tells him of the New Sion and the extermination of the godless."

Mathys, or Jan Mathiesen, was a baker of Haarlem, who, constituted an Anabaptist bishop, was preaching the new gospel through the Netherlands and gathering recruits to the community of God's saints which had been established at Münster. "Full of hope for the future," says Professor Pearson, "Jan sets out for Münster to join the saints. Still young, handsome, imbued with a fiery enthusiasm, actor by nature and even by choice, he has no small influence on the spread of Anabaptism in that city. The youth of twenty-three expounds to the followers of Rottmann the beauties of his ideal kingdom of the good and the true. With his whole soul he preaches to them the redemption of the oppressed, the destruction of tyranny, the community of goods, and the rule of justice and brotherly love. Women and maidens slip away to the secret gatherings of the youthful enthusiast; the glowing young prophet of Leyden becomes the centre of interest in Münster. Dangerous, very dangerous ground, when the pure of heart are not around him; when the spirit 'chosen by God' is to proclaim itself free of the flesh.

"The world has judged Jan harshly, condemned him to endless execration. It were better to have cursed the generations of oppression, the flood of persecution, which forced the toiler to revolt, the Anabaptists to madness. Under other circumstances the noble enthusiasm, with other surroundings the strong will, of Jan of Leyden might have left a different mark on the page of history. Dragged down in this whirlpool of fanaticism, sensuality, and despair, we can only look upon him as a factor of the historic judgment, a necessary actor in that tragedy of Münster, which forms one of the most solemn chapters of the Greater Bible."

Gradually Jan rose to be head of the saints, Mathiesen having been killed, and none other displaying so much strength of purpose or magnetic enthusiasm. And here his mind gave way. Like so many absolute rulers before and since, he could not resist the ecstacies of supremacy. To resume Professor Pearson's narrative: "The sovereign of Sion--although 'since the flesh is dead, gold to him is but as dung'--yet thinks fit to appear in all the pomp of earthly majesty. He appoints a court, of which Knipperdollinch is chancellor, and wherein there are many officers from chamberlain to cook. He forms a body-guard, whose members are dressed in silk. Two pages wait upon the king, one of whom is a son of his grace the bishop of Münster. The great officers of state are somewhat wondrously attired, one breech red, the other grey, and on the sleeves of their coats are embroidered the arms of Sion--the earth-sphere pierced by two crossed swords, a sign of universal sway and its instruments--while a golden finger-ring is token of their authority in Sion. The king himself is magnificently arrayed in gold and purple, and as insignia of his office, he causes sceptre and spurs of gold to be made. Gold ducats are melted down to form crowns for the queen and himself; and lastly a golden globe pierced by two swords and surmounted by a cross with the words, 'A King of Righteousness o'er all' is borne before him. The attendants of the Chancellor Knipperdollinch are dressed in red with the crest, a hand raising aloft the sword of justice. Nay, even the queen and the fourteen queenlets must have a separate court and brilliant uniforms.

"Thrice a week the king goes in glorious array to the market-place accompanied by his body-guards and officers of state, while behind ride the fifteen queens. On the market-place stands a magnificent throne with silken cushions and canopy, whereon the tailor-monarch takes his seat, and alongside him sits his chief queen. Knipperdollinch sits at his feet. A page on his left bears the book of the law, the Old Testament; another on his right an unsheathed sword. The book denotes that he sits on the throne of David; the sword that he is the king of the just, who is appointed to exterminate all unrighteousness. Bannock-Bernt is court-chaplain, and preaches in the market-place before the king. The sermon over, justice is administered, often of the most terrible kind; and then in like state the king and his court return home. On the streets he is greeted with cries of: 'Hail in the name of the Lord. God be praised!'"

Meanwhile underneath all this riot of splendour and power and sensuality, the pangs of starvation were beginning to be felt. For the army of the bishop of Münster was outside the city and the siege was very studiously maintained. The privations became more and more terrible, and more and more terrible the means of allaying them. The bodies of citizens that had died were eaten; and then men and women and children were killed in order that they might be eaten too. Under such conditions, is it any wonder that Münster became a city of the mad, mad beyond the sane man's wildest dreams of excess?

A few of the least demented of Jan's followers at length determined that the tragedy must cease, and the city was delivered into the bishop's hands. "What judgment," writes Professor Pearson, "his grace the bishop thinks fit to pass on the leaders of Sion at least deserves record. Rottmann has fallen by St. Martin's Church, fighting sword in hand, but Jan of Leyden and Knipperdollinch are brought prisoners before this shepherd of the folk.

Scoffingly he asks Jan: 'Art thou a king?' Simple, yet endlessly deep the reply: 'Art thou a bishop?' Both alike false to their callings--as father of men and shepherd of souls. Yet the one cold, self-seeking sceptic, the other ignorant, passionate, fanatic idealist. 'Why hast thou destroyed the town and my folk?' 'Priest, I have not destroyed one little maid of thine. Thou hast again thy town, and I can repay thee a hundredfold.' The bishop demands with much curiosity how this miserable captive can possibly repay him. 'I know we must die, and die terribly, yet before we die, shut us up in an iron cage, and send us round through the land, charge the curious folk a few pence to see us, and thou wilt soon gather together all thy heart's desire.' The jest is grim, but the king of Sion has the advantage of his grace the bishop. Then follows torture, but there is little to extract, for the king still holds himself an instrument sent by God--though it were for the punishment of the world. Sentence is read on these men--placed in an iron cage they shall be shown round the bishop's diocese, a terrible warning to his subjects, and then brought back to Münster; there with glowing pincers their flesh shall be torn from the bones, till the death-stroke be given with red-hot dagger in throat and heart. For the rest let the mangled remains be placed in iron cages swung from the tower of St. Lambert's Church.

"On the 26th of January, 1536, Jan Bockelson and Knipperdollinch meet their fate. A high scaffolding is erected in the market-place, and before it a lofty throne for his grace the bishop, that he may glut his vengeance to the full. Let the rest pass in silence. The most reliable authorities tell us that the Anabaptists remained calm and firm to the last. 'Art thou a king?' 'Art thou a bishop?' The iron cages still hang on the church tower at Münster; placed as a warning, they have become a show; perhaps some day they will be treasured as weird mentors of the truth which the world has yet to learn from the story of the Kingdom of God in Münster."

A living German artist of great power, named Joseph Sattler, too much of whose time has recently been given to designing book-plates, produced some few years ago an extraordinary illustrated history of the Anabaptists in Münster. Many artists have essayed to portray madness, but I know of no work more terrible than his. We have travelled far from Leyden's peaceful studios. It is time to look at the work of Gerard Dou. Rembrandt we have seen was the son of a miller, Jan Steen of a brewer; the elder Dou was a glazier. His son Gerard was born in Leyden in 1613. The father was so far interested in the boy's gifts that he apprenticed him to an engraver when he was nine. At the age of eleven he passed to the studio of a painter on glass, and on St. Valentine's day, 1628, he became a pupil of Rembrandt. From Rembrandt, however, he seems to have learned only the charm of contrasts of light and shade. None of the great rugged strength of the master is to be seen in his minute and patient work, in which the genius of taking pains is always apparent. "He would frequently," says Ireland, "paint six or seven days on a hand, and, still more wonderful, twice the time on the handle of a broom.... The minuteness of his performance so affected his sight that he wore spectacles at the age of thirty."

Gerard Dou's success was not only artistic; it was also financial. Rembrandt's prices did not compare with those of his pupil, whose art coming more within the sympathetic range and understanding of the ordinary man naturally was more sought after than the Titanic and less comfortable canvasses of the greater craftsman.

Dou did exceedingly well, one of his patrons even paying him a yearly honorarium of a thousand florins for the privilege of having the refusal of each new picture. "The Poulterer's Shop" at our National Gallery is a perfect example of his fastidious minuteness and charm. But he painted pictures also with a tenderer brush. I give on the opposite page a reproduction of the most charming picture by Gerard Dou that I know--"The Young Housekeeper" at The Hague. This is a very miracle of painting in every inch, and yet the pains that have been expended upon the cabbage and the fish are not for a moment disproportionate: the cabbage and the fish, for all their finish, remain subordinate and appropriate details. The picture is the picture of the mother and the children. "The Night School"--No. 795 in the Ryks Museum at Amsterdam--is, I believe, more generally admired, but "The Young Housekeeper" is the better. "The Night School" might be described as the work of a pocket Rembrandt; "The Young Housekeeper" is the work of an artist of rare individuality and sympathy. At the Wallace Collection may be seen a hermit by Dou quite in his best nocturnal manner.

Gerard Dou died at Leyden, where he had spent nearly all his quiet life, in 1676. He is buried at St. Peter's, but his grave does not seem to be known there.

Dou had many imitators, some of whom studied under him. One of the chief was Godfried Schalcken of Dort, whose picture of an "Old Woman Scouring a Pan" may be seen in the National Gallery, while the Wallace Collection has several examples of his skill. Schalcken seems to have been a man of great brusquerie, if two stories told by Ireland of his sojourn in England are true. William III., for example, when sitting for his picture, with a candle in his hand, was suffered by Schalcken to burn his fingers. "One is at a loss," says Ireland, "to determine which was most to blame, the monarch for want of feeling, or the painter of politeness. The following circumstance, however, will place the deficiency of the latter beyond controversy. A lady sitting for her portrait, who was more admired for a beautiful hand than a handsome face, after the head was finished, asked him if she should take off her glove, that he might insert the hand in the picture, to which he replied, he always painted the hands from those of his valet." The most attractive picture by Schalcken that I have seen is a girl sewing by candle light, in the Wallace Collection. It pairs off with the charming little Gerard Dou at the Ryks--No. 796.

Dou said that the "Prince of his pupils" was Frans van Mieris of Delft, who combined the manner and predilections of his master with those of Terburg. He was very popular with collectors, but I do not experience any great joy in the presence of his work, which, with all its miraculous deftness, is yet lacking in personal feeling. Mieris, says Ireland, "was frequently paid a ducat per hour for his works. His intimacy and friendship for Jan Steen, that excellent painter and bon vivant, seems to have led him into much inconvenience. After a night's debauch, quitting Jan Steen, he fell into a common drain; whence he was extricated by a poor cobbler and his wife, and, treated by them with much kindness, he repaid the obligation by presenting them with a small picture, which, by his recommendation, was sold for a considerable sum."

The amazingly minute picture of "The Poulterer's Shop" which hangs in the National Gallery as a pendant to Dou's work with the same title, is by William van Mieris, the son of Dou's favourite pupil. He also was born at Leyden, that teeming mother of painters. Frans van Mieris, his father, died at Leyden in 1681; William died at Leyden in 1747.

Above the work of Frans van Mieris I would put that of Gabriel Metsu, another of Dou's pupils, and also a son of Leyden, where he was born in 1630. Upon Metsu's work Terburg, however, exercised more influence than did Gerard Dou. "The Music Lesson" and "The Duet" at the National Gallery are good examples of his pleasant painting. Even better is his work at the Wallace Collection. He died in 1667 in Amsterdam, where one of his best pictures "The Breakfast"--No. 1553 at the Ryks--may be seen. There are many fine examples at the Louvre. He was always graceful, always charming, with a favourite model--perhaps his wife--the pleasant plump woman who occurs again and again in his work. She is in "The Breakfast" (see the opposite page).

Mention of Gerard Dou and his pupils reminds me of a little-known satire on art-criticism written by "Vathek" Beckford. Biographical Memoirs of Extraordinary Painters it is called, among the painters being Sucrewasser of Vienna, and Watersouchy of Amsterdam. It is Watersouchy who concerns us, for he was a Dutch figure painter who carried the art of detail farther than it had been carried before. I quote a little from Beckford's account of this genius, since it helps to bring back a day when the one thing most desired by the English collector was a Dutch picture--still life, boors, cows, ruins, or domestic interior--no matter what subject or how mechanically painted so long as it was done minutely enough.

"Whilst he remained at Amsterdam, young Watersouchy was continually improving, and arrived to such perfection in copying point lace, that Mierhop entreated his father to cultivate these talents, and to place his son under the patronage of Gerard Dow, ever renowned for the exquisite finish of his pieces. Old Watersouchy stared at the proposal, and solemnly asked his wife, to whose opinion he always paid a deference, whether painting was a genteel profession for their son. Mierhop, who overheard their conversation, smiled disdainfully at the question, and Madam Watersouchy answered, that she believed it was one of your liberal arts. In few words, the father was persuaded, and Gerard Dow, then resident at Leyden, prevailed upon to receive the son as a disciple.

"Our young artist had no sooner his foot within his master's apartment, than he found every object in harmony with his own disposition. The colours finely ground, and ranged in the neatest boxes, the pencils so delicate as to be almost imperceptible, the varnish in elegant phials, the easel just where it ought to be, filled him with agreeable sensations, and exalted ideas of his master's merit. Gerard Dow on his side was equally pleased, when he saw him moving about with all due circumspection, and noticing his little prettinesses at every step. He therefore began his pupil's initiation with great alacrity, first teaching him cautiously to open the cabinet door, lest any particles of dust should be dislodged and fix upon his canvas, and advising him never to take up his pencil without sitting motionless a few minutes, till every mote casually floating in the air should be settled. Such instructions were not thrown away upon Watersouchy: he treasured them up, and refined, if possible, upon such refinements."

In course of time Watersouchy gained the patronage of a rich but frugal banker named Baise-la-Main, who seeing his value, arranged for the painter to occupy a room in his house, "Nobody," Beckford continues, "but the master of the house was allowed to enter this sanctuary. Here our artist remained six weeks in grinding his colours, composing an admirable varnish, and preparing his canvass, for a performance he intended as his chef d'oeuvre. A fortnight more passed before he decided upon a subject. At last he determined to commemorate the opulence of Monsieur

Baise-la-Main, by a perspective of his counting-house. He chose an interesting moment, when heaps of gold lay glittering on the counter, and citizens of distinction were soliciting a secure repository for their plate and jewels. A Muscovite wrapped in fur, and an Italian glistening in brocade, occupied the foreground. The eye glancing over these figures highly finished, was directed through the windows of the shop into the area in front of the cathedral; of which, however, nothing was discovered, except two sheds before its entrance, where several barbers were represented at their different occupations. An effect of sunshine upon the counter discovered every coin that was scattered upon its surface. On these the painter had bestowed such intense labour, that their very legends were distinguishable.

"It would be in vain to attempt conveying, by words, an idea adequate to this chef d'oeuvre, which must have been seen to have been duly admired. In three months it was far advanced; during which time our artist employed his leisure hours in practising jigs and minuets on the violin, and writing the first chapter of Genesis on a watchpaper, which he adorned with a miniature of Adam and Eve, so exquisitely finished, that every ligament in their fig-leaves was visible. This little jeu d'esprit he presented to Madam Merian."

Leyden's earliest painter was Lucas Jacobz, known as Lucas van Leyden, who was born in 1494. He painted in oil, in distemper and on glass; he took his subjects from nature and from scripture; he engraved better than he painted; and he was the friend of Dürer. Leyden possesses his triptych, "The Last Judgment," which to me is interesting rather as a piece of pioneering than as a work apart. After settling for a while at Middelburg and Antwerp, he returned to Leyden, where he died in 1533.

In spite of her record as the mother of great painters, Leyden treats pictures with some indifference. The Municipal Museum has little that is of value.

Of most interest perhaps is the Peter van Veen, opposite "The Last Judgment," representing a scene in the siege of Leyden by the Spaniards under Valdez in 1574, which has a companion upstairs by Van Bree, depicting the Burgomaster's heroic feat of opportunism in the same period of stress.

Adrian Van der Werf was this Burgomaster's name (his monument stands in the Van der Werf park), and nothing but his courage and address at a critical moment saved the city. Motley tells the story in a fine passage. "Meantime, the besieged city was at its last gasp. The burghers had been in a state of uncertainty for many days; being aware that the fleet had set forth for their relief, but knowing full well the thousand obstacles which it had to surmount. They had guessed its progress by the illumination from the blazing villages; they had heard its salvos of artillery on its arrival at North Aa; but since then, all had been dark and mournful again, hope and fear, in sickening alternation, distracting every breast. They knew that the wind was unfavourable, and, at the dawn of each day, every eye was turned wistfully to the vanes of the steeples. So long as the easterly breeze prevailed, they felt, as they anxiously stood on towers and house-tops that they must look in vain for the welcome ocean. Yet, while thus patiently waiting, they were literally starving; for even the misery endured at Harlem had not reached that depth and intensity of agony to which Leyden was now reduced. Bread, maltcake, horse-flesh, had entirely disappeared; dogs, cats, rats, and other vermin were esteemed luxuries. A small number of cows, kept as long as possible, for their milk, still remained; but a few were killed from day to day, and distributed in minute proportions, hardly sufficient to support life among the famishing population. Starving wretches swarmed daily around the shambles where these cattle were slaughtered, contending for any morsel which might fall, and lapping eagerly the blood as it ran along the pavement; while the hides, chopped and boiled, were greedily devoured.

"Women and children, all day long, were seen searching gutters and dung hills for morsels of food, which they disputed fiercely with the famishing dogs. The green leaves were stripped from the trees, every living herb was converted into human food, but these expedients could not avert starvation. The daily mortality was frightful,--infants starved to death on the maternal breasts, which famine had parched and withered; mothers dropped dead in the streets, with their dead children in their arms.

"In many a house the watchmen, in their rounds, found a whole family of corpses, father, mother and children, side by side; for a disorder called the plague, naturally engendered of hardship and famine, now came, as if in kindness, to abridge the agony of the people. The pestilence stalked at noonday through the city, and the doomed inhabitants fell like grass beneath it scythe. From six thousand to eight thousand human beings sank before this scourge alone, yet the people resolutely held out--women and men mutually encouraging each other to resist the entrance of their foreign foe--an evil more horrible than pest or famine. [3]

"The missives from Valdez, who saw more vividly than the besieged could do, the uncertainty of his own position, now poured daily into the city, the enemy becoming more prodigal of his vows, as he felt that the ocean might yet save the victims from his grasp. The inhabitants, in their ignorance, had gradually abandoned their hopes of relief, but they spurned the summons to surrender. Leyden was sublime in its despair. A few murmurs were, however, occasionally heard at the steadfastness of the magistrates, and a dead body was placed at the door of the burgomaster, as a silent witness against his inflexibility. A party of the more faint-hearted even assailed the heroic Adrian Van der Werf with threats and reproaches as he passed through the streets.

"A crowd had gathered around him, as he reached a triangular place in the centre of the town, into which many of the principal streets emptied themselves, and upon one side of which stood the church of St. Pancras, with its high brick tower surmounted by two pointed turrets, and with two ancient lime trees at its entrance. There stood the burgomaster, a tall, haggard, imposing figure, with dark visage, and a tranquil but commanding eye. He waved his broad-leaved felt hat for silence, and then exclaimed, in language which has been almost literally preserved, 'What would ye, my friends? Why do ye murmur that we do not break our vows and surrender our city to the Spaniards?--a fate more horrible than the agony which she now endures. I tell you I have made an oath to hold this city, and may God give me strength to keep my oath! I can die but once; whether by your hands, the enemy's, or by the hand of God. My own fate is indifferent to me, not so that of the city intrusted to my care. I know that we shall starve if not soon relieved; but starvation is preferable to the dishonoured death which is the only alternative. Your menaces move me not; my life is at your disposal; here is my sword, plunge it into my breast, and divide my flesh among you. Take my body to appease your hunger, but expect no surrender, so long as I remain alive.'" Leyden was at last relieved by William of Orange, who from his sick-bed had arranged for the piercing of the dykes and letting in enough water to swim his ships and rout the Spaniards.

Out of tribulation comes good. For their constancy and endurance in the siege the Prince offered the people of Leyden one of two benefits--exemption from taxes or the establishment of a University. They took the University.

# CHAPTER IX

Haarlem

Tulip culture--Early speculation--The song of the tulip--Dutch gardening new and old--A horticultural pilgrimage--The Haarlem dunes--Gardens without secrets--Zaandvoort--Through Noord-Holland and its charms--The church of St. Bavo--Whitewash v. Mystery--The true father of the Reformation--Printing paves the way--The Hout--Laocoön and his sons--The siege of Haarlem--Dutch fortitude--The real Dutch courage--The implacable Alva--Broken promises--A tonic for Philip--The women of Haarlem--A pledge to mothers--The great organ--Three curious inhabitants--The Teyler Museum--Frans Hals--A king of

abundance--Regent pieces--The secondary pictures in the Museum--Dirck Hals--Van der Helst--Adrian Brouwer--Nicolas Berchem--Ruisdael--The lost mastery--Echoes of the past.

Haarlem being the capital of the tulip country, the time to visit it is the spring. To travel from Leyden to Haarlem by rail in April is to pass through floods of colour, reaching their finest quality about Hillegom. The beds are too formal, too exactly parallel, to be beautiful, except as sheets of scarlet or yellow; for careless beauty one must look to the heaps of blossoms piled up in the corners (later to be used on the beds as a fertiliser), which are always beautiful, and doubly so when reflected in a canal. From a balloon, in the flowering season, the tulip gardens must look like patchwork quilts.

Tulip Sunday, which represents the height of the season (corresponding to Chestnut Sunday at Bushey Park) is about the third Sunday in April. One should be in Holland then. It is no country for hot weather: it has no shade, the trains become unbearable, and the canals are very unpleasant. But in spring it is always fresh.

Tulip cultivation is now a steady humdrum business, very different from the early days of the fashion for the flower, in the seventeenth century, when speculators lost their heads over bulbs as thoroughly as over South-Sea stock in the great Bubble period. Thousands of florins were given for a single bulb. The bulb, however, did not always change hands, often serving merely as a gambling basis; it even may not have existed at all. Among genuine connoisseurs genuine sales would of course be made, and it is recorded that a "Semper Augustus" bulb was once bought for 13,000 florins. At last the Government interfered; gambling was put down; and "Semper Augustus" fell to fifty florins.

It was to Haarlem, it will be remembered, that the fair Frisian travelled with Cornelius van Baerle's solitary flower in La Tulipe Noire, and won the prize of 100,000 florins offered for a blossom of pure nigritude by the Horticultural Society of Haarlem. Hence the addition of the Tulipa Nigra Rosa Baerleensis to the list of desirable bulbs. Dumas puts into the mouth of Cornelius a very charming song of the tulip:--

Nous sommes les filles du feu secret, Du feu qui circule dans les veines de la terre; Nous sommes les filles de l'aurore et de la rosée, Nous sommes les filles de l'air, Nous sommes les filles de l'eau; Mais nous sommes avant tout les filles du ciel.

The Dutch are now wholly practical. Their reputation as gardeners has become a commercial one, resting upon the fortunate discovery that the tulip and the hyacinth thrive in the sandy soil about Haarlem. For flowers as flowers they seem to me to care little or nothing. Their cottages have no pretty confusion of blossoms as in our villages. You never see the cottager at work among his roses; once his necessary labours are over, he smokes and talks to his neighbours: to grow flowers for æsthetic reasons were too ornamental, too unproductive a hobby. Æsthetically the Dutch are dead, or are alive only in the matter of green paint, which they use with such charming effect on their houses, their mills and their boats. What is pretty is old-- as indeed is the case in our own country, if we except gardens. Modern Dutch architecture is without attraction, modern Delft porcelain a thing to cry over.

If any one would know how an old formal Dutch garden looked, there is a model one at the back of the Ryks Museum in Amsterdam. But the art is no more practised. A few circular beds in the lawn, surrounded by high wire netting--that is for the most part the modern notion of gardening. In an interesting report of a visit paid to the Netherlands and France in 1817 by the secretary of the Caledonia Horticultural Society and some congenial companions, may be read excellent descriptions of old Dutch gardening, which even then was a thing of the past. Here is the account of a typical formal garden, near Utrecht: "The large divisions of the garden are made by tall and thick hedges of beech, hornbeam, and oak, variously shaped, having been tied to frames and thus trained, with the aid of the shears, to the desired form. The smaller divisions are made by hedges of yew and box, which in thickness and density resemble walls of brick. Grottoes and fountains are some of the principal ornaments. The grottoes are adorned with masses of calcareous stuff, corals and shells, some of them apparently from the East Indies, others natives of our own seas. The principal grotto is large, and studded with thousands of crystals and shells. We were told that its construction was the labour of twelve years. The fountains are of various devices, and though old, some of them were still capable of being put in action. Frogs and lizards placed at the edgings of the walks, and spouting water to the risk of passengers, were not quite so agreeable; and other figures were still in worse taste.

"There is a long berceau walk of beech, with numerous windows or openings in the leafy side wall, and many statues and busts, chiefly of Italian marble, some of them of exquisite workmanship. Several large urns and vases certainly do honour to the sculptor. The subjects of the bas-relief ornaments are the histories of Saul and David, and of Esther and Ahasuerus."

I saw no old Dutch garden in Holland which seemed to me so attractive as that at Levens in Westmorland.

It is important at Haarlem to take a drive over the dunes--the billowy, grassy sand hills which stretch between the city and the sea. If it is in April one can begin the drive by passing among every variety of tulip and hyacinth, through air made sweet and heavy by these flowers. Just outside Haarlem the road passes the tiniest deer park that ever I saw--with a great house, great trees, a lawn and a handful of deer all packed as close as they can be. Now and then one sees a stork's nest high on a pole before a house.

On leaving the green and luxuriant flat country a climbing pavé road winds in and out among the pines on the edge of the dunes; past little villas, belonging chiefly to Amsterdam business men, each surrounded by a naked garden with the merest suggestion of a boundary. For the Dutch do not like walls or hedges. This level open land having no natural secrecy, it seems as if its inhabitants had decided there should be no artificial secrecy either.

When they sit in their gardens they like to be seen. An Englishman's first care when he plans a country estate is not to be overlooked; a Dutchman would cut down every tree that intervened between his garden chair and the high road.

Fun has often been made of the names which the Dutch merchants give to their country houses, but they seem to me often to be chosen with more thought than those of similar villas in our country. Here are a few specimens: Buiten Gedachten (Beyond Expectation), Ons Genoegen (Our Contentment), Lust en Rust (Pleasure and Rest), Niet Zoo Quaalyk (Not so Bad), Myn Genegenhied is Voldaan (My Desire is Satisfied), Mijn Lust en Leven (My Pleasure and Life), Vriendschap en Gezelschap (Friendship and Sociability), Vreugde bij Vrede (Joy with Peace), Groot Genoeg (Large Enough), Buiten Zorg (Without Care). These names at any rate convey sentiments which we may take to express their owners' true feelings in their owners' own language; and as such I prefer them to the "Chatsworths" and "Belle-vues," "Cedars" and "Towers," with which the suburbs of London teem. In a small inland street in Brighton the other day I noticed a "Wave Crest".

The dunes extend for miles: an empty wilderness of sand with the grey North Sea beyond. From the high points one sees inland not only Haarlem, just below, but the domes and spires of Amsterdam beyond.

One may return to Haarlem by way of Bloemendaal, a green valley with shady walks and a good hotel; or extend the drive to Haarlem's watering-place Zaandvoort, which otherwise can be gained by steam-tram, and where, says the author of Through Noord-Holland, "the billowing is strong and strengthening". The same author tells us also that "the ponnies and asses have a separated standing-place, whilst severe stipulations warrant the bathers for trouble of the animals and their driver".

Of this book I ought perhaps to say more, for I am greatly indebted to it. Most of the larger towns of Holland have guides, and for the most part they are written in good English, albeit of Dutch extraction; but Through Noord-Holland is an agreeable exception in that it covers all the ground between Amsterdam and the Helder, and is constructed in a peculiar sport of Babel. In Dutch it is I have no doubt an ordinary guide-book; in English it is something far more precious. The following extract from the preface to the second edition ought to be quoted before I borrow further from its pages:--

Being completed with the necessary alterations and corrections I send it into the world for the second time. As it will be published besides in Dutch also in French and English, the aim of the edition will surely be favoured, and our poor misappreciated country that so often is regarded with contempt by our countrymen as well as by foreigners will soon be an attraction for tourists. For were not it those large extensive quiet heatheries those rustling green woods and those quiet low meadows which inspired our great painters to bring their fascinating landscapes on the cloth? Had not that bloomy sky and that sunny mysterious light, those soft green meadows with their multi-coloured flowers, through which the river is streaming as a silver band, had not all this a quieting influence to the agitated mind of many of us, did not it give the quiet rest and did not it whisper to you; here ... here is it good? And for this our country we want to be a reliable guide by the directions of which we can savely start.

With Zaandvoort we may associate Dirck van Santvoort who painted the portrait of the curious girl--No. 2133 at the Ryks Museum--reproduced opposite page 236. Of the painter very little is known. He belongs to the great period, flourishing in the middle of the seventeenth century--and that is all. But he had a very cunning hand and an interesting mind, as the few pictures to his name attest. In the same room at the Ryks Museum where the portrait hangs is a large group of ladies and gentlemen, all wearing some of the lace which he dearly loved to paint. And in one of the recesses of the Gallery of Honour is a quaint little lady from his delicate brush--No. 2131--well worth study.

Haarlem's great church, which is dedicated to St. Bavo, is one of the finest in Holland. All that is needed to make it perfect is an infusion of that warmth and colour which once it possessed but of which so few traces have been allowed to remain. The Dutch Protestants, as I remarked at Utrecht, have shown singular efficiency in denuding religion of its external graces and charm. There is no church so beautiful but they would reduce it to bleak and arid cheerlessness. Place even the cathedral of Chartres in a Dutch market-place, and it would be a whitewashed desert in a week, while little shops and houses would be built against its sacred walls. There is hardly a great church in Holland but has some secular domicile clinging like a barnacle to its sides.

The attitude of the Dutch to their churches is in fact very much that of Quakers to their meeting-houses--even to the retention of hats. But whereas it is reasonable for a Quaker, having made for himself as plain a rectangular building as he can, to attach no sanctity to it, there is an incongruity when the same attitude is maintained amid beautiful Gothic arches. The result is that Dutch churches are more than chilling. In the simplest English village church one receives some impression of the friendliness of religion; but in Holland--of course I speak as a stranger and a foreigner--religion seems to be a cold if not a repellent thing.

One result is that on looking back over one's travels through Holland it is almost impossible to disentangle in the memory one whitewashed church from another. They have a common monotony of internal aridity: one distinguishes them, if at all, by some accidental possession--Gouda, for example, by its stained glass; Haarlem by its organ, and the swinging ships; Delft by the tomb of William the Silent; Utrecht by the startling absence of an entrance fee.

At Haarlem, as it happens, one is peculiarly able to study cause and effect in this matter of Protestant bleakness, since there stands before the door of this wonderful church, once a Roman Catholic temple, drenched, I doubt not, in mystery and colour, a certain significant statue.

To Erasmus of Rotterdam is generally given the parentage of the Reformation. Whatever his motives, Erasmus stands as the forerunner of Luther. But Erasmus had his forerunner too, the discoverer of printing. For had not a means of rapidly multiplying and cheapening books been devised, the people, who were after all the back-bone of the Reformation, would never have had the opportunity of themselves reading the Bible--either the Vulgate or Erasmus's New Testament--and thus seeing for themselves how wide was the gulf fixed between Christ and the Christians. It was the discovery of this discrepancy which prepared them to stand by the reformers, and, by supporting them and urging them on, assist them to victory.

Stimulated by the desire to be level with Rome for his own early fetters, and desiring also an antagonist worthy of his satirical powers, Erasmus (or so I think) hit independently upon the need for a revised Bible. But Luther to a large extent was the outcome of his times and of popular feeling. A spokesman was needed, and Luther stepped forward. The inventor of printing made the way possible; Erasmus showed the way; Luther took it.

Now the honour of inventing printing lies between two claimants, Laurens Janszoon Coster, of Haarlem (the original of this statue) and Gutenburg of Mayence. The Dutch like to think that Coster was the man, and that his secret was sold to Gutenburg by his servant Faust. Be that as it may--and the weight of evidence is in favour of Gutenburg--it is interesting as one stands by the statue of Coster under the shadow of Haarlem's great church to think that this was perhaps the true parent of that great upheaval, the true pavior of the way.

Whatever Coster's claim to priority may be, he certainly was a printer, and it is only fitting that Haarlem should possess so fine a library of early books and MSS. as it does. Another monument to Coster is to be seen in the Hout, a wood of which Haarlem is very proud. It has a fine avenue called the Spanjaards Laan, and is a very pleasant shady place in summer, hardly inferior to the Bosch at The Hague. "The delightful walks of the Hout," says the author of Through Noord-Holland, "and the caressing song of the nightingale and other birds, do not only invite the Haarlemmers to it, but the citizens of the neighbouring towns as well."

On the border of the wood is a pavilion which holds the collections of Colonial curiosities. In front of the pavilion (I quote again from Through Noord-Holland, which is invaluable), "stands a casting of Laskson and his sons to a knot, which has been manufactured in the last centuries before Christ. The original has been digged up at Rome in 1500." Shade of Lessing!

The cannon-ball embedded in the wall of the church, which the sacristan shows with so much interest, recalls Haarlem's great siege in 1572--a siege notable in the history of warfare for the courage and endurance of the townspeople against terrible odds. The story is worth telling in full, but I have not space and Motley is very accessible. But I sketch, with his assistance, its salient features.

The attack began in mid-winter, when Haarlem Mere, a great lake in the east which has since been drained and poldered, was frozen over. For some time a dense fog covered it, enabling loads of provisions and arms to be safely conveyed into the city.

Don Frederic, the son of the Duke of Alva, who commanded the Spanish, began with a success that augured well, a force of 4,000 men which marched from Leyden under De la Marck being completely routed. Among the captives taken by the Spaniards, says Motley, was "a gallant officer, Baptist Van Trier, for whom De la Marck in vain offered two thousand crowns and nineteen Spanish prisoners. The proposition was refused with contempt. Van Trier was hanged upon the gallows by one leg until he was dead, in return for which barbarity the nineteen Spaniards were immediately gibbeted by De la Marck. With this interchange of cruelties the siege may be said to have opened.

"Don Frederic had stationed himself in a position opposite to the gate of the Cross, which was not very strong, but fortified by a ravelin. Intending to make a very short siege of it, he established his batteries immediately, and on the 18th, 19th, and 20th December directed a furious cannonade against the Cross-gate, the St. John's gate, and the curtain between the two. Six hundred and eighty shots were discharged on the first, and nearly as many on each of the two succeeding days. The walls were much shattered, but men, women, and children worked night and day within the city, repairing the breaches as fast as made. They brought bags of sand, blocks of stone, cart-loads of earth from every quarter, and they stripped the churches of all their statues, which they threw by heaps into the gaps. They sought thus a more practical advantage from those sculptured saints than they could have gained by only imploring their interposition

The fact, however, excited horror among the besiegers. Men who were daily butchering their fellow-beings, and hanging their prisoners in cold blood, affected to shudder at the enormity of the offence thus exercised against graven images.

"After three days' cannonade, the assault was ordered, Don Frederic only intending a rapid massacre, to crown his achievements at Zutphen and Naarden. The place, he thought, would fall in a week, and after another week of sacking, killing, and ravishing, he might sweep on to 'pastures new' until Holland was overwhelmed. Romero advanced to the breach, followed by a numerous storming party, but met with a resistance which astonished the Spaniards. The church bells rang the alarm throughout the city, and the whole population swarmed to the walls. The besiegers were encountered not only with sword and musket, but with every implement which the burghers' hands could find. Heavy stones, boiling oil, live coals, were hurled upon the heads of the soldiers; hoops, smeared with pitch and set on fire, were dexterously thrown upon their necks. Even Spanish courage and Spanish ferocity were obliged to shrink before the steady determination of a whole population animated by a single spirit. Romero lost an eye in the conflict, many officers were killed and wounded, and three or four hundred soldiers left dead in the breach, while only three or four of the townsmen lost their lives. The signal of recall was reluctantly given, and the Spaniards abandoned the assault.

"Don Frederic was now aware that Haarlem would not fall at his feet at the first sound of his trumpet. It was obvious that a siege must precede the massacre. He gave orders, therefore, that the ravelin should be undermined, and doubted not that, with a few days' delay, the place would be in his hands."

The Prince of Orange then made, from Sassenheim, another attempt to relieve the town, sending 2,000 men. But a fog falling, they lost their way and fell into the enemy's hands. "De Koning," says Motley, "second in command, was among the prisoners. The Spaniards cut off his head and threw it over the walls into the city, with this inscription: 'This is the head of Captain De Koning, who is on his way with reinforcements for the good city of Haarlem'. The citizens retorted with a practical jest, which was still more barbarous. They cut off the heads of eleven prisoners and put them into a barrel, which they threw into the Spanish camp. A label upon the barrel contained these words: 'Deliver these ten heads to Duke Alva in payment of his tenpenny tax, with one additional head for interest'."

Day after day the attack continued and was repulsed. Meanwhile, unknown to the Spaniards, the besieged burghers were silently and swiftly building inside the ravelin a solid half-moon shaped battlement. On the 31st of December, the last day of 1572, the great assault was made. "The attack was unexpected, but the forty or fifty sentinels defended the walls while they sounded the alarm. The tocsin bells tolled, and the citizens, whose sleep was not apt to be heavy during that perilous winter, soon manned the ramparts again. The daylight came upon them while the fierce struggle was still at its height. The besieged, as before, defended themselves with musket and rapier, with melted pitch, with firebrands, with clubs and stones.

Meantime, after morning prayers in the Spanish camp, the trumpet for a general assault was sounded. A tremendous onset was made upon the gate of the Cross, and the ravelin was carried at last. The Spaniards poured into this fort, so long the object of their attack, expecting instantly to sweep into the city with sword and fire. As they mounted its wall they became for the first time aware of the new and stronger fortification which had been secretly constructed on the inner side. The reason why the ravelin had been at last conceded was revealed. The half moon, whose existence they had not suspected, rose before them bristling with cannon, A sharp fire was instantly opened upon the besiegers, while at the same instant the ravelin, which the citizens had undermined, blew up with a severe explosion, carrying into the air all the soldiers who had just entered it so triumphantly. This was the turning point. The retreat was sounded, and the Spaniards fled to their camp, leaving at least three hundred dead beneath the walls. Thus was a second assault, made by an overwhelming force and led by the most accomplished generals of Spain, signally and gloriously repelled by the plain burghers of Haarlem."

Cold and famine now began to assist the Spaniards, and the townsfolk were reduced to every privation. The Spaniards also suffered and Don Frederic wished to raise the siege. He suggested this step to his father, but Alva was made of sterner stuff. He sent from Nymwegen a grim message: "'Tell Don Frederic,' said Alva, 'that if he be not decided to continue the siege till the town be taken, I shall no longer consider him my son, whatever my opinion may formerly have been. Should he fall in the siege, I will myself take the field to maintain it; and when we have both perished, the Duchess, my wife, shall come from Spain to do the same.' Such language was unequivocal, and hostilities were resumed as fiercely as before. The besieged welcomed them with rapture, and, as usual, made daily the most desperate sallies. In one outbreak the Haarlemers, under cover of a thick fog, marched up to the enemy's chief battery, and attempted to spike the guns before his face. They were all slain at the cannon's mouth, whither patriotism, not vainglory, had led them, and lay dead around the battery, with their hammers and spikes in their hands. The same spirit was daily manifested. As the spring advanced, the kine went daily out of the gates to their peaceful pasture, notwithstanding all the turmoil within and around; nor was it possible for the Spaniards to capture a single one of these creatures, without paying at least a dozen soldiers as its price. 'These citizens,' wrote Don Frederic, 'do as much as the best soldiers in the world could do.'" The whole story is too dreadful to be told; but events proved the implacable old soldier to be right. Month after month passed, assault after assault was repulsed by the wretched but indomitable burghers; but time was all on the side of the enemy. On July 12th, after the frustration again and again of hopes of relief from the Prince of Orange, whose plans were doomed to failure on every occasion, the city surrendered on the promise of complete forgiveness by Don Frederic.

The Don, however, was only a subordinate; the Duke of Alva had other views. He quickly arrived on the scene, and as quickly his presence made itself felt. "The garrison, during the siege, had been reduced from four thousand to eighteen hundred. Of these the Germans, six hundred in number, were, by Alva's order, dismissed, on a pledge to serve no more against the King. All the rest of the garrison were immediately butchered, with at least as many citizens.... Five executioners, with their attendants, were kept constantly at work; and when at last they were exhausted with fatigue, or perhaps sickened with horror, three hundred wretches were tied two and two, back to back, and drowned in the Haarlem Lake. At last, after twenty-three hundred human creatures had been murdered in cold blood, within a city where so many thousands had previously perished by violent or by lingering deaths; the blasphemous farce of a pardon was enacted.

Fifty-seven of the most prominent burghers of the place were, however, excepted from the act of amnesty, and taken into custody as security for the future good conduct of the other citizens. Of these hostages some were soon executed, some died in prison, and all would have been eventually sacrificed, had not the naval defeat of Bossu soon afterwards enabled the Prince of Orange to rescue the remaining prisoners. Ten thousand two hundred and fifty-six shots had been discharged against the walk during the siege. Twelve thousand of the besieging army had died of wounds or disease during the seven months and two days between the investment and the surrender. In the earlier part of August, after the executions had been satisfactorily accomplished, Don Frederic made his triumphal entry, and the first chapter in the invasion of Holland was closed. Such was the memorable siege of Haarlem, an event in which we are called upon to wonder equally at human capacity to inflict and to endure misery. "Philip was lying dangerously ill at the wood of Segovia, when the happy tidings of the reduction of Haarlem, with its accompanying butchery, arrived. The account of all this misery, minutely detailed to him by Alva, acted like magic. The blood of twenty-three hundred of his fellow-creatures--coldly murdered by his orders, in a single city--proved for the sanguinary monarch the elixir of life: he drank and was refreshed. 'The principal medicine which has cured his Majesty,' wrote Secretary Cayas from Madrid to Alva, 'is the joy caused to him by the good news which you have communicated of the surrender of Haarlem.'"

I know nothing of the women of Haarlem to-day, but in the sixteenth century they were among the bravest and most efficient in the world, and it was largely their efforts and example which enabled the city to hold out so long. Motley describes them as a corps of three hundred fighting women, "all females of respectable character, armed with sword, musket, and dagger. Their chief, Kenau Hasselaer, was a widow of distinguished family, and unblemished reputation, about forty-seven years of age, who, at the head of her amazons, participated in many of the most fiercely contested actions of the siege, both within and without the walls. When such a spirit animated the maids and matrons of the city, it might be expected that the men would hardly surrender the place without a struggle."

Haarlem still preserves the pretty custom of hanging lace by the doors of houses which the stork is expected to visit or has just visited. Its origin was the humanity of the Spanish general, during this great siege, in receiving a deputation of matrons from the town and promising protection from his soldiery of all women in childbed. Every house was to go unharmed upon which a piece of lace signifying a confinement was displayed. This was a promise with which the Duke of Alva seems not to have interfered.

The author of Through Noord-Holland thus eloquently describes the effect of Haarlem's great organ--for long the finest in the world: "Vibrating rolls the tone through the church-building, followed by sweet melodies, running through each register of it; now one hears the sound of trumpets or soft whistling tunes then again piano music or melancholical hautboy tunes chiming as well is deceivingly imitated." Free recitals are given on Tuesdays and Thursdays from one to two. On other days the organist can be persuaded to play for a fee. Charles Lamb's friend Fell paid a ducat to the organist and half a crown to the blower, and heard as much as he wanted. He found the vox humana "the voice of a psalm-singing clerk". Other travellers have been more fortunate. Ireland tells us that when Handel played this organ the organist took him either for an angel or a devil.

Among Haarlem's architectural attractions is the very interesting Meat Market, hard by the great church, one of the most agreeable pieces of floridity between the Middelburg stadhuis and the Leeuwarden chancellerie. There is also the fine Amsterdam Gate, on the road to Amsterdam.

In the Teyler Museum, on the Spaarne, is a poor collection of modern oil paintings, some good modern water colours and a very fine collection of drawings by the masters, including several Rembrandts. In this room one may well plan to spend much time. One of the best Israels that I saw in Holland is a little water-colour interior that is hung here. I asked one of the attendants if they had anything by Matthew Maris, but he denied his existence. James he knew, and William; but there was no Matthew. "But he is your most distinguished artist," I said. It was great heresy and not to be tolerated. To the ordinary Dutchman art begins with Rembrandt and ends with Israels. This perhaps is why Matthew Maris has taken refuge in St.

John's Wood.

And now we come to Haarlem's chief glory--which is not Coster the printer, and not the church of Bavo the Saint, and not the tulip gardens, and not the florid and beautiful Meat Market; but the painter Frans Hals, whose masterpieces hang in the Town Hall.

I have called Hals the glory of Haarlem, yet he was only an adopted son, having been born in Antwerp about 1580. But his parents were true Haarlemers, and Frans was a resident there before he reached man's estate.

The painter's first marriage was not happy; he was even publicly reprimanded for cruelty to his wife. In spite of the birth of his eldest child just thirty-four weeks earlier than the proprieties require, his second marriage seems to have been fortunate enough. Some think that we see Mynheer and Myvrouw Hals in the picture--No. 1084 in the Ryks Museum--which is reproduced on the opposite page. If this jovial and roguish pair are really the painter and his wife, they were a merry couple. Children they had in abundance; seven sons, five of whom were painters, and three daughters. Abundance indeed was Hals' special characteristic; you see it in all his work--vigorous, careless abundance and power. He lived to be eighty-five or so. Mrs. Hals, after a married life of fifty years, continued to flourish, with the assistance of some relief from the town, for a considerable period.

In the Haarlem Museum may be seen a picture of Hals' studio, painted by Berck Heyde, in 1652, containing portraits of Hals himself, then about seventy, and several of his old pupils--Wouvermans, Dirck Hals, his brother, four of his sons, the artist himself and others. Hals taught also Van der Helst, whose work at times comes nearest to his own, Verspronk, Terburg and Adrian van Ostade.

To see the work of Hals at his best it is necessary to visit Holland, for we have but little here. The "Laughing Cavalier" in the Wallace Collection is perhaps his best picture in a public gallery in England. But the Haarlem Museum is a temple dedicated to his fame, and there you may revel in his lusty powers.

The room in which his great groups hang is perhaps in effect more filled with faces than any in the world. Entering the door one is immediately beneath the bold and laughing scrutiny of a host of genial masterful arquebusiers, who make merry on the walls for all time. Such a riot of vivid portraiture never was! Other men have painted single heads as well or better: but Hals stands alone in his gusto, his abundance, his surpassing brio. It is a thousand pities that neither Lamb nor Hazlitt ever made the journey to Haarlem, because only they among our writers on art could have brought a commensurate gusto to the praise of his brush. I have reproduced one of the groups opposite page 150, but the result is no more than a memento of the original. It conveys, however, an impression of the skill in composition by which the group is made not only a collection of portraits but a picture too. If such groups there must be, this is the way to paint them. The Dutch in the seventeenth century had a perfect mania for these commemorative canvases, and there is not a stadhuis but has one or more. Rembrandt's "Night Watch" and Hals'

Haarlem groups are the greatest; but one is always surprised by the general level of excellence maintained, and now and then a lesser man such as Van der Helst climbs very nigh the rose, as in his "De Schuttersmaaltyd" in the "Night Watch" room in the Ryks Museum. The Corporation pieces of Jan van Ravesteyn in the Municipal Museum at The Hague are also exceedingly vivid; while Jan de Bray's canvases at Haarlem, in direct competition with Hals', would be very good indeed in the absence of their rivals.

Among other painters who can be studied here is our Utrecht friend Jan van Scorel, who has a large "Adam and Eve" in the passage and a famous "Baptism of Christ"; Jan Verspronk of Haarlem, Hals' pupil, who has a very quiet and effective portrait (No. 210) and a fine rich group of the lady managers of an orphanage; and Cornelius Cornellessen, also of Haarlem, painter of an excellent Corporation Banquet. In the collection are also a very charming little Terburg (No. 194) and a fascinating unsigned portrait of William III. as a pale and wistful boy.

Haarlem was the mother or instructor of many painters. There is Dirck Hals, the brother of Frans, who was born there at the end of the sixteenth century, and painted richly coloured scenes of fashionable convivial life. He died at Haarlem ten years before Frans. A greater was Bartholomew van der Helst, who was Hals' most assimilative pupil. He was born at Haarlem about 1612, and is supposed to have studied also under Nicolas Elias. His finest large work is undoubtedly the "Banquet" to which I have just referred, but I always associate him with his portrait of Gerard Bicker, Landrichter of Muiden, that splendid tun of a man, No. 1140 in the Gallery of Honour at the Ryks Museum (see opposite page 86). One of his most beautiful paintings is a portrait of a woman in our National Gallery, on a screen in the large Netherlands room: a picture which shows the influence of Elias not a little, as any one can see who recalls Nos. 897 and 899 in the Ryks Museum--two very beautiful portraits of a man and his wife.

Haarlem and Oudenarde both claim the birth of Adrian Brouwer, a painter of Dutch topers. As to his life little is known. Tradition says that he drank and dissipated his earnings, while his work is evidence that he knew inn life with some particularity; but his epitaph calls him "a man of great mind who rejected every splendour of the world and who despised gain and riches".

Brouwer, who was born about 1606, was put by his mother, a dressmaker at Haarlem, into the studio of Frans Hals. Hals bullied him, as he bullied his first wife. Escaping to Amsterdam, Brouwer became a famous painter, his pictures being acquired, among others, by Rembrandt in his wealthy days, and by Rubens. He died at Antwerp when only thirty-three. We have nothing of his in the National Gallery, but he is represented at the Wallace Collection.

At Haarlem was born also, in 1620, Nicolas Berchem, painter of charming scenes of broken arches and columns (which he certainly never saw in his own country), made human and domestic by the presence of people and cows, and suffused with gentle light. We have five of his pictures in the National Gallery. Berchem's real name was Van Haarlem. One day, however, when he was a pupil in Van Goyen's studio, his father pursued him for some fault. Van Goyen, who was a kindly creature, as became the father-in-law of Jan Steen, called out to his other pupils--"Berg hem" (Hide him!) and the phrase stuck, and became his best-known name. Nicolas married a termagant, but never allowed her to impair his cheerful disposition.

Haarlem was the birthplace also of Jacob van Ruisdael, greatest of Dutch landscape painters. He was born about 1620. His idea was to be a doctor, but Nicolas Berchem induced him to try painting, and we cannot be too thankful for the change. His landscapes have a deep and grave beauty: the clouds really seem to be floating across the sky; the water can almost be heard tumbling over the stones. Ruisdael did not find his typical scenery in his native land: he travelled in Germany and Italy, and possibly in Norway; but whenever he painted a strictly Dutch scene he excelled. He died at Haarlem in 1682; and one of his most exquisite pictures hangs in the Museum. I do not give any reproductions of Ruisdael because his work loses so much in the process. At the National Gallery and at the Wallace Collection he is well represented.

Walking up and down beneath the laughing confidence of these many bold faces in the great Hals' room at Haarlem I found myself repeating Longfellow's lines:--

He has singed the beard of the King of Spain, And carried away the Dean of Jaen And sold him in Algiers.

Surely the hero, Simon Danz, was something such a man as Hals painted. How does the ballad run?--

A DUTCH PICTURE.

Simon Danz has come home again, From cruising about with his buccaneers; He has singed the beard of the King of Spain, And carried away the Dean of Jaen And sold him in Algiers.

In his house by the Maese, with its roof of tiles And weathercocks flying aloft in air, There are silver tankards of antique styles, Plunder of convent and castle, and piles Of carpets rich and rare.

In his tulip garden there by the town Overlooking the sluggish stream, With his Moorish cap and dressing-gown The old sea-captain, hale and brown, Walks in a waking dream.

A smile in his gray mustachio lurks Whenever he thinks of the King of Spain. And the listed tulips look like Turks, And the silent gardener as he works Is changed to the Dean of Jaen.

The windmills on the outermost Verge of the landscape in the haze, To him are towers on the Spanish coast, With whisker'd sentinels at their post, Though this is the river Maese. But when the winter rains begin, He sits and smokes by the blazing brands, And old sea-faring men come in, Goat-bearded, gray, and with double chin, And rings upon their hands.

They sit there in the shadow and shine Of the flickering fire of the winter night, Figures in colour and design Like those by Rembrandt of the Rhine, Half darkness and half light.

And they talk of their ventures lost or won, And their talk is ever and ever the same, While they drink the red wine of Tarragon, From the cellars of some Spanish Don, Or convent set on flame.

Restless at times, with heavy strides He paces his parlour to and fro; He is like a ship that at anchor rides, And swings with the rising and falling tides And tugs at her anchor-tow.

Voices mysterious far and near, Sound of the wind and sound of the sea, Are calling and whispering in his ear, "Simon Danz! Why stayest thou here? Come forth and follow me!"

So he thinks he shall take to the sea again, For one more cruise with his buccaneers; To singe the beard of the King of Spain, And capture another Dean of Jaen And sell him in Algiers.

One thought leads to another. It is impossible also to remain long in the great Hals' room of the Museum without meditating a little upon the difference between these arquebusiers and the Dutch of the present day. Passing among these people, once so mighty and ambitious, so great in government and colonisation, in seamanship and painting, and seeing them now so material and self-centred, so bound within their own small limits, so careless of literature and art, so intent upon the profits of the day and the pleasures of next Sunday, one has a vision of what perhaps may be our own lot. For the Dutch are very near us in kin, and once were nigh as great as we have been. Are we, in our day of decadence, to shrivel thus? "There but for the grace of God goes England"--is that a reasonable utterance? One sees the difference concretely as one passes from these many Corporation and Regent pieces in the galleries of Holland to the living Dutchmen of the streets. I saw it particularly at Haarlem on a streaming wet day, after hurrying from the Museum to the Café Brinkmann through some inches of water. At a table opposite, sipping their coffee, were two men strikingly like two of Frans Hals' arquebusiers. Yet how unlike. For the air of masterful recklessness had gone, that good-humoured glint of power in the eye was no more. Hals had painted conquerors, or at any rate warriors for country; these coffee drinkers were meditating profit and loss. Where once was authority is now calculation.

I quote a little poem by Mr. Van Lennep of Zeist, near Utrecht, which shows that the Dutch, whatever their present condition, have not forgotten:--

The shell, when put to child-like ears, Yet murmurs of its bygone years, In echoes of the sea; The Dutch-born youngster likes the sound, And ponders o'er its mystic ground And wondrous memory.

Thus, in Dutch hearts, an echo dwells, Which, like the ever-mindful shells, Yet murmurs of the sea: That sea, of ours in times of yore, And, when De Ruyter went before, Our road to victory.

# CHAPTER X

Amsterdam

The Venice of the North--The beauty of gravity--No place for George Dyer--The Keizersgracht--Kalverstraat and Warmoes Straat--The

Ghetto--Pile-driving--Erasmus's sarcasm--The new Bourse--Learning the city--Tramway perplexities The unnecessary guide--The Royal

Palace--The New Church--Stained glass--The Old Church--The five carpets--Wedding customs--Dutch wives to-day and in the past--The Begijnenhof--The new religion and the old--The Burgerweesmeisjes--The Eight Orange Blossoms--Dutch music halls--A Dutch Hamlet--The fish market--Rembrandt's grave--A nation of shopkeepers--Max Havelaar--Mr. Drystubble's device--Lothario and Betsy--The English in Holland and the Dutch in England--Athleticism--A people on skates--The chaperon's perplexity--Love on the level.

Amsterdam is notable for two possessions above others: its old canals and its old pictures. Truly has it been called the Venice of the North; but very different is its sombre quietude from the sunny Italian city among the waters. There is a beauty of gaiety and a beauty of gravity; and Amsterdam in its older parts--on the Keizersgracht and the Heerengracht--has the beauty of gravity. In Venice the canal is of course also the street: gondolas and barcas are continually gliding hither and thither; but in the Keizersgracht and the Heerengracht the water is little used. One day, however, I watched a costermonger steering a boat-load of flowers under a bridge, and no words of mine can describe the loveliness of their reflection. I remember the incident particularly because flowers are not much carried in Holland, and it is very pleasant to have this impression of them--this note of happy gaiety in so dark a setting.

An unprotected roadway runs on either side of the water, which makes the houses beside these canals no place for Charles Lamb's friend, George Dyer, to visit in. Accidents are not numerous, but a company exists in Amsterdam whose business it is to rescue such odd dippers as horses and carriages by means of elaborate machinery devised for the purpose. Only travellers born under a luckier star than I are privileged to witness such sport.

In the main Amsterdam is a city of trade, of hurrying business men, of ceaseless clanging tramcars and crowded streets; but on the Keizersgracht and the Heerengracht you are always certain to find the old essential Dutch gravity and peace. No tide moves the sullen waters of these canals, which are lined with trees that in spring form before the narrow, dark, discreet houses the most delicate green tracery imaginable; and in summer screen them altogether. These houses are for the most part black and brown, with white window frames, and they rise to a great height, culminating in that curious stepped gable (with a crane and pulley in it) which is, to many eyes, the symbol of the city. I know no houses that so keep their secrets. In every one, I doubt not, is furniture worthy of the exterior: old paintings of Dutch gentlemen and gentlewomen, a landscape or two, a girl with a lute and a few tavern scenes; old silver windmills; and plate upon plate of serene blue Delft. (You may see what I mean in the Suasso rooms at the Stedelijk Museum.) I have walked and idled in the Keizersgracht at all times of the day, but have never seen any real signs of life. Mats have been banged on its doorsteps by clean Dutch maidservants armed with wicker beaters; milk has been brought in huge cans of brass and copper shining like the sun; but of its life proper the gracht has given no sign. Its true life is houseridden, behind those spotless and very beautiful lace curtains, and there it remains.

One of the wittiest of the old writers on Holland (of whom I said something in the second chapter), Owen Feltham the moralist, describes in his Brief Character of the Low Countries an Amsterdam house of the middle of the seventeenth century. Thus:--

When you are entered the house, the first thing you encounter is a

Looking-glasse. No question but a true Embleme of politick hospitality; for though it reflect yourself in your own figure, 'tis yet no longer than while you are there before it. When you are gone once, it flatters the next commer, without the least remembrance that you ere were there. The next are the vessels of the house marshalled about the room like watchmen. All as neat as if you were in a Citizen's Wife's Cabinet; for unless it be themselves, they let none of God's creatures lose any thing of their native beauty.

Their houses, especially in their Cities, are the best eye-beauties of their Country. For cost and sight they far exceed our English, but they want their magnificence. Their lining is yet more rich than their outside; not in hangings, but pictures, which even the poorest are there furnisht with. Not a cobler but has his toyes for ornament. Were the knacks of all their houses set together, there would not be such another Bartholmew-Faire in Europe....

Their beds are no other than land-cabines, high enough to need a ladder or stairs. Up once, you are walled in with Wainscot, and that is good discretion to avoid the trouble of making your will every night; for once falling out else would break your neck perfectly. But if you die in it, this comfort you shall leave your friends, that you dy'd in clean linnen.

Whatsoever their estates be, their houses must be fair. Therefore from Amsterdam they have banisht seacoale, lest it soyl their buildings, of which the statelier sort are sometimes sententious, and in the front carry some conceit of the Owner. As to give you a taste in these.

Christus Adjutor Meus; Hoc abdicato Perenne Quero; Hic Medio tuitus Itur.

Every door seems studded with Diamonds. The nails and hinges hold a constant brightnesse, as if rust there was not a quality incident to Iron. Their houses they keep cleaner than their bodies; their bodies than their souls. Goe to one, you shall find the Andirons shut up in net-work. At a second, the Warming-pan muffled in Italian Cutworke. At a third the Sconce clad in Cambrick.

The absence of any lively traffic on the canals, as in Venice, has this compensation, that the surface is left untroubled the more minutely to mirror the houses and trees, and, at night, the tramcars on the bridges. The lights of these cars form the most vivid reflections that I can recollect. But the quiet reproduction of the stately black façades is the more beautiful thing. An added dignity and repose are noticeable. I said just now that one desired to learn the secret of the calm life of these ancient grachts. But the secret of the actual houses of fact is as nothing compared with the secret of those other houses, more sombre, more mysterious, more reserved, that one sees in the water. To penetrate their impressive doors were an achievement, a distinction, indeed! With such a purpose suicide would lose half its terrors.

For the greatest contrast to these black canals, you must seek the Kalverstraat and Warmoes Straat. Kalverstraat, running south from the Dam, is by day filled with shoppers and by night with gossipers. No street in the world can be more consistently busy. Damrak is of course always a scene of life, but Damrak is a thoroughfare--its population moving continually either to or from the station. But those who use the Kalverstraat may be said almost to live in it. To be there is an end in itself. Warmoes Straat, parallel with Damrak on the other side of the Bourse, behind the Bible Hotel, is famous for its gigantic restaurant--the hugest in Europe, I believe--the Krasnapolsky, a palace of bewildering mirrors, and for concert halls and other accessories of the gayer life. But this book is no place in which to enlarge upon the natural history of Warmoes Straat and its southern continuation, the Nes.

For the principal cafés, as distinguished from restaurants, you must seek the Rembrandt's Plein, in the midst of which stands the master's statue. The pavement of this plein on Sunday evening in summer is almost impassable for the tables and chairs that spread over it and the crowds overflowing from Kalverstraat.

But there is still to be mentioned a district of Amsterdam which from the evening of Friday until the evening of Saturday is more populous even than Kalverstraat. This is the Jews' quarter, which has, I should imagine, more parents and children to the square foot than any residential region in Europe. I struggled through it at sundown one fine Saturday--to say I walked through it would be too misleading--and the impression I gathered of seething vivacity is still with me. These people surely will inherit the earth.

Spinoza was a child of this Ghetto: his birthplace at 41 Waterloo Plein is still shown; and Rembrandt lived at No. 4 Jodenbree Straat for sixteen years.

A large number of the Amsterdam Jews are diamond cutters and polishers. You may see in certain cafés dealers in these stones turning over priceless little heaps of them with the long little finger-nail which they preserve as a scoop.

Amsterdam may be a city builded on the sand; but none the less will it endure. Indeed the sand saves it; for it is in the sand that the wooden piles on which every house rests find their footing, squelching through the black mud to this comparative solidity. Some of the piles are as long as 52 ft., and watching them being driven in, it is impossible to believe that stability can ever be attained, every blow of the monkey accounting for so very many inches. When one watches pile-driving in England it is difficult to see the effect of each blow; but during the five or fewer minutes that I spent one day on Damrak observing the preparation for the foundations of a new house, the pile must have gone in nearly a foot each time, and it was very near the end of its journey too. In course of years the black brackish mud petrifies not only the piles but the wooden girders that are laid upon them.

Pile-driving on an extensive scale can be a very picturesque sight. Breitner has painted several pile-driving scenes, one of which hangs in the Stedelijk Museum at Amsterdam.

Statistics are always impressive. I have seen somewhere the number of piles which support the new Bourse and the Central Station; but I cannot now find them. The Royal Palace stands on 13,659. Erasmus of Rotterdam made merry quite in the manner of an English humorist over Amsterdam's wooden foundations. He twitted the inhabitants with living on the tops of trees, like rooks. But as I lay awake from daybreak to a civilised hour for two mornings in the

Hotel Weimar at Rotterdam--prevented from sleeping by the pile-driving for the hotel extension--I thought of the apologue of the pot and the kettle.

I referred just now to the new Bourse. When I was at Amsterdam in 1897, the water beside Damrak extended much farther towards the Dam than it does now. Where now is the new Bourse was then shipping. But the new Bourse looks stable enough to-day. As to its architectural charms, opinions differ. My own feeling is that it is not a style that will wear well. For a permanent public building something more classic is probably desirable; and at Amsterdam, that city of sombre colouring, I would have had darker hues than the red and yellow that have been employed. The site of the old Bourse is now an open space.

It is stated that the kindly custom of allowing the children of Amsterdam the run of the Bourse as a playground for a week every year is some compensation for the suppression of the Kermis, but another story makes the sanction a perpetual reward for an heroic deed against the Spaniards performed by a child in 1622.

My advice to any one visiting Amsterdam is first to study a map of the city--Bædeker gives a very useful one--and thus to begin with a general idea of the lie of the land and the water. With this knowledge, and the assistance of the trams, it should not appear a very bewildering place. The Dam is its heart: a fact the acquisition of which will help very sensibly. All roads in Amsterdam lead to the Dam, and all lead from it. The Dam gives the city its name--Amstel dam, the dam which stops the river Amstel on its course to the Zuyder Zee. It also gives English and American visitors opportunities for facetiousness which I tingle to recall. Every tram sooner or later reaches the Dam: that is another simplifying piece of information. The course of each tram may not be very easily acquired, but with a common destination like this you cannot be carried very far wrong.

One soon learns that the trams stop only at fixed points, and waits accordingly. The next lesson, which is not quite so simple, is that some of these points belong exclusively to trams going one way and some exclusively to trams going the other. If there is one thing calculated to reduce a perplexed foreigner in Amsterdam to rage and despair, it is, after a tiring day among pictures, to hail a half empty tram at a fixed point, with Tram-halte written on it, and be treated to a pitying smile from the driver as it rushes by. Upon such mortifications is education based; for one then looks again more narrowly at the sign and sees that underneath it is a little arrow pointing in the opposite direction to which one wished to go. One then walks on to the next point, at which the arrow will be pointing homewards, and waits there. Sometimes--O happy moment--a double arrow is found, facing both ways.

It is on the Dam that guides will come and pester you. The guide carries an umbrella and offers to show Amsterdam in such a way as to save you much money. He is quite useless, and the quickest means of getting free is to say that you have come to the city for no other purpose than to pay extravagantly for everything. So stupendous an idea checks even his importunity for a moment, and while he still reels you can escape. The guides outside the Ryks Museum who offer to point out the beauties of the pictures are less persistent. It would seem as if they were aware of the unsoundness of their case. There is no need to reply to these at all.

On the Dam also is the Royal Palace, which once was the stadhuis, but in 1808 (when Amsterdam was the third city of the French Empire) was offered to Louis Napoleon for a residence. Queen Wilhelmina occasionaly stays there, but The Hague holds her true home. The apartments are florid and not very interesting; but if the ascent of the tower is permitted one should certainly make it. It is interesting to have Amsterdam at one's feet. Only thus can its peculiar position and shape be understood: its old part an almost perfect semicircle, with canal-arcs within arcs, and its northern shore washed by the Y.

Also on the Dam is the New Church, which is to be seen more for the tomb of De Ruyter than for any architectural graces. The old sea dog, whose dark and determined features confront one in Bol's canvases again and again in Holland, reposes in full dress on a cannon amid symbols of his victories.

Close by, in the Royal Palace, are some of the flags which he wrested from the English. Other admirals also lie there, the Dutch naval commander never having wanted for honour in his own country.

The New Church, where the monarchs of Holland are crowned, has a very large new stained-glass window representing the coronation of Queen Wilhemina--one of the most satisfying new windows that I know, but quite lacking in any religious suggestion. That poet who considered a church the best retreat, because it is good to contemplate God through stained glass, would have fared badly in Holland.

The New Church is new only by comparison with the Old. It was built in 1410, rebuilt in 1452 and 1645. Amsterdam's Old Church, on the other side of Warmoes Straat, dates from 1300. The visitor to the New Church is handed a brief historical leaflet in exchange for his twenty-five cents, and is left to his own devices; but the Old Church has a koster who takes a pride in showing his lions and who deprecates gifts of money. An elderly, clean-shaved man with a humorous mouth, he might be taken for Holland's leading comedian. Instead, he displays ecclesiastical treasures, of which in 1904 there were fewer than usual, two of the three fine old windows representing the life of the Virgin being under repair behind a screen. The tombs and monuments are not interesting--admirals of the second rank and such small fry.

It is in the Old Church that most of the weddings of Amsterdam are celebrated. Thursday is the day, for then the fees are practically nothing; on other days to be married is an expense. The koster deplores the modern materialism which leads so many young men to be satisfied with the civil function; but the little enclosure, like a small arena, in which the church blesses unions, had to me a hardly less business-like appearance than a registry office. The comedian overflows with details. For the covering of the floor, he explains, there are five distinct carpets, ranging in price from five guelders to twenty-five for the hire, according to the means or ostentation of the party. Thursdays are no holiday for the church officials, one couple being hardly united before the horses of the next are pawing the paving stones at the door. I saw on one Thursday three bridal parties in as many minutes. The happy bride sat on the back seat of the brougham, immediately before her being two mirrors in the shape of a heart supporting a bouquet of white flowers. Contemplating this simple imagery she rattles to the ecclesiastical arena and the sanctities of the five, ten, fifteen, twenty or twenty-five guelder carpet. After, a banquet and jokes.

This is the second banquet, for when the precise preliminaries of a Dutch engagement are settled a betrothal feast is held. Friends are bidden to the wedding by the receipt of a box of sweets and a bottle of wine known as "Bride's tears". For the wedding day itself there is a particular brand of wine which contains little grains of gold. The Dutch also have special cake and wine for the celebration of births.

The position of the Dutch wife is now very much that of the wife in England; but in Holland's great days she ruled. Something of her quality is to be seen in the stories of Barneveldt's widow and Grotius's wife, and the heroism and address of the widow Kenau Hasselaer during the siege of Haarlem. Davies has an interesting page or two on this subject: "To be master of his own house is an idea which seems never to have occurred to the mind of a genuine Dutchman; nor did he often commence any undertaking, whether public or private, without first consulting the partner of his cares; and it is even said, that some of the statesmen most distinguished for their influence in the affairs of their own country and Europe in general, were accustomed to receive instructions at home to which they ventured not to go counter. But the dominion of these lordly dames, all despotic though it were, was ever exerted for the benefit of those who obeyed. It was the earnest and undaunted spirit of their women, which encouraged the Dutch to dare, and their calm fortitude to endure, the toils, privations, and sufferings of the first years of the war of independence against Spain; it was their activity and thrift in the management of their private incomes, that supplied them with the means of defraying an amount of national expenditure wholly unexampled in history; and to their influence is to be ascribed above all, the decorum of manners, and the purity of morals, for which the society of Holland has at all times been remarkable. But though they preserved their virtue and modesty uncontaminated amid the general corruption, they were no longer able to maintain their sway. The habit which the Dutch youth had acquired, among other foreign customs, of seeking amusement abroad, rendered them less dependent for happiness on the comforts of a married life; while, accustomed to the more dazzling allurements of the women of France and Italy, they were apt to overlook or despise the quiet and unobtrusive beauties of those of their own country. Whether they did not better consult their own dignity in emancipating themselves from this subjection may be a question; but the fact, that the decline of the republic and of the female sex went hand in hand, is indubitable."

To return to Amsterdam's sights, the church which I remember with most pleasure is the English Reformed Church, which many visitors never succeed in finding at all, but to which I was taken by a Dutch lady who knew my tastes. You seek the Spui, where the electric trams start for Haarlem, and enter a very small doorway on the north side. It seems to lead to a private house, but instead you find yourself in a very beautiful little enclosure of old and quaint buildings, exquisitely kept, each with a screen of pollarded chestnuts before it; in the midst of which is a toy white church with a gay little spire that might have wandered out of a fairy tale. The enclosure is called The Begijnenhof, or Court of the Begijnen, a little sisterhood named after St. Begga, daughter of Pipinus, Duke of Brabant,--a saint who lived at the end of the seventh century and whose day in the Roman Catholic Calendar is December 17.

The church was originally the church of these nuns, but when the old religion was overthrown in Amsterdam, in 1578, it was taken from them, although they were allowed--as happily they still are--to retain possession of the court around it.

In 1607 the church passed into the possession of a settlement of Scotch weavers who had been invited to Amsterdam by the merchants, and who had made it a condition of acceptance that they should have a conventicle of their own. It is now a resort of English church-going visitors on Sunday. Most of Holland's churches--as of England's--once belonged to Rome, and it is impossible to forget their ancient ownership; but I remember no other case where the new religion is practised, as in the Begijnenhof, in the heart of the enemy's camp. In the very midst of the homes of the quiet sweet Begijnen sisters are the voices of the usurping Reformers heard in prayer and praise.

One little concession, however, was made by the appropriators of the chapel. Until as recently as 1865 a special part of the building the original Roman consecration of which had not been nullified was retained by the sisterhood in which to bury their dead. The ceremony was very impressive. Twelve of the nuns carried their dead companion three times round the court before entering the church. But all that is over, and now they must seek burial elsewhere, without their borders.

One may leave the Begijnenhof by the other passage into Kalverstraat, and walking up that busy street towards the Dam, turn down the St. Lucien Steeg, on the left, to another of Amsterdam's homes of ancient peace--the municipal orphanage, which was once the Convent of St. Lucien. The Dutch are exceedingly kind to their poor, and the orphanages and almshouses (Oudemannen and Oudevrouwen houses as they are called) are very numerous. The Municipal Orphanage of Amsterdam is among the most interesting; and it is to this refuge that the girls and boys belong whom one sees so often in the streets of the city in curious parti-coloured costume--red and black vertically divided. The Amsterdamsche burgerweesmeisjes, as the girls are called, make in procession a very pretty and impressive sight--with their white tippets and caps above their dresses of black and red.

This reminds me that one of the most agreeable performances that I saw in any of the Dutch music halls (which are not good, and which are rendered very tedious to English people by reason of the interminable interval called the Pause in the middle of the evening), was a series of folk songs and dances by eight girls known as the Orange Blossoms, dressed in different traditional costumes of the north and south--Friesland, Marken, and Zeeland. They were quite charming. They sang and danced very prettily, as housewives, as fisher girls, but particularly as Amsterdamsche burgerweesmeisjes.

In the music halls both at Amsterdam and Rotterdam I listened to comic singers inexorably endowed with too many songs apiece; but I saw also some of those amazing feats of acrobatic skill and exhibitions of clean strength which alone should cause people to encourage these places of entertainment, where the standard of excellence in such displays is now so high. I did not go to the theatre in Holland. My Dutch was too elementary for that. My predecessor Ireland, however, did so, and saw an amusing piece of literalness introduced into Hamlet. In the impassioned scene, he tells us, between the prince and his mother, "when the hero starts at the imagined appearance of his father, his wig, by means of a concealed spring, jumped from 'the seat of his distracted brain,' and left poor Hamlet as bare as a Dutch willow in winter."

The Oude Kerk has very beautiful bells, but Amsterdam is no place in which to hear such sweet sounds. The little towns for bells. Near the church is the New Market, with the very charming old weigh-house with little extinguisher spires called the St. Anthonysveeg. Here the fish market is held; and the fish market of a city like Amsterdam should certainly be visited. The Old Market is on the western side of the Dam, under the western church. "It is said," remarks the author of Through Noord-Holland, "that Rembrandt has been buried in this church, though his grave has never been found."

Napoleon's sarcasm upon the English--that they were a nation of shopkeepers--never seemed to me very shrewd: but in Holland one realises that if any nation is to be thus signally stigmatised it is not the English. As a matter of fact we are very indifferent shopkeepers. We lack several of the needful qualities: we lack foresight, the sense of order and organised industry, and the strength of mind to resist the temptations following upon a great coup. A nation of shopkeepers would not go back on the shop so completely as we do. No nation that is essentially snobbish can be accurately summed up as a nation of shopkeepers. The French for all their distracting gifts of art and mockery are better shopkeepers than we, largely because they are more sensibly contented. They take short views and live each day more fully. But the Dutch are better still; the Dutch are truly a nation of shopkeepers. [4]

If one would see the Amsterdam merchant as the satirist sees him, the locus classicus is Multatuli's famous novel Max Havelaar, where he stands delightfully nude in the person of Mr. Drystubble, head of the firm of Last and Co., Coffee-brokers, No. 37 Laurier Canal. Max Havelaar was published in the early sixties to draw attention to certain scandals in Dutch colonial administration, and it has lived on, and will live, by reason of a curious blend of vivacity and intensity. Here is a little piece of Mr.

Drystubble's mind:--

Business is slack on the Coffee Exchange. The Spring Auction will make it right again. Don't suppose, however, that we have nothing to do. At Busselinck and Waterman's trade is slacker still. It is a strange world this: one gets a deal of experience by frequenting the Exchange for twenty years. Only fancy that they have tried--I mean Busselinck and Waterman--to do me out of the custom of Ludwig Stern. As I do not know whether you are familiar with the Exchange, I will tell you that Stern is an eminent coffee-merchant in Hamburg, who always employed Last and Co. Quite accidentally I found that out--I mean that bungling business of Busselinck and Waterman. They had offered to reduce the brokerage by one-fourth per cent. They are low fellows--nothing else. And now look what I have done to stop them. Any one in my place would perhaps have written to Ludwig Stern, "that we too would diminish the brokerage, and that we hoped for consideration on account of the long services of Last and Co."

I have calculated that our firm, during the last fifty years, has gained four hundred thousand guilders by Stern. Our connexion dates from the beginning of the continental system, when we smuggled Colonial produce and such like things from Heligoland. No, I won't reduce the brokerage.

I went to the Polen coffee-house, ordered pen and paper, and wrote:-- "That because of the many honoured commissions received from North Germany, our business transactions had been extended"--(it is the simple truth)--"and that this necessitated an augmentation of our staff"--(it is the truth: no more than yesterday evening our bookkeeper was in the office after eleven o'clock to look for his spectacles);--"that, above all things, we were in want of respectable, educated young men to conduct the German correspondence. That, certainly, there were many young Germans in Amsterdam, who possessed the requisite qualifications, but that a respectable firm"--(it is the very truth),--"seeing the frivolity and immorality of young men, and the daily increasing number of adventurers, and with an eye to the necessity of making correctness of conduct go hand in hand with correctness in the execution of orders"--(it is the truth, I observe, and nothing but the truth),--"that such a firm--I mean Last and Co., coffee-brokers, 37 Laurier Canal--could not be anxious enough in engaging new hands."

All that is the simple truth, reader. Do you know that the young German who always stood at the Exchange, near the seventeenth pillar, has eloped with the daughter of Busselinck and Waterman? Our Mary, like her, will be thirteen years old in September.

"That I had the honour to hear from Mr. Saffeler"--(Saffeler travels for Stern)--"that the honoured head of the firm, Ludwig Stern, had a son, Mr. Ernest Stern, who wished for employment for some time in a Dutch house.

"That I, mindful of this"--(here I referred again to the immorality of employés, and also the history of that daughter of Busselinck and Waterman; it won't do any harm to tell it)--"that I, mindful of this, wished, with all my heart, to offer Mr. Ernest Stern the German correspondence of our firm."

From delicacy I avoided all allusion to honorarium or salary; yet I said:--

"That if Mr. Ernest Stern would like to stay with us, at 37 Laurier Canal, my wife would care for him as a mother, and have his linen mended in the house"--(that is the very truth, for Mary sews and knits very well),--and in conclusion I said, "that we were a religious family."

The last sentence may do good, for the Sterns are Lutherans. I posted that letter. You understand that old Mr. Stern could not very well give his custom to Busselinck and Waterman, if his son were in our office.

When Max Havelaar gets to Java the narrative is less satisfactory, so tangential does it become, but there are enough passages in the manner of that which I have quoted to keep one happy, and to show how entertaining a satirist of his own countrymen at home "Multatuli" (whose real name was Edward Douwes Dekker) might have been had he been possessed by no grievance.

The book, which is very well worth reading, belongs to the literature of humanity and protest. Its author had to suffer much acrimonious attack, and was probably called a Little Hollander, but the fragment from an unpublished play which he placed as a motto to his book shows him to have lacked no satirical power to meet the enemy:--

Officer.--My Lord, this is the man who murdered Betsy.

Judge.--He must hang for it. How did he do it?

Officer.--He cut up her body in little pieces, and salted them.

Judge.--He is a great criminal. He must hang for it.

Lothario.--My Lord, I did not murder Betsy: I fed and clothed and cherished her. I can call witnesses who will prove me to be a good man, and no murderer.

Judge.--You must hang. You blacken your crime by your self-sufficiency. It ill becomes one who ... is accused of anything to set up for a good man.

Lothario,--But, my Lord, ... there are witnesses to prove it; and as I am now accused of murder.... Judge.--You must hang for it. You cut up Betsy--you salted the pieces--and you are satisfied with your conduct--three capital counts--who are you, my good woman?

Woman.--I am Betsy.

Lothario.--Thank God! You see, my Lord, that I did not murder her.

85

Judge.--Humph!--ay--what!--What about the salting?

Betsy.--No, my Lord, he did not salt me:--on the contrary, he did many things for me ... he is a worthy man!

Lothario.--You hear, my Lord, she says I am an honest man!

Judge.--Humph!--the third count remains. Officer, remove the prisoner, he must hang for it; he is guilty of self-conceit.

Shopkeeping--to return to Amsterdam--is the Dutch people's life. An idle rich class they may have, but it does not assert itself. It is hidden away at The Hague or at Arnheim. In Amsterdam every one is busy in one trade or another. There is no Pall Mall, no Rotten Row. There is no Bond Street or Rue de la Paix, for this is a country where money tries to procure money's worth, a country of essentials. Nor has Holland a Lord's or an Oval, Epsom Downs or Hurlingham.

Perhaps the quickest way to visualise the differences of nations is to imagine them exchanging countries. If the English were to move to Holland the whole face of the land would immediately be changed. In summer the flat meadows near the towns, now given up to cows and plovers, would be dotted with cricketers; in winter with football-players. Outriggers and canoes, punts and house-boats, would break out on the canals. In the villages such strange phenomena as idle gentlemen in knickerbockers and idle ladies with parasols would suddenly appear. To continue the list of changes (but not for too long) the trains would begin to be late; from the waiting-rooms all free newspapers would be stolen; churches would be made more comfortable; hundreds of newspapers would exist where now only a handful are sufficient; the hour of breakfast would be later; business would begin later; drunken men would be seen in the streets, dirt in the cottages.

If the Dutch came to England the converse would happen. The athletic grounds would become pasture land; the dirt of our slums and the gentry of our villages would alike vanish; Westminster Abbey would be whitewashed; and ... But I have said enough.

It must not be thought that the Dutch play no games. As a matter of fact they were playing golf, as old pictures tell, before it had found its way to England at all; and there are now many golf clubs in Holland. The Dutch are excellent also at lawn tennis; and I saw the youth of Franeker very busy in a curious variety of rounders. There are horse-racing meetings and trotting competitions too. But the nation is not naturally athletic or sporting. It does not even walk except on business.

In winter, however, the Dutch are completely transformed. No sooner does the ice bear than the whole people begin to glide, and swirl, and live their lives to the poetry of motion. The canals then become the real streets of Amsterdam. A Dutch lady--a mother and a grandmother--threw up her hands as she told me about the skating parties to the Zuyder Zee. The skate, it seems, is as much the enemy of the chaperon as the bicycle, although its reign is briefer. Upon this subject I am personally ignorant, but I take that gesture of alarm as final.

And yet M. Havard, who had a Frenchman's eye and therefore knew, says that if Etna in full eruption were taken to Holland, at the end of the week it would have ceased even to smoke, so destructive to enthusiasm is the well-disciplined nature of the Dutch woman.

M. Havard referred rather to the women of the open country than the dwellers in the town. I can understand the rural coolness, for Holland is a land without mystery. Everything is plain and bare: a man in a balloon would know the amours of the whole populace. What chance has Cupid when there are no groves? But let Holland be afforested and her daughters would keep Etna burning warmly enough; for I am persuaded that it is not that they are cold but that the physical development of the country is against them.

# CHAPTER XI

Amsterdam's Pictures

Dutch art in the palmy days--The Renaissance--A miracle--What Holland did for painting--The "Night Watch"--Rembrandt's isolation--Captain Franz Banning Cocq--Elizabeth Bas--The Staalmeesters--If one might choose one picture--Vermeer of Delft again--Whistler--"Paternal

Advice"--Terburg--The romantic Frenchmen again--The Dutch painter's ideal--The two Maris--Old Dutch rooms--The Six Collection--"Six's Bridge" and the wager--The Fodor Museum.

The superlative excellence of Dutch painting in the seventeenth century has never been explained, and probably never will be. The ordinary story is that on settling down to a period of independence and comparative peace and prosperity after the cessation of the Spanish war, the Dutch people called for good art, and good art came. But that is too simple. That a poet, a statesman or a novelist should be produced in response to a national desire is not inconceivable; for poets, statesmen and novelists find their material in the air, as we say, in the ideas of the moment. They are for the most part products of their time. But the great Dutch painters of the seventeenth century were expressing no real idea. Nor, even supposing they had done so, is it to be understood how the demand for them should yield such a supply of unsurpassed technical power: how a perfectly disciplined hand should be instantly at the public service.

That Holland in an expansive mood of satisfaction at her success should have wished to see groups of her gallant arquebusiers and portraits of her eminent burghers is not to be wondered at, and we can understand that respectable painters of such pictures should arise in some force to supply the need--just as wherever in this country at the present day there are cricketers and actresses, there also are photographers. That painters of ordinary merit should be forthcoming is, as I have said, no wonder: the mystery is that masters of technique whose equal has never been before or since should have arisen in such numbers; that in the space of a few years--between say 1590 and 1635--should have been born in a country never before given to the cultivation of the arts Rembrandt and Jan Steen, Vermeer and De Hooch, Van der Helst and Gerard Dou, Fabritius and Maes, Ostade and Van Goyen, Potter and Ruisdael, Terburg and Cuyp.

That is the staggering thing.

Another curious circumstance is that by 1700 it was practically all over, and Dutch art had become a convention. The gods had gone. Not until very recently has Holland had any but half gods since.

It may of course be urged that Italy had witnessed a somewhat similar phenomenon. But the spiritual stimulus of the Renaissance among the naturally artistic southerners cannot, I think, be compared with the stimulus given by the establishment of prosperity to these cold and material northerners. The making of great Italian art was a gradual process: the Dutch masters sprang forth fully armed at the first word of command. In the preceding generation the Rembrandts had been millers; the Steens brewers; the Dous glaziers; and so forth. But the demand for pictures having sounded, their sons were prepared to be painters of the first magnitude. Why try to explain this amazing event? Let there rather be miracles.

I have said that the great Dutch painters expressed no idea; and yet this is not perfectly true. They expressed no constructive idea, in the way that a poet or statesman does; but all had this in common, that they were informed by the desire to represent things--intimate and local things--as they are. The great Italians had gone to religion and mythology for their subjects: nearer at hand, in Antwerp, Rubens was pursuing, according to his lights, the same tradition. The great Dutchmen were the first painters to bend their genius exclusively to the honour of their own country, its worthies, its excesses, its domestic virtues, its trivial dailiness. Hals and Rembrandt lavished their power on Dutch arquebusiers and governors of hospitals, Dutch burgomasters and physicians; Ostade and Brouwer saw no indignity in painting Dutch sots as well as Dutch sots could be painted; De Hooch introduced miracles of sunlight into Dutch cottages; Maes painted old Dutch housewives, and Metsu young Dutch housewives, to the life; Vermeer and Terburg immortalised Dutch ladies at their spinets; Albert Cuyp toiled to suffuse Dutch meadows and Dutch cows with a golden glow; Jan Steen glorified the humblest Dutch family scenes; Gerard Dou spent whole weeks upon the fingers of a common Dutch hand. In short, art that so long had been at the service only of the Church and the proud, became suddenly, without losing any of its divinity, a fireside friend. That is what Holland did for painting.

It would have been a great enjoyment to me to have made this chapter a companion to the Ryks Museum: to have said a few words about all the pictures which I like best. But had I done so the rest of the book would have had to go, for all my space would have been exhausted. And therefore, as I cannot say all I want to say, I propose to say very little, keeping only to the most importunate pictures. Here and there in this book, particularly in the chapters on Dordrecht, Haarlem, and Leyden's painters, I have already touched on many of them.

The particular shining glory of the Ryks Museum is Rembrandt's "Night Watch," and it is well, I think, to make for that picture at once. The direct approach is down the Gallery of Honour, where one has this wonderful canvas before one all the way, as near life as perhaps any picture ever painted. It is possible at first to be disappointed: expectation perhaps had been running too high; the figure of the lieutenant (in the yellow jerkin) may strike one as a little mean. But do not let this distress you. Settle down on one of the seats and take Rembrandt easily, "as the leaf upon the tree"; settle down on another, and from the new point of view take him easily, "as the grass upon the weir". Look at Van der Helst's fine company of arquebusiers on one of the side walls; look at Franz Hals' company of arquebusiers on the other; then look at Rembrandt again. Every minute his astounding power is winning upon you. Walk again up the Gallery of Honour and turning quickly at the end, see how much light there is in the "Night Watch". Advance upon it slowly.... This is certainly the finest technical triumph of pigment that you have seen. What a glow and greatness.

After a while it becomes evident that Rembrandt was the only man who ought to have painted arquebusiers at all. Van der Heist and Frans Hals are sinking to the level of gifted amateurs. Why did not Rembrandt paint all the pictures? you begin to wonder. And yet the Hals and the Van der Helsts were so good a little while ago.

Hals and Van der Helst are, however, to recover their own again; for the "Night Watch," I am told, is to be moved to a building especially erected for it, where the lighting will be more satisfactory than connoisseurs now consider it. Perhaps it is as well. It is hard to be so near the rose; and there are few pictures in the recesses of the Gallery of Honour which the "Night Watch" does not weaken; some indeed it makes quite foolish.

It is not of course really a night watch at all. Captain Franz Banning Cocq's arquebusiers are leaving their Doelen in broad day; the centralisation of sunlight from a high window led to the mistake, and nothing now will ever change the title.

How little these careless gallant arquebusiers, who paid the painter-man a hundred florins apiece to be included in the picture, can have thought of the destiny of the work! Of Captain Franz Banning Cocq as a soldier we know nothing, but as a sitter he is hardly second to any in the world.

But it is not the "Night Watch" that I recall with the greatest pleasure when I think of the Ryks Rembrandts. It is that wise and serene old lady in the Van der Poll room--Elizabeth Bas--who sits there for all time, unsurpassed among portraits. This picture alone is worth a visit to Holland. I recall also, not with more pleasure than the "Night Watch," but with little less, the superb group of syndics in the Staalmeester room. It is this picture--with the "School of Anatomy" at The Hague--that in particular makes one wish it had been possible for all the Corporation pieces to have been from Rembrandt's brush. It is this picture which deprives even Hals of some of his divinity, and makes Van der Helst a dull dog. If ever a picture of Dutch gentlemen was painted by a Dutch gentleman it is this.

Having seen the "Night Watch" again, it is a good plan to study the Gallery of Honour. To pick out one's favourite picture is here not difficult: it is No. 1501, "The Endless Prayer," by Nicolas Maes, of which I have said something in the chapter on Dordrecht, the painter's birthplace. Its place is very little below that of Elizabeth Bas, by Maes's master.

It is always interesting in a fine gallery to ask oneself which single picture one would choose before all others if such a privilege were offered. The answer if honest is a sure revelation of temperament, for one would select of a certainty a picture satisfying one's prevailing moods rather than a picture of any sensational character. In other words, the picture would have to be good to live with. To choose from thousands of masterpieces one only is a very delicate test.

If the Dutch Government, stimulated to gratitude for the encomiastic character of the present book, were to offer me my choice of the Ryks Museum pictures I should not hesitate a moment. I should take No.

2527--"Woman Reading a Letter" (damaged), by Vermeer of Delft. You will see a reproduction in black and white on the opposite page; but how wide a gulf between the picture and the process block. The jacket, for example, is the most lovely cool blue imaginable.

This picture, apart from its beauty, is interesting as an illustration of the innovating courage of Vermeer. Who else at that date would have placed the woman's head against a map almost its own colour? Many persons think that such daring began with Whistler. It is, however, Terburg who most often suggests Whistler. Vermeer had, I think, a rarer distinction than Terburg. Vermeer would never have painted such a crowded group (however masterly) as that of Terburg's "Peace of Munster" in our National Gallery; he could not have brought himself so to pack humanity. Among all the Dutch masters I find no such fastidious aristocrat.

He, Vermeer, has another picture at the Ryks--"De brief" (No.

2528)--which technically is wonderful; but the whole effect is artificial and sophisticated, very different from his best transparent mood.

Any mortification, by the way, which I might suffer from the knowledge that No. 2527 can never be mine is allayed by the knowledge, equally certain, that it can never be any one else's. Money is powerless here. To the offer of a Rothschild the Government would return as emphatic a negative as to a request from me.

The room in which is Vermeer's "Reader" contains also Maes's "Spinning Woman" (see page 230), two or three Peter de Hoochs and the best Jan Steen in the Ryks. It is indeed a room to linger in, and to return to, indefinitely. De Hooch's "Store Room" (No. 1248), of which I have already spoken, is in one of the little "Cabinet piece" rooms, which are not too well lighted. Here also one may spend many hours, and then many hours more.

The "Peace of Munster" has been called Terburg's masterpiece: but the girl in his "Paternal Advice," No. 570 at the Ryks, seems to me a finer achievement. The grace and beauty and truth of her pose and the miraculous painting of her dress are unrivalled. Yet judged as a picture it is, I think, dull. The colouring is dingy, time has not dealt kindly with the background; but the figure of the girl is perfect. I give a reproduction opposite page 190. It was this picture, in one of its replicas, that Goethe describes in his Elective Affinities: a description which procured for it the probably inaccurate title "Parental Advice".

We have a fine Terburg in our National Gallery--"The Music Lesson"--and here too is his "Peace of Munster," which certainly was a great feat of painting, but which does not, I think, reproduce his peculiar characteristics and charm. These may be found somewhere between "The Music Lesson" and the portrait next the Vermeer in the smallest of the three Dutch rooms. Even more ingratiating than "The Music Lesson" is "The Toilet" at the Wallace Collection. Terburg might be called a pocket Velasquez--a description of him which will be appreciated at the Ryks Museum in the presence of his tiny and captivating "Helena van der Schalcke," No. 573, one of the gems of the Cabinet pieces (see opposite page 290), and his companion pictures of a man and his wife, each standing by a piece of red furniture--I think Nos. 574 and 575. The execution of the woman's muslin collar is among the most dexterous things in Dutch art.

From the Ryks Museum it is but a little way (past the model Dutch garden) to the Stedelijk Museum, where modern painting may be studied--Israels and Bosboom, Mesdag and James Maris, Breitner and Jan van Beers, Blommers and Weissenbruch.

There is also one room dedicated to paintings of the Barbizon school, and of this I would advise instant search. I rested my eyes here for an hour. A vast scene of cattle by Troyon (who, such is the poverty of the Dutch alphabet, comes out monstrously upon the frame as Troijon); a mysterious valley of trees by Corot; a wave by Courbet; a mere at evening by Daubigny--these are like cool firm hands upon one's forehead.

The statement

Nothing graceful, wise, or sainted,-- That is how the Dutchman painted,

is so sweeping as to be untrue. Indeed it is wholly absurd. The truth simply is that one goes to Dutch art for the celebration of fact without mystery or magic. In other words, Dutch painting is painting without poetry; and it is this absence of poetry which makes the romantic

Frenchmen appear to be such exotics when one finds them in Holland, and why it is so pleasant in Holland now and then to taste their quality, as one may at the Stedelijk Museum and in the Mesdag Collection at The Hague.

We must not forget, however, that under the French influence certain modern Dutch painters have been quickened to celebrate the fact with poetry. In a little room adjoining the great French room at the Stedelijk Museum will be found some perfect things by living or very recent artists for whom Corot did not work in vain: a mere by James Maris, with a man in a blue coat sitting in a boat; a marsh under a white sky by Matthew Maris; a village scene by the same exquisite craftsman. These three pictures, but especially the last two, are in their way as notable and beautiful as anything by the great names in Dutch art.

On the ground floor of the Stedelijk Museum is the series of rooms named after the Suasso family which should on no account be missed, but of which no notice is given by the Museum authorities. These rooms are furnished exactly as they would have been by the best Dutch families, their furniture and hangings having been brought from old houses in the Keizersgracht and the Heerengracht. The kitchen is one of the prettiest things in Holland--with its shining brass and copper, its delicate and dainty tiles and its air of cheerful brightness. Some of the carving in the other rooms is superb; the silver, the china, the clocks are all of the choicest. The custodian has a childlike interest in secret drawers and unexpected recesses, which he exhibits with a gusto not habitual in the Dutch cicerone. For the run of these old rooms a guelder is asked; one sees the three rooms on the other side of the entrance hall for twenty-five cents, the church and museum unit of Holland. But they are uninteresting beside the larger suite. They consist of an old Dutch apothecary's shop and laboratory; a madhouse cell; and the bedroom of a Dutch lady who has just presented her lord with an infant. We see the mother in bed, a doctor at her side, and in the foreground a nurse holding the baby. Except that the costumes and accessories are authentic the tableau is in no way superior to an ordinary waxwork.

At the beginning of the last chapter I said that the Keizersgracht and Heerengracht do not divulge their secrets; they present an impassive and inscrutable front, grave and sombre, often black as night, beyond which the foreigner may not penetrate. But by the courtesy of the descendants of Rembrandt's friend Jan Six, in order that pleasure in their collection of the old masters may be shared, No. 511 Heerengracht is shown on the presentation of a visiting card at suitable hours. Here may be seen two more of the rare pictures of Vermeer of Delft--his famous "Milk Woman" and a Dutch façade in the manner of Peter de Hooch, with an added touch of grave delicacy and distinction. Peter de Hooch is himself represented in this little gallery, but the picture is in bad condition. There is also an interesting and uncharacteristically dramatic Nicolas Maes called "The Listener". But the pride of the house is the little group of portraits by Rembrandt.

It was, by the way, at Burgomaster Six's house at Elsbroek that Rembrandt's little etching called "Six's Bridge" was executed. Rembrandt and his friend had just sat down to dinner when it was discovered that there was no mustard. On a servant being sent to buy or borrow some, Rembrandt made a bet that he would complete an etching of the bridge before the man's return. The artist won.

Another little private collection, which has now become a regular resort, with fixed hours, is that known as the Fodor Museum, at No. 609 Keizersgracht; but I do not recommend a visit unless one is absolutely a glutton for paint.

# CHAPTER XII

Around Amsterdam: South and South-East

Dutch railways--Amsterdam as a centre--Town and country--Milking time--Scotch scenery in Holland--Hilversum--Laren--Anton

Mauve--Buckwheat Sunday--Dress in Holland--Naarden's hour of agony--The indomitable Dutch--Through Noord-Holland again--Muiderberg--Muiden's Castle.

The Dutch have several things to learn from the English; and there are certain lessons which we might acquire from them. To them we might impart the uses of the salt-spoon, and ask in return the secret of punctuality on the railways.

The Dutch railways are admirable. The trains come in to the minute and go out to the minute. The officials are intelligent and polite. The carriages are good. Every station has its waiting-room, where you may sit and read, and drink a cup of coffee that is not only hot and fresh but is recognisably the product of the berry. It is impossible to travel in the wrong train. It is very difficult not to get out at the right station. The fares are very reasonable.

The stationmasters are the only visible and tangible members of the Dutch aristocracy. The disposition of one's luggage is very simple when once it has been mastered. The time tables are models of clarity.

The only blot on the system is the detestable double fastening to the carriage doors, and the curious fancy, prevalent on the Continent, that a platform is a vanity. It is a perpetual wonder to me that some of the wider Dutch ever succeed in climbing into their trains at all; and yet after accomplishing one's own ascent one discovers them seated there comfortably and numerously enough, showing no signs of the struggle.

Travellers who find the Dutch tendency to closed windows a trial beyond endurance may be interested to know that it is law in Holland that if any passenger wish it the window on the lee side may be open. With the knowledge of this enactment all difficulty should be over-- provided that one has sufficient strength of purpose (and acquaintance with the Dutch language) to enforce it.

All this preamble concerning railways is by way of introduction to the statement (hinted at in the first chapter) that if the traveller in Holland likes, he can see a great part of the country by staying at Amsterdam--making the city his headquarters, and every day journeying here and there and back again by train or canal.

A few little neighbouring towns it is practically necessary to visit from Amsterdam; and for the most part, I take it, Leyden and Haarlem are made the object of excursions either from Amsterdam or The Hague, rather than places of sojourn, although both have excellent quiet inns much more to my taste than anything in the largest city. Indeed I found Amsterdam's hotels exceedingly unsatisfactory; so much so that the next time I go, when the electric railway to Haarlem is open, I am proposing to invert completely the usual process, and, staying at Haarlem, study Amsterdam from there.

For the time being, however, we must consider ourselves at Amsterdam, branching out north or south, east or west, every morning.

A very interesting excursion may be made to Hilversum, returning by the steam-tram through Laren, Naarden and Muiden. The rail runs at first through flat and very verdant meadows, where thousands of cows that supply Amsterdam with milk are grazing; and one notices again the suddenness with which the Dutch city ends and the Dutch country begins. Our English towns have straggling outposts: new houses, scaffold poles, cottages, allotments, all break the transition from city to country; the urban gives place to suburban, and suburban to rural, gradually, every inch being contested. But the Dutch towns--even the great cities--end suddenly; the country begins suddenly.

In England for the most part the cow comes to the milker; but in Holland the milker goes to the cow. His first duty is to bind the animal's hind legs together, and then he sets his stool at his side and begins. Anton Mauve has often painted the scene--so often that at milking time one looks from the carriage windows at a very gallery of Mauves. I noticed this particularly on an afternoon journey from Amsterdam to Hilversum, between the city and Weesp, where the meadows (cricket grounds manqués) are flat as billiard tables.

The train later runs between great meres, some day perhaps to be reclaimed, and then dashes into country that resembles very closely our Government land about Woking and Bisley--the first sand and firs that we have seen in Holland. It has an odd and unexpected appearance; but as a matter of fact hundreds of square miles of Holland in the south and east have this character; while there are stretches of Dutch heather in which one can feel in Scotland.

All about Naarden and Hilversum are sanatoria, country-seats and pleasure grounds, the softening effect of the pines upon the strong air of the Zuyder Zee being very beneficial. Many of the heights have towers or pavilions, some of which move the author of Through Noord-Holland to ecstasies. As thus, of the Larenberg: "The most charming is the tower, where one can enjoy a perspective that only rarely presents itself. We can see here the towers of Nijkerk, Harderwijk, Utrecht, Amersfoort, Bunschoten, Amsterdam and many others." And again, of a wood at Heideheuvel: "The perspective beauty here formed cannot be said in words".

Hilversum is the Chislehurst of Holland--a discreet and wealthy suburb, where business men have their villas amid the trees. It is a pleasant spot, excellent from which to explore.

The author of Through Noord-Holland thus describes Laren, which lies a few miles from Hilversum and is reached by tram: "Surrounded by arable land and hilly heathery it is richly provided with picturesque spots; country-seats, villas, ordinary houses and farms are following one another. For those who are searching for rest and calmness is this village very recommendable." But to say only that is to omit Laren's principal claim to distinction--its fame as the home of Anton Mauve. No great painter of nature probably ever adapted less than Mauve. His pictures, oils and water-colours alike, are the real thing, very true, very beautiful, low-toned, always with a touch of wistfulness and melancholy. He found his subjects everywhere, and justified them by the sympathy and truth of his exquisite modest art.

Chiefly he painted peasants and cows. What a spot of red was to Corot, the blue linen jacket of the Dutch peasant was to his disciple. I never hear the name of Mauve without instantly seeing a black and white cow and a boy in a blue jacket amid Holland's evening green.

At Laren Mauve's fame is kept sweet by a little colony of artists, who like to draw their inspiration where the great painter drew his.

North of Laren, on the sea coast, is the fishing village of Huizen, where the women have a neat but very sedate costume. They wear white caps with curved sides that add grace to a pretty cheek. Having, however, the odd fancy that a flat chest is more desirable than a rounded one, they compress their busts into narrow compass, striving as far as possible to preserve vertical lines. At the waist a plethora of petticoats begins, spreading the skirts to inordinate width and emphasising the meagreness above.

The sombre attire of the Huizen women is a contrast to most of the traditional costumes of Holland, which are charming, full of gay colour and happy design. The art of dress seems otherwise to be dead in Holland

to-day; In the towns the ordinary conventional dress is dull; and in the country it is without any charm. Holland as a whole, omitting the costumes, cannot be said to have any more knowledge of clothes than we have. It is only by the blue linen jackets of the men in the fields that the situation is saved and the Dutch are proved our superiors. How cool and grateful to the eyes this blue jacket can be all admirers of Mauve's pictures know.

Naarden and Muiden are curiously mediæval. The steam-tram has been rushing along for some miles, past beer gardens and villas, when suddenly it slows to walking pace as we twist in and out over the bridges of a moat, and creeping through the tunnel of a rampart are in the narrow streets of a fortified town. Both Naarden and Muiden are surrounded by moats and fortifications.

Naarden's crowning hour of agony was in 1572, since it had the misfortune to stand in the path of Don Frederic on his way from Zutphen, where not a citizen had been left alive, to Amsterdam. The story of the surrender of the city to Don Romero under the pledge that life and property should be respected, and of the dastardly and fiendish disregard of this pledge by the Spaniards, is the most ghastly in the whole war. From Motley I take the account of the tragedy:--

"On the 22nd of November a company of one hundred troopers was sent to the city gates to demand its surrender. The small garrison which had been left by the Prince was not disposed to resist, but the spirit of the burghers was stouter than their walls. They answered the summons by a declaration that they had thus far held the city for the King and the Prince of Orange, and, with God's help, would continue so to do. As the horsemen departed with this reply, a lunatic, called Adrian Krankhoeft, mounted the ramparts, and discharged a culverine among them. No man was injured, but the words of defiance, and the shot fired by a madman's hand, were destined to be fearfully answered.

"Meanwhile, the inhabitants of the place, which was at best far from strong, and ill provided with arms, ammunition, or soldiers, despatched importunate messages to Sonoy, and to other patriot generals nearest to them, soliciting reinforcements. Their messengers came back almost empty-handed. They brought a little powder and a great many promises, but not a single man-at-arms, not a ducat, not a piece of artillery. The most influential commanders, moreover, advised an honourable capitulation, if it were still possible.

"Thus baffled, the burghers of the little city found their proud position quite untenable. They accordingly, on the 1st of December, despatched the burgomaster and a senator to Amersfoort, to make terms, if possible, with Don Frederic. When these envoys reached the place, they were refused admission to the general's presence. The army had already been ordered to move forward to Naarden, and they were directed to accompany the advance guard, and to expect their reply at the gates of their own city. This command was sufficently ominous. The impression which it made upon them was confirmed by the warning voices of their friends in Amersfoort, who entreated them not to return to Naarden. The advice was not lost upon one of the two envoys. After they had advanced a little distance on their journey, the burgomaster, Laurentszoon, slid privately out of the sledge in which they were travelling, leaving his cloak behind him. 'Adieu; I think I will not venture back to Naarden at present,' said he calmly, as he abandoned his companion to his fate. The other, who could not so easily desert his children, his wife, and his fellow-citizens in the hour of danger, went forward as calmly to share in their impending doom.

"The army reached Bussum, half a league distant from Naarden, in the evening. Here Don Frederic established his headquarters, and proceeded to invest the city. Senator Gerrit was then directed to return to Naarden, and to bring out a more numerous deputation on the following morning, duly empowered to surrender the place. The envoy accordingly returned next day, accompanied by Lambert Hortensius, rector of a Latin academy, together with four other citizens. Before this deputation had reached Bussum, they were met by Julian Romero, who informed them that he was commissioned to treat with them on the part of Don Frederic. He demanded the keys of the city, and gave the deputation a solemn pledge that the lives and property of all the inhabitants should be sacredly respected. To attest this assurance, Don Julian gave his hand three several times to Lambert Hortensius. A soldier's word thus plighted, the commissioners, without exchanging any written documents, surrendered the keys, and immediately afterwards accompanied Romero into the city, who was soon followed by five or six hundred musketeers.

"To give these guests an hospitable reception, all the housewives of the city at once set about preparations for a sumptuous feast, to which the Spaniards did ample justice, while the colonel and his officers were entertained by Senator Gerrit at his own house. As soon as this conviviality had come to an end, Romero, accompanied by his host, walked into the square. The great bell had been meantime ringing, and the citizens had been summoned to assemble in the Gast Huis Church, then used as a town hall. In the course of a few minutes 500 had entered the building, and stood quietly awaiting whatever measures might be offered for their deliberation. Suddenly a priest, who had been pacing to and fro before the church door, entered the building and bade them all prepare for death; but the announcement, the preparation, and the death, were simultaneous. The door was flung open, and a band of armed Spaniards rushed across the sacred threshold. They fired a single volley upon the defenceless herd, and then sprang in upon them with sword and dagger. A yell of despair arose as the miserable victims saw how hopelessly they were engaged, and beheld the ferocious faces of their butchers. The carnage within that narrow space was compact and rapid. Within a few minutes all were despatched, and among them Senator Gerrit, from whose table the Spanish commander had but just risen. The church was then set on fire, and the dead and dying were consumed to ashes together.

"Inflamed but not satiated, the Spaniards then rushed into the streets, thirsty for fresh horrors. The houses were all rifled of their contents, and men were forced to carry the booty to the camp, who were then struck dead as their reward. The town was then fired in every direction, that the skulking citizens might be forced from their hiding-places. As fast as they came forth they were put to death by their impatient foes. Some were pierced with rapiers, some were chopped to pieces with axes, some were surrounded in the blazing streets by troops of laughing soldiers, intoxicated, not with wine but with blood, who tossed them to and fro with their lances, and derived a wild amusement from their dying agonies. Those who attempted resistance were crimped alive like fishes, and left to gasp themselves to death in lingering torture. The soldiers becoming more and more insane, as the foul work went on, opened the veins of some of their victims, and drank their blood as if it were wine. Some of the burghers were for a time spared, that they might witness the violation of their wives and, daughters, and were then butchered in company with these still more unfortunate victims. Miracles of brutality were accomplished. Neither church nor hearth was sacred. Men were slain, women outraged at the altars, in the streets, in their blazing homes. The life of Lambert Hortensius was spared out of regard to his learning and genius, but he hardly could thank his foes for the boon, for they struck his only son dead, and tore his heart out before his father's eyes. Hardly any man or woman survived, except by accident. A body of some hundred burghers made their escape across the snow into the open country. They were, however, overtaken, stripped stark naked, and hung upon the trees by the feet, to freeze, or to perish by a more lingering death. Most of them soon died, but twenty, who happened to be wealthy, succeeded, after enduring much torture, in purchasing their lives of their inhuman persecutors. The principal burgomaster, Heinrich Lambertszoon, was less fortunate. Known to be affluent, he was tortured by exposing the soles of his feet to a fire until they were almost consumed. On promise that his life should be spared he then agreed to pay a heavy ransom; but hardly had he furnished the stipulated sum when, by express order of Don Frederic himself, he was hanged in his own doorway, and his dissevered limbs afterwards nailed to the gates of the city.

"Nearly all the inhabitants of Naarden, soldiers and citizens, were thus destroyed; and now Don Frederic issued peremptory orders that no one, on pain of death, should give lodging or food to any fugitive. He likewise forbade to the dead all that could now be forbidden them-- a grave. Three weeks long did these unburied bodies pollute the streets, nor could the few wretched women who still cowered within such houses as had escaped the flames ever move from their lurking-places without treading upon the festering remains of what had been their husbands, their fathers, or their brethren. Such was the express command of him whom the flatterers called the 'most divine genius ever known'. Shortly afterwards came an order to dismantle the fortifications, which had certainly proved sufficiently feeble in the hour of need, and to raze what was left of the city from the surface of the earth. The work was faithfully accomplished, and for a long time Naarden ceased to exist."

The Naarden of to-day sprang from the ruins. Mendoza's comment upon the siege ran thus: "The sack of Naarden was a chastisement which must be believed to have taken place by express permission of a Divine Providence; a punishment for having been the first of the Holland towns in which heresy built its nest, whence it has taken flight to all the neighbouring cities". None the less, "the hearts of the Hollanders," says Motley, "were rather steeled to resistance than awed into submission by the fate of Naarden"; as Don Frederic found when he passed on to besiege Haarlem and later Alkmaar.

To Muiderburg, between Naarden and Muiden, I have not been, and therefore with the more readiness quote my indispensable author:--

In summer is Muiderberg by its situation at the Zuiderzee a favourite little spot and very recommendable for nervous people. The number of those who sought cure and found it here is enormous. It is the vacation-place by excellence. There is a church with square tower and organ. About the tower, the spire of which is failing, various opinions go round how this occured, by war, by shooting or storm.

The beautiful beech-grove in the center of the village, where a lot of forest-giants are rising in the sky in severe rows, is a favorite place, in the middle of which is a hill with fine pond.

A couple of years ago Geertruida Carelsen wrote in her Berlin letters that Muiderberg perhaps is the only bathing-place where sea and wood are united. There are three well-known graveyards.

Of Muiden's very picturesque moated castle--the ideal castle of a romance--Peter Cornellissen Hooft, the poet and historian, was once custodian. It was built in the thirteenth century and restored by Florence V., who was subsequently incarcerated there. As the Noord-Holland guide-book sardonically remarks, "He will never have thought that he built his own prison by it".

# CHAPTER XIII

Around Amsterdam: North

To Marken--An opera-bouffe island--Cultivated and profitable

simplicity--Broek-in-Waterland--Cow-damp--The two doors--Gingerbread and love--Dead cities--Monnickendam--The overturned camera--Dutch phlegm--Brabant the quarrelsome--Edam--Holland's great

churches--Edam's roll of honour--A beard of note--A Dutch Daniel Lambert--A virgin colossus--A ship-owner indeed—The mermaid--Volendam--Taciturnity and tobacco--Purmerend--The land of windmills--Zaandam--Green paint at its highest power--A riverside inn--Peter the Great.

An excursion which every one will say is indispensable takes one to Marken (pronounced Marriker); but I have my doubts. The island may be reached from Amsterdam either by boat, going by way of canal and returning by sea, or one may take the steam-tram to Monnickendam or Edam, and then fall into the hands of a Marken mariner. To escape his invitations to sail thither is a piece of good fortune that few visitors succeed in achieving.

Marken in winter wears perhaps a genuine air; in the season of tourists it has too much the suggestion of opera bouffe. The men's costume is comic beyond reason; the inhabitants are picturesque of set design; the old women at their doorways are too consciously the owners of quaint habitations, glimpses of which catch the eye by well-studied accident. I must confess to being glad to leave: for either one was intruding upon a simple folk entirely surrounded by water; or the simple folk, knowing human nature, had made itself up and sent out its importunate young from strictly mercenary motives. In either case Marken is no place for a sensitive traveller. The theory that the Marken people are savages is certainly a wrong one; they have carried certain of the privileges of civilisation very far and can take care of themselves with unusual cleverness. Moreover, no savage would cover his legs with such garments as the men adhere to. What is wrong with Marken is that for the most part it subsists on sight-seers, which is bad; and it too generally suggests that a stage-manager, employed by a huge Trust, is somewhere in the background. It cannot be well with a community that encourages its children to beg of visitors.

The women, however, look sensible: fine upstanding creatures with a long curl of yellow hair on each side of their faces. One meets them now and then in Amsterdam streets, by no means dismayed by the traffic and bustle. Their head-dresses are striking and gay, and the front of their bodices is elaborately embroidered, the prevailing colours being red and pink. Bright hues are also very popular within doors on this island, perhaps by way of counteracting the external monotony, the Marken walls being washed with yellow and hung with Delft plates, while the furniture and hangings all have a cheerful gaiety.

The island is flat save for the mounds on which its villages are built, each house standing on poles to allow the frequent inundations of the winter free way. If one has the time and money it is certainly better to visit Marken in a fishing-boat than in the steamer--provided that one can trust oneself to navigators masquerading in such bloomers.

The steamers from Amsterdam pause for a while at Broek and Monnickendam. Broek-in-Waterland, to give it its full title, is one of the quaintest of Dutch villages. But unfortunately Broek also has become to some extent a professional "sight". Its cleanliness, however, for which it is famous, is not an artificial effect attained to impress visitors, but a genuine enough characteristic. The houses are gained by little bridges which, with various other idiosyncrasies, help to make Broek a delight to children. If a company of children were to be allowed to manage a small republic entirely alone, the whimsical millionaire who fathered the project might do worse than buy up this village for the experiment.

In the model dairy farm of Broek, through which visitors file during the time allowed by the steam-boat's captain, things happen as they should: the cows' tails are tied to the roof, and all is spick and span. The author of Through Noord-Holland tells us that among the dairy's illustrious visitors was an Italian duchess from Livorno who ordered cheese for herself, for the Princess Borghese and for the Duke of Ceri. Everything in the farm, he adds, "is glimmering and glittering".

One of the phenomena of Broek is thus explained by the same ingenious author: "By beholding the dark-tinted columns attentively one sees something dull here and there. In the year 1825, when the great flood inundated whole Broek, men as well as cattle flied into the church, which lies so much higher and remained quite free of water. By the exhalations of the cows, the cow-damp, has the wood been blemished and made dull at many places, chamois nor polish could help, the dullness remained." The church has beauties to set against the phenomenon of cow-damp, and among them a very elaborate carved pulpit in various precious woods, and some fine lamps.

Ireland tells us that the front doors of many of Broek's houses are opened only twice in their owners' lives--when they marry and when they die. For the rest the back door must serve. The custom is not confined to Broek, but is found all over North Holland. These ceremonial front doors are often very ornate. It was also at Broek that Ireland picked up his information as to the best means of winning the Dutch heart. "Laughable as it may seem, a safe expedient to insure the affections of the lower class of these lasses, is to arm yourself well with gingerbread. The first question the lover is asked after knocking at the door, when the parents are supposed to be in bed, is, 'Have you any gingerbread?' If he replies in the affirmative, he finds little difficulty in gaining admission. A second visit ensures his success, and the lady yields."

I can add a little to this. When a young man thinks of courting he first speaks to the parents, and if they are willing to encourage him he is asked to spend the evening with their daughter. They then discreetly retire to bed and leave the world to him. Under his arm is a large cake, not necessarily of gingerbread, and this he deposits on the table, with or without words. If he is acceptable in the girl's eyes she at once puts some more peat on the fire.

He then knows that all is well with him: the cake is cut, and Romance is king. But if the fire is not replenished he must gather up his cake and return to his home. A very favourite Dutch picture represents "The Cutting of the Cake". I have heard that the Dutch wife takes her husband's left arm; the Dutch fiancee her lover's right.

Monnickendam, on the shores of the Zuyder Zee, is now a desolate sleepy spot; once it was one of the great towns of Holland, at the time when The Hague was a village. I say Zuyder Zee, but strictly speaking it is on the Gouwzee, the name of the straits between Monnickendam and Marken. It is here, in winter, when the ice holds, that a fair is held, to which come all Amsterdam on skates, to eat poffertjes and wafelen,

Monnickendam affords our first sight of what are called very misleadingly the "Dead Cities of the Zuyder Zee," meaning merely towns which once were larger and busier. Monnickendam was sufficiently important to fit out a fleet against the Spanish in 1573, under Cornelius Dirckszoon (whose tomb we saw at Delft) and capture Bossu in the battle of Hoorn.

To-day Monnickendam suggests nothing so little as a naval engagement. People live there, it is true, but one sees very few of them. Only in an old English market town on a hot day--such a town as Petworth, for example, in Sussex--do you get such desertion and quiet and imperturbability.

Monnickendam has, however, a treasure that few English towns can boast--its charming little stadhuis tower, one of the prettiest in Holland, with a happy peal of bells, and mechanical horses in action once an hour; while the tram line running right down the main street periodically awakens the populace.

When last I visited Monnickendam it was by steam-tram; and at a little half-way station, where it is necessary to wait for another tram, our engine driver, stoker and guard were elaborately photographed by an artist who seemed to be there for no other purpose. He placed his tripod on the platform; grouped the officials; gave them--and incidentally a score of heads protruding from the carriages--a sufficient exposure, and was preparing another plate when an incoming tram dashed up so unexpectedly as to cause him to jump, and, in jumping, to overturn his tripod and precipitate the camera under the carriage wheels. Now here was a tragedy worthy of serious treatment. A Frenchman would have danced with rage; an Englishman would have wanted to know whose fault it was and have threatened reprisals. But the Dutchman merely looked a little pained, a little surprised, and in a minute or two was preparing a friendly group of the officials of the tram which had caused the accident. I do not put the incident forward as typical; but certainly one may travel far in Holland without seeing exhibitions of temper. I mentioned the nation's equability to the young Dutchman in the canal boat between Rotterdam and Delft. "Ah!" he said, "you should go to Brabant. They fight enough there!" I did go to Brabant, but I saw no anger or quarrelsomeness; yet I suppose he had his reasons.

The steam-tram to Monnickendam runs on to Edam, whence one may command both Volegdam and Purmerend. Edam is famous for its cheese, but the traveller in Holland as a rule reserves for Alkmaar cheese market his interest in this industry; and we will do the same. Broadly speaking Edam sends forth the red cheeses, Alkmaar the yellow; but no hard and fast line can be drawn. Were it not for its cheese market Edam would be as "dead" as Monnickendam, but cheese saves it. It was once a power and the water-gate of Amsterdam, at a time when the only way to the Dutch capital was by the Zuyder Zee and the Y. Edam is at the mouth of the Y, its name really being Ydam. The size of its Groote Kerk indicates something of this past importance, for it is immense: a Gothic building of the fourteenth century, cold and drear enough, but a little humanised by some coloured glass from Gouda, often in very bad condition. In the days when this church was built Edam had twenty-five thousand inhabitants: now there are only five thousand.

It is difficult to lose the feeling of disproportion between the size of the Dutch churches and that of the villages and congregations. The villages are so small, the churches so vast. It is as though the churches were built to compensate for the absence of hills. From any one spire in

Holland one must be able to see almost all the others. The stained glass in Edam's great church has reference rather to Holland's temporal prosperity than to religion. More interesting is the room over the southern door, which was used first for a prison, and later for a school, the library of which still may be seen. Edam possesses in addition to the immense church of St. Nicholas a little church of the Virgin, with a spire full of bells, badly out of the perpendicular. The town has also some interesting old houses, one or two of great beauty, and many enriched by quaint bas-reliefs.

The stadhuis is comparatively modern and not externally attractive. Within, however, Edam does honour to three fantastic figures who once were to be seen in her streets--Peter Dircksz, Jan Cornellissen and Trijntje Kever, portraits of whom grace the town hall. Their claims to fame are certainly genuine, although unexpected. Peter's idiosyncrasy was a beard which had to be looped up to prevent it trailing in the mud; Jan, at the age of

forty-two, when the artist set to work upon him, weighed thirty-two stones and six pounds; while Trijntje was a maiden nine feet tall and otherwise ample. Peter and Trijntje were, I believe, true children of Edam, but Jan was a mere import, having conveyed his bulk thither from Friesland. Like our own Daniel Lambert, he kept an inn. One of Trijntje's shoes is also preserved--liker to a boat than anything else.

I have by no means exhausted Edam's roll of honour. Shipowner Osterlen must be added--a burgher, who, in 1682, when his portrait was painted, could point (and in the canvas does point, with no uncertain finger,) to ninety-two ships of which he was the possessor. And a legend of Edam tells how once in 1403, when the country was inundated by the sea, some girls taking fresh water to the cows saw and captured a mermaid. Her (like the lady in Mr. Wells's story) they dressed and civilised, and taught to sow and spin, but could never make talk. Possibly it is this mermaid who, caught in a fisherman's net, is represented in bas-relief (as the fish that pleases all tastes) on one of the facades of Edam, with accompanying verses which must not be translated, embodying comments upon the nature of the haul by various typical and very plain-spoken members of society--a soldier and a schoolmaster, a monk and a fowler, for example. Edam has yet another hero. On the Dam bridge are iron-backed benches which never grow rusty. "One owes this particularity," says Through Noord-Holland, "to the invention of an Edamer about 1569, who also took his secret with him into the grave."

To the little fishing village of Volendain, paradise of quaint costumes and gay prettinesses, artists invariably resort. Like much of Monnickendam, and indeed almost all Dutch seaside settlements, the village is, if not below sea-level, almost invisible from the water, on account of an obliterating dyke. At the Helder one can consider the rampart reasonable, but here, where there is no foe but the Zuyder Zee, it may seem fantastic. If we lived there in winter, however, the precaution would soon be justified, for the Zuyder Zee can on occasion roar like a lion. It is odd to reflect that Volendam, Monnickendam and Marken may become ordinary inland hamlets in the midst of green fields if the great scheme for draining the Zuyder Zee is carried through.

If the people and village of Volendam are to be described in a phrase, they may be called better Markeners in a better Marken. The decoration of the pointed red-roofed houses is similar; there is the same prevailing and very ingratiating passion for blue Delft--and a very beautiful blue too; the clothes of the men and women have a family resemblance. But Volendam is in every way better--although its open drain is a sore trial: it is more human, more natural. The men hold the record for Dutch taciturnity. They also smoke more persistently and wear larger sabots than I saw anywhere else, leaving them outside their doors with a religious exactitude that suggests that the good-wives of Volendam know how to be obeyed. The women discard the Marken ringlets and richness of embroidery, but in the matter of petticoats they approach the Scheveningen and Huizen standards. Their jewellery resolves itself into a coral necklace, while the men wear silver buttons--both coming down from mother to daughter, and father to son.

The fishing fleet of Volendam sails as far as the North Sea, but it is always in Volendam by Saturday morning. Hence if you would see the Volendam fishermen in their greatest strength the time to visit the little town is at the end of the week or on Sunday.

The day for Purmerend is Tuesday, because then the market is held, in the castle plein, among mediæval surroundings. To this market the neighbourhood seems to send its whole population, by road and water, in gay cart and comfortable wherry. According to my unfailing informant in these regions, the Purmerend stadhuis, in order "to aggrandise the cheese market," was in 1633 "set back a few meters by screwing-force".

The excursion to Marken and the excursion to Edam and its neighbourhood take each a day; but between Amsterdam and Zaandam, just off the great North Canal, steamers ply continually, and one may be there in half an hour. The journey must be made, because Zaandam is superficially the gayest town in Holland and the capital of windmill land. In an hour's drive (obviously no excursion for Don Quixote) one may pass hundreds. These mills do everything except grind corn. For the most part the Dutch mills pump: but they also saw wood, and cut tobacco, and make paper, and indeed perform all the tasks for which in countries less windy and less leisurely steam or water power is employed. The one windmill in Holland which always springs to my mind when the subject is mentioned is, however, not among Zaandam's legions: it is that solitary and imposing erection which rises from the water in the Coolsingel in Rotterdam. That is my standard Dutch mill. Another which I always recall stands outside Bergen-op-Zoom, on the way to Tholen--all white.

The Dutch mill differs from the English mill in three important respects: it is painted more gaily (although for England white paint is certainly best); it has canvas on its sails; and it is often thatched. Dutch thatching is very smooth and pretty, like an antelope's skin; and never more so than on the windmills.

Zaandam lies on either side of the river Zaan, here broad and placid and north of the dam more like the Thames at Teddington, say, than any stretch of water in Holland. A single street runs beside the river for about a mile on both banks, the houses being models of smiling neatness, picked out with cheerful green paint. At Zaandam green paint is at its greenest. It is the national pigment; but nowhere else in Holland have they quite so sure a hand with it. To the critics who lament that there is no good Dutch painting to-day, I would say "Go to Zaandam". Not only is Zaandam's green the greenest, but its red roofs are the reddest, in Holland. A single row of trees runs down each of its long streets, and on the other side of each are illimitable fields intersected by ditches which on a cloudless afternoon might be strips of the bluest ribbon.

We sat for an hour in the garden of "De Zon," a little inn on the west bank half-way between the dam and the bridge. The landlady brought us coffee, and with it letters from other travellers who had liked her garden and had written to tell her so. These she read and purred over, as a good landlady is entitled to do, while we watched the barges float past and disappear as the distant lock opened and swallowed them.

South of the dam the interest is centred in the hut where for a while in 1697 Peter the Great lived to see how the Dutchmen built their ships. The belief that no other motive than the inspection of this very uninteresting cottage could bring a stranger hither is a tenet of faith to which the Zaandamer is bound with shackles of iron. The moment one disembarks the way to Peter's residence begins to be pointed out. Little boys run before; sturdy men walk beside; old men (one with a wooden leg) struggle behind. It was later that the Czar crossed to England and worked in the same way at Deptford; but no visitor to Deptford to-day is required to see his lodging there.

The real interest of Zaandam is not its connection with Peter the Great but the circumstance that it was the birthplace of Anton Mauve, in 1838. He died at Arnheim in 1888, Neither Zaandam nor Arnheim honours him.

# CHAPTER XIV

Alkmaar and Hoorn, The Helder and Enkhuisen

To Alkmaar by canal--The Cheese Market--The Weigh House

clock--Buyers and sellers--The siege of Alkmaar--To Hoorn by sea--A Peaceful harbour--Hoorn's explorer sons--John Haring's bravery--The defeat of De Bossu--Negro heroes--Hoorn's streets--and museum--Market day--and Kermis--Nieuwediep--The Helder--The Lighthouse--Hotel characters--The praise of the porter--Texel--Medemblik--King Radbod's hesitancy--Enkhuisen--Paul Potter--Sir William Temple and the old philosopher--The Dromedary.

If the weather is fine one should certainly go to Alkmaar by canal. The journey by water, on a steamer, is always interesting and intensely invigorating. It is only one remove from the open sea, so flat is the country, so free the air.

Alkmaar's magnet is its cheese market, which draws little companies of travellers thither every Friday in the season. To see it rightly one must reach Alkmaar on the preceding afternoon, to watch the arrival of the boats from the neighbouring farms, and see them unload their yellow freight on the market quay. The men who catch the cheeses are exceedingly adroit--it is the nearest thing to an English game that is played in Holland. Before they are finally placed in position the cheeses are liberally greased, until they glow and glitter like orange fires. All the afternoon the boats come in, with their collections from the various dairies on the water. By road also come cheeses in wagons of light polished wood painted blue within; and all the while the carillon of the beautiful grave Weigh House is ringing out its little tunes--the wedding march from "Lohengrin" among them--and the little mechanical horsemen are charging in the tourney to the blast of the little mechanical trumpeter. At one o'clock they run only a single course; but at noon the glories of Ashby-de-la-Zouche are enacted.

By nine o'clock on the Friday morning the market square is covered with rectangular yellow heaps arranged with Dutch systematic order and symmetry, many of them protected by tarpaulins, and the square is filled also with phlegmatic sellers and buyers, smoking, smoking, unceasingly smoking, and discussing the weather and the cheese, the cheese and the Government.

Not till ten may business begin. Instantly the first stroke of ten sounds the aspect of the place is changed. The Government and the weather recede; cheese emerges triumphant. Tarpaulins are stripped off; a new expression settles upon the features both of buyers and sellers; the dealers begin to move swiftly from one heap to another. They feel the cheeses, pat them, listen to them, plunge in their scoops and remove a long pink stick which they roll in their fingers, smell or taste and then neatly replace. Meanwhile, the seller stands by with an air part self-satisfaction, part contempt, part pity, part detachment, as who should say "It matters nothing to me whether this fussy fellow thinks the cheese good or not, buys it or not; but whether he thinks it good or bad, or whether he buys, or leaves it, it is still the best cheese in Alkmaar market, and some one will give me my price".

The seller gnaws his cigar, the buyer asks him what he asks. The buyer makes an offer. The seller refuses. The buyer increases it. The seller either refuses or accepts. In accepting, or drawing near acceptance, he extends his hand, which the buyer strikes once, and then pausing, strikes again.

Apparently two such movements clench the bargain; but I must confess to being a bad guide here, for I could find no absolute rule to follow. The whole process of Alkmaar chaffering is exceedingly perplexing and elusive. Otherwise the buyer walks away to other cheeses, the seller by no means unconscious of his movements. A little later he returns, and then as likely as not his terms are accepted, unless another has been beforehand with him and bought the lot.

Not until half-past ten strikes may the weighing begin. At that hour the many porters suddenly spring into activity and hasten to the Weigh House with their loads, which are ticketed off by the master of the scales.

The scene is altogether very Dutch and very interesting; and one should make a point of crossing the canal to get a general view of the market, with the river craft in the foreground, the bustling dealers behind, and above all the elaborate tower and facade of the Weigh House.

Alkmaar otherwise is not of great interest. It has a large light church, bare and bleak according to custom, with very attractive green curtains against its whitewash, in which, according to the author of Through

Noord-Holland, is a tomb containing "the entrails of Count Florence the Fifth". Here also is a model of one of De Ruyter's ships. Alkmaar also possesses a charming Oude Mannen en Oude Vrouwen Huis (or alms house, as we say) with white walls and a very pretty tower; quiet, pleasant streets; and on its outskirts a fine wood called the Alkmaarder Hout.

In the Museum, which is not too interesting, is a picture of the siege of Alkmaar, an episode of which the town has every right to be proud. It was the point of attack by the Duke of Alva and his son after the conquest of Haarlem--that hollow victory for Spain which was more costly than many defeats. Philip had issued a decree threatening the total depopulation of Holland unless its cities submitted to the charms of his attractive religion. The citizens of Alkmaar were the first to defy this proclamation. Once again Motley comes to our aid with his vivid narrative: "The Spaniards advanced, burned the village of Egmont to the ground as soon as the patriots had left it, and on the 21st of August Don Frederic, appearing before the walls, proceeded formally to invest Alkmaar. In a few days this had been so thoroughly accomplished, that, in Alva's language, 'it was impossible for a sparrow to enter or go out of the city'. The odds were somewhat unequal. Sixteen thousand veteran troops constituted the besieging force. Within the city were a garrison of eight hundred soldiers, together with thirteen hundred burghers, capable of bearing arms. The rest of the population consisted of a very few refugees, besides the women and children. Two thousand one hundred able-bodied men, of whom only about one-third were soldiers, to resist sixteen thousand regulars!

"Nor was there any doubt as to the fate which was reserved for them, should they succumb. The Duke was vociferous at the ingratitude with which his clemency had hitherto been requited. He complained bitterly of the ill success which had attended his monitory circulars; reproached himself with incredible vehemence, for his previous mildness, and protested that, after having executed only twenty-three hundred persons at the surrender of Haarlem, besides a few additional burghers since, he had met with no correspondent demonstrations of affection. He promised himself, however, an ample compensation for all this ingratitude in the wholesale vengeance which he purposed to wreck upon Alkmaar. Already he gloated in anticipation over

106

the havoc which would soon be let loose within those walls. Such ravings, if invented by the pen of fiction, would seem a puerile caricature; proceeding, authentically, from his own, they still appear almost too exaggerated for belief. 'If I take Alkmaar,' he wrote to Philip, 'I am resolved not to leave a single creature alive; the knife shall be put to every throat. Since the example of Harlem has proved of no use, perhaps an example of cruelty will bring the other cities to their senses,' He took occasion also to read a lecture to the party of conciliation in Madrid, whose counsels, as he believed, his sovereign was beginning to heed.

Nothing, he maintained, could be more senseless than the idea of pardon and clemency. This had been sufficiently proved by recent events. It was easy for people at a distance to talk about gentleness; but those upon the spot knew better. Gentleness had produced nothing, so far; violence alone could succeed in future. 'Let your Majesty,' he said, 'be disabused of the impression, that with kindness anything can be done with these people.

Already have matters reached such a point that many of those born in the country, who have hitherto advocated clemency, are now undeceived, and acknowledge their mistake. They are of opinion that not a living soul should be left in Alkmaar, but that every individual should be put to the sword.'...

"Affairs soon approached a crisis within the beleaguered city. Daily skirmishes, without decisive result, had taken place outside the walls. At last, on the 18th of September, after a steady cannonade of nearly twelve hours, Don Frederic at three in the afternoon, ordered an assault.

Notwithstanding his seven months' experience at Haarlem, he still believed it certain that he should carry Alkmaar by storm. The attack took place at once upon the Frisian gate, and upon the red tower on the opposite side.

Two choice regiments, recently arrived from Lombardy, led the onset, rending the air with their shouts, and confident of an easy victory. They were sustained by what seemed an overwhelming force of disciplined troops. Yet never, even in the recent history of Haarlem, had an attack been received by more dauntless breasts. Every living man was on the walls, The storming parties were assailed with cannon, with musketry, with pistols.

Boiling water, pitch and oil, molten lead, and unslaked lime, were poured upon them every moment. Hundreds of tarred and burning hoops were skilfully quoited around the necks of the soldiers, who struggled in vain to extricate themselves from these fiery ruffs, while as fast as any of the invaders planted foot upon the breach, they were confronted face to face with sword and dagger by the burghers, who hurled them headlong into the moat below.

"Thrice was the attack renewed with ever-increasing rage--thrice repulsed with unflinching fortitude. The storm continued four hours long. During all that period, not one of the defenders left his post, till he dropped from it dead or wounded. The women and children, unscared by the balls flying in every direction, or by the hand-to-hand conflicts on the ramparts, passed steadily to and fro from the arsenals to the fortifications, constantly supplying their fathers, husbands, and brothers with powder and ball. Thus, every human being in the city that could walk had become a soldier. At last darkness fell upon the scene. The trumpet of recall was sounded, and the Spaniards, utterly discomfited, retired from the walls, leaving at least one thousand dead in the trenches, while only thirteen burghers and twenty-four of the garrison lost their lives. Thus was Alkmaar preserved for a little longer--thus a large and well-appointed army signally defeated by a handful of men fighting for their firesides and altars. Ensign Solis, who had mounted the breach for an instant, and miraculously escaped with life, after having been hurled from the battlements, reported that he had seen 'neither helmet nor harness,' as he looked down into the city; only some plain-looking people, generally dressed like fishermen. Yet these plain-looking fishermen had defeated the veterans of Alva....

"The day following the assault, a fresh cannonade was opened upon the city. Seven hundred shots having been discharged, the attack was ordered. It was in vain; neither threats nor entreaties could induce the Spaniards, hitherto so indomitable, to mount the breach. The place seemed to their imagination protected by more than mortal powers, otherwise how was it possible that a few half-starved fishermen could already have so triumphantly overthrown the time-honoured legions of Spain. It was thought, no doubt, that the Devil, whom they worshipped, would continue to protect his children. Neither the entreaties nor the menaces of Don Frederic were of any avail. Several soldiers allowed themselves to be run through the body by their own officers, rather than advance to the walls, and the assault was accordingly postponed to an indefinite period."

What seemed at first an unfortunate accident turned the scale. A messenger bearing despatches from the Prince of Orange fell into Spanish hands and Don Frederic learned that the sea was to be let in. Motley continues: "The resolution taken by Orange, of which Don Frederic was thus unintentionally made aware, to flood the country far and near rather than fail to protect Alkmaar, made a profound impression upon his mind. It was obvious that he was dealing with a determined leader, and with desperate men. His attempt to carry the place by storm had signally failed, and he could not deceive himself as to the temper and disposition of his troops ever since that repulse. When it should become known that they were threatened with submersion in the ocean, in addition to all the other horrors of war, he had reason to believe that they would retire ignominiously from that remote and desolate sand hook, where, by remaining, they could only find a watery grave. These views having been discussed in a council of officers, the result was reached that sufficient had been already accomplished for the glory of the Spanish arms. Neither honour nor loyalty, it was thought, required that sixteen thousand soldiers should be sacrificed in a contest, not with man, but with the ocean.

"On the 8th of October, accordingly, the siege, which had lasted seven weeks, was raised, and Don Frederic rejoined his father in Amsterdam. Ready to die in the last ditch, and to overwhelm both themselves and their foes in a common catastrophe, the Hollanders had at last compelled their haughty enemy to fly from a position which he had so insolently assumed."

Every one is agreed that Hoorn should be approached by water, because it rises from the sea like an enchanted city of the East, with its spires and its Harbour Tower beautifully unreal. And as the ship comes nearer there is the additional interest of wondering how the apparently landlocked harbour is to be entered, a long green bar seeming to stretch unbrokenly from side to side. At the last minute the passage is revealed, and one glides into this romantic port. I put Hoorn next to Middelburg in the matter of charm, but seen from the sea it is of greater fascination. In many ways Hoorn is more remarkable as a town, but more of my heart belongs to Middelburg.

I sat on the coping of the harbour at sundown and watched a merry party dining in the saloon of a white and exceedingly comfortable-looking yacht, some thirty or forty yards away. Two neat maids continually passed from the galley to the saloon, and laughter came over the water. The yacht was from Arnheim, its owner having all the appearance of a retired East Indian official. In the distance was a tiny sailing boat with its sail set to catch what few puffs of wind were moving. Its only occupant was a man in crimson trousers, the reflection from which made little splashes of warm colour in the pearl grey sea. At Hoorn there seems to be a tendency to sail for pleasure, for as we came away a party of chattering girls glided out in the care of an elderly man--bound for a cruise in the Zuyder Zee.

It is conjectured that Hoorn took its name from the mole protecting the harbour, which might be considered to have the shape of a horn. The city as she used to be (now dwindled to something less, although the cheese industry makes her prosperous enough and happy enough) was called by the poet Vondel the trumpet and capital of the Zuyder Zee, the blessed Horn. He referred particularly to the days of Tromp, whose ravaging and victorious navy was composed largely of Hoorn ships.

Cape Horn, at the foot of South America, is the name-child of the Dutch port, for the first to discover the passage round that headland and to give it its style was Willem Schouten, a Hoorn sailor. It was another Hoorn sailor, Abel Tasman, who discovered Van Diemen's Land (now called after him) and also New Zealand; and a third, Jan Pieters Coen (whose statue may be seen at Hoorn) who founded the Dutch dominions in the East Indies, and thus changed the whole character of his own country, leading to that orientalising to which I have so often referred. A more picturesque hero was John Haring of Hoorn, who performed a great feat in 1572, when De Sonoy, the Prince of Orange's general, was fighting De Bossu, the Spanish Admiral, off the Y, just at the beginning of the siege of Haarlem. An unexpected force of Spaniards from Amsterdam overwhelmed the few men whom De Sonoy had mustered for the defence of the Diemerdyk. I quote Motley's account: "Sonoy, who was on his way to their rescue, was frustrated in his design by the unexpected faint-heartedness of the volunteers whom he had enlisted at Edam. Braving a thousand perils, he advanced, almost unattended, in his little vessel, but only to witness the overthrow and expulsion of his band. It was too late for him singly to attempt to rally the retreating troops. They had fought well, but had been forced to yield before superior numbers, one individual of the little army having performed prodigies of valour. John Haring, of Hoorn, had planted himself entirely alone upon the dyke, where it was so narrow between the Y on the one side and Diemer Lake on the other, that two men could hardly stand abreast. Here, armed with sword and shield, he had actually opposed and held in check one thousand of the enemy, during a period long enough to enable his own men, if they had been willing, to rally, and effectively to repel the attack. It was too late, the battle was too far lost to be restored; but still the brave soldier held the post, till, by his devotion, he had enabled all those of his compatriots who still remained in the entrenchments to make good their retreat. He then plunged into the sea, and, untouched by spear or bullet, effected his escape. Had he been a Greek or a Roman, a Horatius or a Chabras, his name would have been famous in history--his statue erected in the market-place; for the bold Dutchman on his dyke had manifested as much valour in a sacred cause as the most classic heroes of antiquity."

Then came the siege of Haarlem, and then the siege of Alkmaar. Hoorn's turn followed, but Hoorn was gloriously equal to it in the hands of Admiral Dirckzoon, whose sword is in the Alkmaar museum, and whose tomb is at Delft. Motley shall tell the story: "On the 11th October, however, the whole patriot fleet, favored by a strong easterly breeze, bore down upon the Spanish armada, which, numbering now thirty sail of all denominations, was lying off and on in the neighbourhood of Hoorn and Enkhuyzen. After a short and general engagement, nearly all the Spanish fleet retired with precipitation, closely pursued by most of the patriot Dutch vessels. Five of the King's ships were eventually taken, the rest effected their escape. Only the Admiral remained, who scorned to yield, although his forces had thus basely deserted him. His ship, the 'Inquisition,' for such was her insolent appellation, was far the largest and best manned of both the fleets. Most of the enemy had gone in pursuit of the fugitives, but four vessels of inferior size had attacked the 'Inquisition' at the commencement of the action. Of these, one had soon been silenced, while the other three had grappled themselves inextricably to her sides and prow. The four drifted together, before wind and tide, a severe and savage action going on incessantly, during which the navigation of the ships was entirely abandoned. No scientific gunnery, no military or naval tactics were displayed or required in such a conflict. It was a life-and-death combat, such as always occurred when Spaniard and Netherlander met, whether on land or water. Bossu and his men, armed in bullet-proof coats of mail, stood with shield and sword on the deck of the 'Inquisition,' ready to repel all attempts to board. The Hollander, as usual, attacked with pitch hoops, boiling oil, and molten lead. Repeatedly they effected their entrance to the Admiral's ship, and as often they were repulsed and slain in heaps, or hurled into the sea.

"The battle began at three in the afternoon, and continued without intermission through the whole night. The vessels, drifting together, struck on the shoal called the Nek, near Wydeness. In the heat of the action the occurrence was hardly heeded. In the morning twilight, John Haring, of Hoorn, the hero who had kept one thousand soldiers at bay upon the Diemer dyke, clambered on board the 'Inquisition,' and hauled her colors down. The gallant but premature achievement cost him his life. He was shot through the body and died on the deck of the ship, which was not quite ready to strike her flag. In the course of the forenoon, however, it became obvious to Bossu that further resistance was idle. The ships were aground near a hostile coast, his own fleet was hopelessly dispersed, three-quarters of his crew were dead or disabled, while the vessels with which he was engaged were constantly recruited by boats from the shore, which brought fresh men and ammunition, and removed their killed and wounded. At eleven o'clock Admiral Bossu surrendered, and with three hundred prisoners was carried into Holland. Bossu was himself imprisoned at Hoorn, in which city he was received, on his arrival, with great demonstrations of popular hatred."

De Bossu remained in prison for three years. Later he fought for the States. His goblet is preserved at Hoorn. His collar is at Monnickendam and his sword at Enkhuisen.

The room in the Protestant orphanage where De Bossu was imprisoned is still to be seen; and you may see also at the corner of the Grooteoost the houses from which the good wives and housekeepers watched the progress of the battle, and on which a bas-relief representation of the battle was afterwards placed in commemoration.

Two more heroes of Hoorn may be seen in effigy on the façade of the State College, opposite the Weigh House, guarding an English shield. The shield is placed there, among the others, on account of a daring feat performed by two negro sailors in De Ruyter's fleet in the Thames, who ravished from an English ship in distress the shield at her stern and presented it to Hoorn, their adopted town, where it is now supported by bronze figures of its captors.

Hoorn's streets are long and cheerful, with houses graciously bending forwards, many of them dignified by black paint and yet not made too grave by it. This black paint blending with the many trees on the canal sides has the same curious charm as at Amsterdam, although there the blackness is richer and more absolute. Even the Hoorn warehouses are things of beauty: one in particular, by the Harbour Tower, with bright green shutters, is indescribably gay, almost coquettish. Hoorn also has the most satisfying little houses I saw in Holland--streets of them.

110

And of all the costumes of Holland I remember most vividly the dead black dress and lace cap of a woman who suddenly turned a corner here--as if she had walked straight from a picture by Elias.

The Harbour Tower is perhaps Hoorn's finest building, its charm being intensified rather than diminished by the hideous barracks close by. St. Jan's Gasthuis has a façade of beautiful gravity, and the gateway of the home for Ouden Vrouwen is perfect. The museum in the Tribunalshof is the most intimate and human collection of curiosities which I saw in Holland--not a fossil, not a stuffed bird, in the building. Among the pictures are the usual groups of soldiers and burgomasters, and the usual fine determined De Ruyter by Bol. We were shown Hoorn's treasures by a pleasant girl who allowed no shade of tedium to cross her smiling courteous face, although the display of these ancient pictures and implements, ornaments and domestic articles must have been her daily work for years. In the top room of all is a curious piece of carved stone on which may be read these inscriptions:--

This most illustrious Prince, Henry Lord Darnley, King of Scotland, Father to our Soveraigne Lord King James. He died at the age of 21.

The most excellent Princesse Marie, Queen of Scotland, Mother of our Soveraigne, Lord King James. She died 1586, and entombed at West Minster.

It would be interesting to know more of this memorial.

In another room are two carved doors from a house in Hoorn that had been disfurnished which give one a very vivid idea of the old good taste of this people and the little palaces of grave art in which they lived.

Thursday is Hoorn's market day, and it is important to be there then if one would see the market carts of North Holland in abundance. We had particularly good fortune since our Thursday was not only market day but the Kermis too. I noticed that the principal attraction of the fair, for boys, was the stalls (unknown at the Kermis both at Middelburg and Leyden) on which a variety of flat cake was chopped with a hatchet. The chopper, who I understand is entitled only to what he can sever with one blow, often fails to get any.

Nieuwediep and The Helder, at the extreme north of Holland, are one, and interesting only to those to whom naval works are interesting. For they are the Portsmouth and Woolwich of the country. My memories of these twin towns are not too agreeable, for when I was there in 1897 the voyage from Amsterdam by the North Holland canal had chilled me through and through, and in 1904 it rained without ceasing. Nieuwediep is all shipping and sailors, cadet schools and hospitals. The Helder is a dull town, with the least attractive architecture I had seen, cowering beneath a huge dyke but for which, one is assured, it would lie at the bottom of the North Sea. Under rain it is a drearier town than any I know; and ordinarily it is bleak and windy, saved only by its kites, which are flown from the dyke and sail over the sea at immense heights. Every boy has a kite--one more link between Holland and China.

I climbed the lighthouse at The Helder just before the lamp was lit. It was an impressive ceremony. The captain and his men stood all ready, the captain watching the sun as it sunk on the horizon. At the instant it disappeared he gave the word, and at one stride came the light. I chanced at the moment to be standing between the lantern and the sea, and I was asked to move with an earnestness of entreaty in which the safety of a whole navy seemed to be involved. The light may be seen forty-eight miles away. It is fine to think of all the eyes within that extent of sea, invisible to us, caught almost simultaneously by this point of flame.

I did not stay at Nieuwediep but at The Helder. Thirty years ago, however, one could have done nothing so inartistic, for then, according to M. Havard, the Hotel Ten Burg at Nieuwediep had for its landlord a poet, and for its head waiter a baritone, and to stay elsewhere would have been a crime.

Here is M. Havard's description of these virtuosi: "No one ever sees the landlord the first day he arrives at the hotel. M.B.R. de Breuk is not accessible to ordinary mortals. He lives up among the clouds, and when he condescends to come down to earth he shuts himself up in his own room, where he indulges in pleasant intercourse with the Muses.

"I have no objection to confessing that, although I am a brother in the art, and have stayed several times at his hotel, I have never once been allowed to catch a glimpse of his features. The head-waiter, happily, is just the contrary. It is he who manages the hotel, receives travellers, and arranges for their well-being. He is a handsome fellow, with a fresh complexion, heavy moustache, and one lock of hair artificially arranged on his forehead. He is perfectly conscious of his own good looks, and wears rings on both his hands. Nature has endowed him with a sonorous baritone voice, the notes of which, whether sharp or melodious, he is careful in expressing, because he is charmed with his art, and has an idea that it is fearfully egotistical to conceal such treasures. One note especially he never fails to utter distinctly, and that is the last-- the note of payment.

"Sometimes he allows himself to become so absorbed in his art that he forgets the presence in the hotel of tired travellers, and disturbs their slumbers by loud roulades and cadences; or perhaps he is asked to fetch a bottle of beer, he stops on the way to the cellar to perfect the harmony of a scale, and does not return till the patience of the customer is exhausted. But who would have the heart to complain of such small grievances when the love of song is stronger than any other?"

I had no such fortune in Holland. No hotel proprietor rhymed for me, no waiter sang. My chief friends were rather the hotel porters, of whom I recall in particular two--the paternal colossus at the Amstel in Amsterdam, who might have sat for the Creator to an old master-- urbane, efficient, a storehouse of good counsel; and the plump and wide cynic into whose capable and kindly hands one falls at the Oude Doelen at The Hague, that shrewd and humorous reader of men and Americans. I see yet his expression of pity, not wholly (yet perhaps sufficiently) softened to polite interest, when consulted as to the best way in which to visit Alkmaar to see the cheese market. That any one staying at The Hague--and more, at the Oude Doelen--should wish to see traffic in cheese at a provincial town still strikes his wise head as tragic, although it happens every week. I honour him for it and for the exquisite tact with which he retains his opinion and allows you to have yours.

A poet landlord and an operatic head waiter, what are they when all is said beside a friendly hotel porter? He is the Deus ex machinâ indeed. The praises of the hotel porter have yet to be sung. O Switzerland! the poet might begin (not, probably, a landlord poet) O Switzerland- -I give but a bald paraphrase of the spirited original--O Switzerland, thou land of peaks and cow bells, of wild strawberries and nonconformist conventions, of grasshoppers and climbing dons, thou hast strange limitations! Thou canst produce no painter, thou possessest no navy; but thou makest the finest hotel porters in the world. Erect, fair-haired, blue-eyed, tactful and informing, they are the true friends of the homeless!--And so on for many strophes.

To Texel I did not cross, although it is hard for any one who has read The Riddle of the Sands to refrain. Had we been there in the nesting season I might have wandered in search of the sea birds' and the plovers' eggs, just for old sake's sake, as I have in the island of Coll, but we were too late, and The Helder had depressed us. It was off the Island of Texel on 31st July, 1653, that Admiral Tromp was killed during his engagement with the English under Monk.

Medemblik, situated on the point of a spur of land between The Helder and Enkhuisen, was once the residence of Radbod and the Kings of Frisia. It is now nothing. One good story at any rate may be recalled there. When Radbod, King of the Frisians, was driven out of Western Frisia in 689 by Pepin of Heristal, Duke and Prince of the Franks (father of Charles Martel and great grandfather of Charlemagne, who completed the conquest of Frisia), the defeated king was considered a convert to Christianity, and the preparations for his baptism were made on a grand scale. Never a whole-hearted convert, Radbod, even as one foot was in the water, had a visitation of doubt. Where, he made bold to ask, were the noble kings his ancestors, who had not, like himself, been offered this inestimable privilege of baptism--in heaven or in hell? The officiating Bishop replied that they were doubtless in hell. "Then," said Radbod, withdrawing his foot, "I think it would be better did I join them there, rather than go alone to Paradise."

Enkhuisen, where one embarks for Friesland, is a Dead City of the Zuyder Zee, with more signs of dissolution than most of them. Once she had a population of sixty thousand; that number must now be divided by ten.

"Above all things," says M. Havard, the discoverer of Dead Cities, "avoid a promenade in this deserted town with an inhabitant familiar with its history, otherwise you will constantly hear the refrain; 'Here was formerly the richest quarter of commerce; there, where the houses are falling into total ruin, was the quarter of our aristocracy,' But more painful still, when we have arrived at what appears the very end of the town, the very last house, we see at a distance a gate of the city. A hundred years ago the houses joined this gate. It took us a walk of twenty minutes across the meadows to arrive at this deserted spot." I did not explore the town, and therefore I cannot speak with any authority of its possessions; but I saw enough to realise what a past it must have had.

At Enkhuisen was born Paul Potter, who painted the famous picture of the bull in the Mauritshuis at The Hague. The year 1625 saw his birth; and it was only twenty-nine years later that he died. While admiring Potter's technical powers, I can imagine few nervous trials more exacting than having to live with his bull intimately in one's room. This only serves to show how temperamental a matter is art criticism, for on each occasion that I have been to the Mauritshuis the bull has had a ring of mute or throbbing worshippers, while Vermeer's "View of Delft" was without a devotee. I have seen, however, little scenes of cattle by Potter which were attractive as well as masterly.

Sir William Temple, in his Observations upon the United Provinces gives a very human page to this old town: "Among the many and various hospitals, that are in every man's curiosity and talk that travels their country, I was affected with none more than that of the aged seamen at Enchuysen, which is contrived, finished, and ordered, as if it were done with a kind intention of some well-natured man, that those, who had passed their whole lives in the hardships and incommodities of the sea, should find a retreat stored with all the eases and conveniences that old age is capable of feeling and enjoying. And here I met with the only rich man that ever I saw in my life: for one of these old seamen entertaining me a good while with the plain stories of his fifty years' voyages and adventures, while I was viewing their hospital, and the church adjoining, I gave him, at parting, a piece of their coin about the value of a crown: he took it smiling, and offered it me again; but, when I refused it, he asked me, What he should do with money? for all, that ever they wanted, was provided for them at their house. I left him to overcome his modesty as he could; but a servant, coming after me, saw him give it to a little girl that opened the church door, as she passed by him: which made me reflect upon the fantastic calculation of riches and poverty that is current in the world, by which a man, that wants a million, is a Prince; he, that wants but a groat, is a beggar; and this a poor man, that wanted nothing at all."

Hoorn's Harbour Tower, as I have said, has a charm beyond description; but Enkhuisen's--known as the Dromedary--is unwieldly and plain. It has, however, this advantage over Hoorn's, its bells are very beautiful. One sees the Dromedary for some miles on the voyage to Stavoren and Friesland.

# CHAPTER XV

Friesland: Stavoren to Leeuwarden

Enkhuisen to Stavoren--Draining the Zuyder Zee--The widow and the sandbank--Frisian births and courtships--Hindeloopen--Quaint rooms and houses--A pious pun--Biers for all trades--Sneek--Barge life—Two giants--Bolsward--The cow--A digression on the weed.

The traveller from Amsterdam enters Free Frisia at Stavoren, once the home of kings and now a mere haven. A little steamer carries the passengers from Enkhuisen, while the cattle trucks and vans of merchandise cross the Zuyder Zee in a huge railway raft. The steamer takes an hour or a little longer--time enough to have lunch on deck if it is fine, and watch Enkhuisen fading into nothingness and Stavoren rising from the sea.

Before the thirteenth century the Zuyder Zee consisted only of Lake Flevo, south of Stavoren and Enkhuisen, so that our passage then would have been made on land. But in 1282 came a great tempest which drove the German ocean over the north-west shores of Holland, insulating Texel and pouring over the low land between Holland and Friesland. The scheme now in contemplation to drain the Zuyder Zee proposes a dam from Enkhuisen to Piaam, thus reclaiming some 1,350,000 acres for meadow land. Since what man has done man can do, there is little doubt but that the Dutch will carry through this great project.

Concerning Stavoren there is now but one thing to say, and no writer on Holland has had the temerity to avoid saying it. That thing is the story of the widow and the sandbank. It seems that at Stavoren in its palmy days was a wealthy widow shipowner, who once gave instructions to one of her captains, bound for a foreign port, that he should bring back the most valuable and precious thing to be found there, in exchange for the outward cargo. The widow expected I know not what--ivory, perhaps, or peacocks, or chrysoprase--and when the captain brought only grain, she was so incensed that, though the poor of Stavoren implored her to give it them, she bade him forthwith throw it overboard. This he did, and the corn being cursed there sprang up on that spot a sandbank which gradually ruined the harbour and the town. The bank is called The Widow's Corn to this day.

It was near Stavoren that M. Havard engaged in a pleasant and improving conversation with a lock-keeper who had fought with France, and from him learned some curious things about Friesland customs. I quote a little: "When a wife has given birth to a boy and added a son to Friesland, all her female friends come to see her and drink in her room the brandewyn, which is handed round in a special cup or goblet. Each woman brings with her a large tart, all of which are laid out in the room--sometimes they number as many as thirty. The more there are and the finer the cakes the better, because that proves the number of friends. A few days later the new-born Frieslander is taken to church, all the girls from twelve years old accompanying the child and carrying it each in turn. As soon as they reach the church the child is handed to the father, who presents it for baptism.

Not a girl in the place would renounce her right to take part in the little procession, for it is a subject of boasting when she marries to be able to say, 'I have accompanied this and that child to its baptism'. Besides, it is supposed to ensure happiness, and that she in her turn will have a goodly number of little ones.

"'Well and how about betrothals?' 'Ah! ha! that's another thing. The girl chooses the lad. You know the old proverb, 'There are only two things a girl chooses herself--her potatoes and her lover'. You can well imagine how such things begin. They see each other at the kermis, or in the street, or fields. Then one fine day the lad feels his heart beating louder than usual. In the evening he puts on his best coat, and goes up to the house where the girl lives.

"The father and mother give him a welcome, which the girls smile at, and nudge each other. No one refers to the reason for his visit, though of course it is well known why he is there. At last, when bedtime comes, the children retire--even the father and mother go to their room-- and the girl is left alone at the fireside with the young man. "They speak of this and that, and everything, but not a word of love is uttered. If the girl lets the fire go down, it is a sign she does not care for the lad, and won't have him for a husband. If, on the contrary, she heaps fuel on the fire, he knows that she loves him and means to accept him for her affianced husband. In the first case, all the poor lad has to do is to open the door and retire, and never put his foot in the house again. But, in the other, he knows it is all right, and from that day forward he is treated as if he belonged to the family.'

"'And how long does the engagement last?'

"'Oh, about as long as everywhere else--two, three years, more or less, and that is the happiest time of their lives. The lad takes his girl about everywhere; they go to the kermis, skate, and amuse themselves, and no one troubles or inquires about them. Even the girl's parents allow her to go about with her lover without asking any questions.'"

A Dutch proverb says, "Take a Brabant sheep, a Guelderland ox, a Flemish capon and a Frisian cow". The taking of the Frisian cow certainly presents few difficulties, for the surface of Friesland is speckled thickly with that gentle animal--ample in size and black and white in hue. The only creatures that one sees from the carriage windows on the railway journey are cows in the fields and plovers above them. Now and then a man in his blue linen coat, now and then a heron; but cows always and plovers always. Never a bullock. The meadows of Holland are a female republic. Perkin Middlewick (in Our Boys) had made so much money out of pork that whenever he met a pig he was tempted to raise his hat; the Dutch, especially of North Holland and Friesland, should do equal homage to their friend the cow. Edam acknowledges the obligation in her municipal escutcheon.

Stavoren may be dull and unalluring, but not so Hindeloopen, the third station on the railway to Leeuwarden, where we shall stay. At Hindeloopen the journey should be broken for two or three hours. Should, nay must.

Hindeloopen (which means stag hunt) has been called the Museum of Holland. All that is most picturesque in Dutch furniture and costume comes from this little town--or professes to do so, for the manufacture of spurious Hindeloopen cradles and stoofjes, chairs and cupboards, is probably a recognised industry.

In the museum at Leeuwarden are two rooms arranged and furnished exactly in the genuine Hindeloopen manner, and they are exceedingly charming and gay. The smaller of the two has the ordinary blue and white Dutch tiles, with scriptural or other subjects, around the walls to the height of six feet; above them are pure white tiles, to the ceiling, with an occasional delicate blue pattern. The floor is of red and brown tiles. All the furniture is painted very gaily upon a cream or white background--with a gaiety that has a touch of the Orient in it. The bed is

116

hidden behind painted woodwork in the wall, like a berth, and is gained by a little flight of movable steps, also radiant. I never saw so happy a room. On the wall is a cabinet of curios and silver ornaments.

The larger room is similiar but more costly. On the wall are fine Delft plates, and seated at the table are wax Hindeloopeners: a man with a clay pipe and tobacco box, wearing a long flowered waistcoat, a crossed white neckcloth and black coat and hat--not unlike a Quaker in festival attire; and his neat and very picturesque women folk are around him. In the cradle, enshrined in ornamentations, is a Hindeloopen baby. More old silver and shining brass here and there, and the same resolute cheerfulness of colouring everywhere. Some of the houses in which such rooms were found still stand at Hindeloopen.

The Dutch once liked puns, and perhaps still do so. Again and again in their old inscriptions one finds experiments in the punning art, On the church of Hindeloopen, for example, are these lines:--

Des heeren woord Met aandacht hoort Komt daartoe met hoopen Als hinden loopen.

The poet must have had a drop of Salvationist blood in his veins, for only in General Booth's splendid followers do we look for such spirited invitations. The verses call upon worshippers to run together like deer to hear the word of God.

Within the great church, among other interesting things, are a large number of biers. These also are decorated according to the pretty Hindeloopen usage, one for the dead of each trade. Order even in death. The Hindeloopen baker who has breathed his last must be carried to the grave on the bakers' bier, or the proprieties will wince.

After Hindeloopen the first town of importance on the way to Leeuwarden is Sneek; and Sneek is not important. But Sneek has a water-gate of quaint symmetrical charm, with two little spires--the least little bit like the infant child of the Amsterdam Gate at Haarlem. In common with so many Frisian towns Sneek has suffered from flood. A disastrous inundation overwhelmed her on the evening of All Saints' Day in 1825, when the dykes were broken and the water rushed in to the height of five feet. Such must be great times of triumph for the floating population, who, like the sailor in the old ballad of the sea, may well pity the unfortunate and insecure dwellers in houses. What the number of Friesland's floating population is I do not know; but it must be very large. Many barges and tjalcks are both the birthplace and deathplace of their owners, who know no other home. The cabins are not less intimately cared for and decorated than the sitting-rooms of Volendam and Marken.

We saw at Edam certain odd characters formed in Nature's wayward moods. Sneek also possessed a giant named Lange Jacob, who was eight feet tall and the husband of Korte Jannetje (Little Jenny), who was just half that height. People came from great distances to see this couple. And at Sneek, in the church of St. Martin, is buried a giant of more renown and prowess--Peter van Heemstra, or "Lange Pier" as he was called from his inches, a sea ravener of notable ferocity, whose two-handed sword is preserved at Leeuwarden--although, as M. Havard says, what useful purpose a two-handed sword can serve to an admiral on a small ship baffles reflection.

Bolsward, Sneek's neighbour, is another amphibious town, with a very charming stadhuis in red and white, crowned by an Oriental bell tower completely out of keeping with the modern Frisian who hears its voice. This constant occurrence of Oriental freakishness in the

117

architecture of Dutch towns, in contrast with Dutch occidental four-square simplicity and plainness of character, is an effect to which one never quite grows accustomed.

Bolsward's church, which is paved with tomb-stones, among them some very rich ones in high relief--too high for the comfort of the desecrating foot--has a fine carved pulpit, some oak stalls of great antiquity and an imposing bell tower.

It is claimed that the Frisians were the first Europeans to smoke pipes. Whether or not that is the case, the Dutch are now the greatest smokers. Recent statistics show that whereas the annual consumption of tobacco by every inhabitant of Great Britain and Ireland is 1.34 lb., and of Germany 3 lb., that of the Dutch is 7 lb. Putting the smoking population at 30 per cent. of the total--allowing thus for women, children and non-smokers--this means that every Dutch smoker consumes about eight ounces of tobacco a week, or a little more than an ounce a day.

I excepted women and children, but that is wrong. The boys smoke too--sometimes pipes, oftenest cigars. At a music hall at The Hague I watched a contest in generosity between two friends in a family party as to which should supply a small boy in sailor suit, evidently the son of the host, with a cigar. Both won.

Fell, writing in 1801, says that the Dutch, although smoke dried, were not then smoking so much as they had done twenty years before. The Dutchmen, he says, "of the lower classes of society, and not a few in the higher walks of life, carry in their pockets the whole apparatus which is necessary for smoking:--a box of enormous size, which frequently contains half a pound of tobacco; a pipe of clay or ivory, according to the fancy or wealth of the possessor; if the latter, instruments to clean it; a pricker to remove obstructions from the tube of the pipe; a cover of brass wire for the bowl, to prevent the ashes or sparks of the tobacco from flying out; and sometimes a tinderbox, or bottle of phosphorus, to procure fire, in case none is at hand.

"The excuse of the Dutch for their lavish attachment to tobacco, in the most offensive form in which it can be exhibited, is, that the smoke of this transatlantic weed preserves them from many disorders to which they are liable from the moisture of the atmosphere of their country, and enables them to bear cold and wet without inconvenience."

Fell supports this curious theory by relating that when, soaked by a storm, he arrived at an inn at Overschie, the landlord offered him a pipe of tobacco to prevent any bad consequences. Fell, however, having none of his friend Charles Lamb's affection for the friendly traitress, declined it with asperity.

Ireland has an ingenious theory to account for the addiction of the Dutch to tobacco. It is, he says, the succedaneum to purify the unwholesome exhalations of the canals. "A Dutchman's taciturnity forbids his complaining; so that all his waking hours are silently employed in casting forth the filthy puff of the weed, to dispel the more filthy stench of the canal."

Ireland's view was probably an invention; but this I know, that the Dutch cigar and the Dutch atmosphere are singularly well adapted to each other. I brought home a box of a brand which was agreeable in Holland, and they were unendurable in the sweet air of Kent.

The cigar is the national medium for consuming tobacco, cigarettes being practically unknown, and pipes rare in the streets. My experience of the Dutch cigar is that it is a very harmless luxury and a very persuasive one. After a little while it becomes second nature to drop into a tobacconist's and slip a dozen cigars into one's pocket, at a cost of a few pence; and the cigars being there, it is another case of second nature to smoke them practically continuously. Of these cigars, which range in price from one or two cents to a few pence each, there are hundreds if not thousands of varieties.

The number of tobacconists in Holland must be very great, and the trade is probably strong enough to resist effectually the impost on the weed which was recently threatened by a daring Minister, if ever it is attempted. The pretty French custom of giving tobacco licences to the widows of soldiers is not adopted here; indeed I do not see that it could be, for the army is only 100,000 strong. In times of stress it might perhaps be advisable to send the tobacconists out to fight, and keep the soldiers to mind as many of their shops as could be managed, shutting up the rest.

# CHAPTER XVI

Leeuwarden and Neighbourhood

An agricultural centre--A city of prosperity and health--The fair

Frisians--Metal head-dresses--Silver work--The Chancellerie--A paradise of blue china--Jumping poles--The sea swallow--A Sunday

excursion--Dogs for England--The idle busybodies--The stork--A critical village--The green crop--The dyke--A linguist--Harlingen--A Dutch picture collector--Franeker--The Planetarium--Dokkum's bad reputation--A discursive guide-book--Bigamy punished--A husband-tamer--Boxum's record--Sjuck's short way--The heroic Bauck--A load of exorcists--Poor Lysse.

In an hour or two the train brings us to Leeuwarden, between flat green meadows unrelieved save for the frequent isolated homesteads, in which farm house, dairy, barn, cow stalls and stable are all under one great roof that starts almost from the ground. On the Essex flats the homesteads have barns and sheltering trees to keep them company: here it is one house and a mere hedge of saplings or none at all. For the rest--cows and plovers, plovers and cows.

Friesland's capital, Leeuwarden, might be described as an English market town, such as Horsham in Sussex, scoured and carried out to its highest power, rather than a small city. The cattle trade of Friesland has here its headquarters, and a farmer needing agricultural implements must fare to Leeuwarden to buy them. The Frisian farmer certainly does need them, for it is his habit to take three crops of short hay off his meadows, rather than one crop of long hay in the English manner.

Not only cattle but also horses are sold in Leeuwarden market. The Frisian horse is a noble animal, truly the friend of man; and the Frisians are fond of horses and indulge both in racing and in trotting--or "hardraverij" as they pleasantly call it. I made a close friend of a Frisian mare on the steamer from Rotterdam to Dort. At Dort I had to leave her, for she was bound for Nymwegen. A most charming creature. Leeuwarden is large and prosperous and healthy. What one misses in it is any sense of intimate cosiness. One seems to be nearer the elements, farther from the ingratiating works of man, than hitherto in any Dutch town. The strong air, the openness of land, the 180 degrees of sky, the northern sharpness, all are far removed from the solace of the chimney corner. It is a Spartan people, preferring hard health to overcoats; and the streets and houses reflect this temperament. They are clean and strong and bare--no huddling or niggling architecture. Everything also is bright, the effect largely of paint, but there must be something very antiseptic in this Frisian atmosphere.

The young women of Leeuwarden--the fair Frisians--are tall and strong and fresh looking; not exactly beautiful but very pleasant. "There go good wives and good mothers," one says. Their Amazonian air is accentuated by the casque of gold or silver which fits tightly over their heads and gleams through its lace covering: perhaps the most curious head-dress in this country of elaborate head-dresses, and never so curious as when, on Sundays, an ordinary black bonnet, bristling with feathers and jet, is mounted on the top of it. That, however, is a refinement practised only by the middle-aged and elderly women: the young women wear either the casque or a hat, never both. If one climbs the Oldehof and looks down on the city on a sunny day--as I did--the glint of a metal casque continually catches the eye. These head-dresses are of some value, and are handed on from mother to daughter for generations. No Dutch woman is ever too poor to lay by a little jewellery; and many a domestic servant carries, I am told, twenty pounds worth of goldsmith's work upon her.

Once Leeuwarden was famous for its goldsmiths and silversmiths, but the interest in precious metal work is not what it was. Many of the little silver ornaments--the windmills, and houses, and wagons, and boats--which once decorated Dutch sitting-rooms as a matter of course, and are now prized by collectors, were made in Leeuwarden.

The city's architectural jewel is the Chancellerie, a very ornate but quite successful building dating from the sixteenth century: first the residence of the Chancellors, recently a prison, and now the Record Office of Friesland. Not until the Middelburg stadhuis shall we see anything more cheerfully gay and decorative. The little Weigh House is in its own way very charming. But for gravity one must go to the Oldehof, a sombre tower on the ramparts of the city. Once the sea washed its very walls.

To the ordinary traveller the most interesting things in the Leeuwarden museum, which is opposite the Chancellerie, are the Hindeloopen rooms which I have described in the last chapter; but to the antiquary it offers great entertainment. Among ancient relics which the spade has revealed are some very early Frisian tobacco pipes. Among the pictures, for the most part very poor, is a dashing Carolus Duran and a very beautiful little Daubigny.

Affiliated to the museum is one of the best collections of Delft china in Holland--a wonderful banquet of blue. This alone makes it necessary to visit Leeuwarden.

All about Leeuwarden the boys have jumping poles for the ditches, and you may see dozens at a time, after school, leaping backwards and forwards over the streams, like frogs. Children abound in Friesland: the towns are filled with boys and girls; but one sees few babies. In Holland the very old and the very young are alike invisible.

One of the first things that I noticed at Leeuwarden was the presence of a new bird. Hitherto I had seen only the familiar birds that we know at home, except for a stork here and there and more herons than one catches sight of in England save in the neighbourhood of one of our infrequent heronries.

But at Leeuwarden you find, sweeping and plaining over the canals, the beautiful tern, otherwise known as the sea swallow, white and powerful and delicately graceful, and possessed of a double portion of the melancholy of birds of the sea. Of the bittern, which is said to boom continually over the Friesland meres, I caught no glimpse and heard no sound.

From Leeuwarden I rode one Sunday morning by the steam-tram to St. Jacobie Parochie, a little village in the extreme north-west, where I proposed to take a walk upon the great dyke. It was a chilly morning, and I was glad to be inside the compartment as we rattled along the road. The only other occupant was a young minister in a white tie, puffing comfortably at his cigar, which in the manner of so many Dutchmen he seemed to eat as he smoked. For a while we were raced--and for a few yards beaten--by two jolly boys in a barrow drawn by a pair of gallant dogs who foamed past us ventre à terre with six inches of flapping tongue.

The introduction into England of dogs as beasts of draught would I suppose never be tolerated. A score of humanitarian societies would spring into being to prevent it: possibly with some reason, for one has little faith in the considerateness of the average English costermonger or barrow-pusher.

And yet the dog-workers of the Netherlands seem to be cheerful beasts, wearing their yoke very easily. I have never seen one, either in Holland or Belgium, obviously distressed or badly treated. Why the English dog should so often be a complete idler, and his brother across the sea the useful ally of man, is an ethnological problem: the reason lying not with the animals but with the nations. The Flemish and Dutch people are essentially humble and industrious, without ambitions beyond their station. The English are a dissatisfied folk who seldom look upon their present position as permanent. The English dog is idle because his master, always hoping for the miracle that shall make him idle too, does not really set his hand to the day's work and make others join him; the Netherlandish dog is busy because his master does not believe in sloth, and having no illusions as to his future, knows that only upon a strenuous youth and middle age can a comfortable old age be built. Countries that have not two nations--the idle and rich and the poor and busy--as we have, are, I think, greatly to be envied. Life is so much more genuine there.

England indeed has three nations: the workers, the idle rich who live only for themselves, and the idle rich or well-to-do who live also for others--in other words the busybodies. The third nation is the real enemy, for an altruist who has time on his hands can do enormous mischief between breakfast and lunch. It is this class that would at once make it impossible for a strong dog to help in drawing a poor man's barrow. The opportunity would be irresistible to them. The resolutions they would pass! The votes of thanks to the lieutenant-colonels in the chair! It was on this little journey to St. Jacobie Parochie that I saw my first stork. Storks' nests there had been in plenty, but all were empty. But at Wier, close to St. Jacobie Parochie, was a nest on a pole beside the road, and on this nest was a stork. The Dutch, I think, have no more endearing trait than their kindness to this bird. Once at any rate their solicitude was grotesque, although serviceable, for Ireland tells of a young stork with a broken leg for which a wooden leg was substituted. Upon this jury limb the bird lived happily for thirty years.

The stork alone among Dutch birds is sacred, but he is not alone in feeling secure. The fowler is no longer a common object of the country, as he seems to have been in Albert Cuyp's day, when he returned in the golden evening laden with game--for Jan Weenix to paint.

St. Jacobie Parochie on a fine Sunday morning is no place for a sensitive man. The whole of the male population of the village had assembled by the church--not, I fancy, with any intention of entering it--and every eye among them probed me like a corkscrew. It is an out of the world spot, to which it is possible no foreigner ever before penetrated, and since their country was a show to me I had no right to object to serve as a show to them. But such scrutiny is not comfortable. I hastened to the sea.

One reaches the sea by a path across the fields to an inner dyke with a high road upon it, and then by another footpath, or paths, beside green ditches, to the ultimate dyke which holds Neptune in check. As I walked I was continually conscious of heavy splashes just ahead of me, which for a while I put down to water-rats. But chancing to stand still I was presently aware of the proximity of a huge green frog, the largest I have ever seen, who sat, solid as a paper weight, close beside me, with one eye glittering upon me and the other upon the security of the water, into which he jumped at a movement of my hand. Walking then more warily I saw that the banks on either side were populous with these monsters; and sometimes it needed only a flourish of the handkerchief to send a dozen simultaneously into the ditch. I am glad we have not such frogs at home. A little frog is an adorable creature, but a frog half-way to realising his bovine ambition is a monster. The sea dyke is many feet high. Its lowest visible stratum is of black stones, beneath the sea-level; then a stratum of large red bricks; then turf. The willow branches are invisible, within. The land hereabout is undoubtedly some distance below sea-level, but it is impossible either here or anywhere in Holland to believe in the old and venerable story of the dyke plugged by an heroic thumb to the exclusion of the ocean and the safety of the nation.

As I lay on the bank in the sun, listening to a thousand larks, with all Friesland on one hand and the pearl grey sea on the other, a passer-by stopped and asked me a question which I failed to understand. My reply conveyed my nationality to him. "Ah," he said, "Eenglish. Do it well with you?" I said that it did excellently well. He walked on until he met half a dozen other men, some hundred yards away, when I saw him pointing to me and telling them of the long conversation he had been enjoying with me in my own difficult tongue. It was quite clear from their interest that the others were conscious of the honour of having a real linguist among them.

Another day I went to Harlingen. I had intended to reach the town by steam-tram, but the time table was deceptive and the engine stopped permanently at a station two or three miles away. Fortunately, however, a curtained brake was passing, and into this I sprang, joining two women and a dominie, and together we ambled very deliberately into the quiet seaport. Harlingen is a double harbour--inland and maritime. Barges from all parts of Friesland lie there, transferring their goods a few yards to the ocean-going ships bound for England and the world, although Friesland does not now export her produce as once she did. Thirty years ago much of our butter and beef and poultry sailed from Harlingen.

The town lies in the savour of the sea. Masts rise above the houses, ship-chandlers' shops send forth the agreeable scent of tar and cordage, sailors and stevedores lounge against posts as only those that follow the sea can do. I had some beef and bread, in the Dutch midday manner, in the upper room of an inn overlooking the harbour, while two shipping-clerks played a dreary game of billiards. Beyond the dyke lay the empty grey sea, with Texel or Vlieland a faint dark line on the horizon. Nothing in the town suggested the twentieth century, or indeed any century. Time was not. I wish that Mr. Bos had been living, that I might have called upon him and seen his pictures, as M. Havard did. But he is no more, and I found no one to tell me of the fate of his collection. Possibly it is still to be seen: certainly other visitors to Harlingen should be more energetic than I was, and make sure. Here is M. Havard's account of Mr. Bos and an evening at his house: "Mr. Bos started in life as a farm-boy--then became an assistant in a shop.

Instead of spending his money at the beer-houses he purchased books. He educated himself, and being provident, steady, industrious, he soon collected sufficient capital to start in business on his own account, which he did as a small cheesemonger; but in time his business prospered, and to such an extent that one day he awoke to find himself one of the greatest and richest merchants of Harlingen.

"Many under these circumstances would have considered rest was not undeserved; but Mr. Bos thought otherwise. He became passionately fond of the arts. Instead of purchasing stock he bought pictures, then the books necessary to understand them, and what with picking up an engraving here and a painting there he soon became possessed of a most interesting collection, and of an artistic knowledge sufficient for all purposes. But to appreciate the virtue (the term is not too strong) of this aimable man, one should know the difficulties he had to surmount before gaining his position. It is no joke when one lives in a town like Harlingen to act differently from other people. Tongues are as well hung there as in any small French town.

Instead of encouraging this brave collector, they laughed at and ridiculed him. His taste for the arts was regarded as a mania. In fact, he was looked upon as a madman, and even to this day, notwithstanding his successful career, he is looked upon as no better than a lunatic. Happily a taste for art gives one joys that makes the remarks of fools and idiots pass like water off a duck's back.

"When we called on Mr. Bos he was absent; but as soon as Madame Bos was made acquainted with our names we received a most cordial reception. She is, however, a most charming woman, combining both amiability and affability, with a venerable appearance; and, notwithstanding her immense fortune and gold plate, still wears the large Frison cap of the good old times. She was anxious to do the honours of the collection in person, and immediately sent for her son, so that we might receive every information.

"Mr. Bos returned home the same evening, and at once came on board, and would not leave until we had promised to spend the evening at his house, which we did in the Frison fashion--that is to say, that whilst examining the pictures we were compelled to devour sundry plates of soeskrahelingen, a kind of pastry eaten with cheese; also to empty several bottles of old wine.

"A slight incident that occurred shortly before our departure touched me greatly. 'You think, sir,' said Mr. Bos, 'that because I do not understand French, I have not read the books you have written on our National Arts. Pray undeceive yourself, for here is a translation of it,' The old gentleman then placed before me a complete manuscript translation of the work, which he had had made specially for himself."

The special lion of Franeker, which I visited on my way back from Harlingen, is the Planetarium of Eisa Eisinga, a mathematician and wool-comber, who constructed it alone in his back parlour between 1774 and 1781. Interest in planetaria is, I should say, an acquired taste; but there can be no doubt as to the industry and ingenuity of this inventor. The wonders of the celestial law are unfolded by a very tired young woman, whose attitude to the solar system is probably similar to that of Miss Jellyby to Africa. After her lecture one stumbles upstairs to see the clock-work which controls the spheres, and is then free once more.

Franeker is proud also of her tombstones in the great church, but it is, I fancy, Eisa Eisinga whom she most admires. She was once the seat of an honourable University, which Napoleon suppressed in 1811. Her learning gone, she remains a very pleasant and clean little town. By some happy arrangement all the painting seems to be done at once--so different from London, where a fresh façade only serves to emphasise a dingy one. But although the quality of the paint can be commended, the painters of Franeker are undoubtedly allowed too much liberty. They should not have been permitted to spread their colour on the statues of the stadhuis. The principal street has an avenue of elm trees down its midst, in the place where a canal would be expected; but canals traverse the town too. Upon the deck of a peat barge I watched a small grave child taking steady and unsmiling exercise on a rocking horse.

I did not go to Dokkum, which lies at the extreme north of Friesland. Mr. Doughty, the author of an interesting book of Dutch travel, called Friesland Meres--he was the first that ever burst into these silent canals in a Norfolk wherry--gives Dokkum a very bad character, and so do other travellers. It seems indeed always to have been an unruly and inhospitable town. As long ago as 853 it was resisting the entry of strangers. The strangers were Saint Boniface and his companion, whom Dokkum straightway massacred. King Pepin was furious and sent an army on a punitive mission; while Heaven supplemented Pepin's efforts by permanently stigmatising the people of the town, all the men thenceforward being marked by a white tuft of hair and all the women by a bald patch.

At Leeuwarden is a patriotic society known as the "Vereenigung tot bevordering van vreemdelingenverkeer," whose ambition, as their title suggests, is to draw strangers to the town; and as part of their campaign they have issued a little guide to Leeuwarden and its environs, in English. It is an excellent book. The preface begins thus:--

The travelling-season, which causes thousands of people to leave their homes and hearths, has come round again. Throughout Europe silk strings are being prepared to catch human birds of passage with. Is Frisia--Old Frisia--to lag behind? Impossible! Natural condition as well as population and history give to our province a right to claim a little attention and to be a hostess. We beg to refer to the words of a Frenchman, M. Malte-Brun (quoted by one of the best Frisian authors), the English translation of which words runs as follows: "Eighteen centuries saw the river Rhine change its course, and the Ocean swallow its shores, but the Frisian nation has remained unchanged, and from an historical point of view deserves being taken an interest in by the descendants of the Franks as well as of the Anglo-Saxons and the Scandinavians." It is not often to a Frenchman that the author of this guide has to go for his purple patches. He is capable of producing them himself, and there seems also always to be a Frisian poet who has said the right thing. Thus (of Leeuwarden): "It is surrounded by splendid fertile meadows, to all of which, though especially to those lying near the roads to Marssum and Stiens, may be applied the words of the Frisian poet Dr. E. Halbertsma:--

'Sjen nou dat lân, hwer jy op geane, Dat ophelle is út gulle sé; Hwer binne brûsender lânsdouwen, Oerspriede mei sok hearlik fé?'

('Behold the soil you are walking on, The soil, snatched from the waves; Where are more luxurious meadows, Where do you find such cattle?')

The farmer, living in the midst of this fine natural scenery, is to be envied indeed: if the struggle for life does not weigh too heavily upon him, his must be a life happier than that of thousands of other people. Living and working with his own family and servants attached to him, he made the right choice when he chose to breed his cattle and improve his grounds to the best of his power. The parlour-windows look out on the fields: the gay sight they grant has its effect on the mood of those inside. The peasant sees and feels the beauty of life, and it makes him thankful, and gives him courage to struggle and to work on, where necessity requires it."

I gather from the account of Leeuwarden that the justices of that city once knew a crime when they saw one--none quicklier. In 1536, for example, they punished Jan Koekebakken in a twinkling for the dastardly offence of marrying a married woman. This was his sentence:--

We command that the said Jan Koekebakken, prisoner, be conducted by the executioner from the Chancery to Brol-bridge, and that he be put into the pillory there. He shall remain standing there for two hours with a spindle under each arm, and with the letter in which he pledged faith to the said Aucke Sijbrant hanging from his neck. He shall remain for ever within the town of Leeuwarden, under penalty of death if he should leave it.

Done and pronounced at Leeuwarden April 29th, 1536. But the best part of the guide-book is its rapid notes on the villages around Leeuwarden, to so many of which are curious legends attached. At Marssum, close at hand, was born the English painter of Roman life, Sir Lawrence Alma-Tadema. Here also was born the ingenious Eisa Eisinga, who constructed the Franeker planetarium in the intervals of wool-combing. At Menaldum lived Mrs. Van Camstra van Haarsma, a husband-tamer and eccentric, of whom a poet wrote:--

She breaks pipe and glass and mug, When he speaks as suits a man; And instead of being cross, He is gentler than a lamb. When in fury glow her eyes, He keeps silent ... isn't he wise?

When not hen-pecking her husband this powerful lady was rearing wild animals or corresponding with the Princess Caroline.

At Boxum, was fought, on 17th January, 1586, hard by the church, the battle of Boxum, between the Spaniards and the Frisians. The Frisians were defeated, and many of them massacred in the church; but their effort was very brave, and "He also has been to Boxum" is to this day a phrase applied to lads of courage. Another saying, given to loud speakers, is "He has the voice of the Vicar of Boxum," whose tones in the pulpit were so dulcet as to frighten the birds from the roof, and, I hope, sinners to repentance.

At Jelsum is buried Balthazar Becker, the antagonist of superstition and author of The Enchanted World. Near by was Martena Castle, where Alderman Sjuck van Burmania once kept a crowd of assailants at bay by standing over a barrel of gunpowder with a lighted brand while he offered them the choice of the explosion or a feast. Hence the excellent proverb, "You must either fight or drink, said Sjuck".

At Berlikum was the castle of Bauck Poppema, a Frisian lady cast in an iron mould, who during her husband's absence in 1496 defended the stronghold against assailants from Groningen. Less successful than Sjuck, after repelling them thrice she was overpowered and thrown into prison.

While there she produced twins, thus proving herself a woman no less than a warrior. "When the people of Holland glorify Kenau," says the proverb, "the Frisians praise their Bauck." Kenau we have met: the heroic widow of Haarlem who during the siege led a band of three hundred women and repelled the enemy on the walls again and again.

Near Roodkerk is a lake called the Boompoel, into which a coach and four containing six inside passengers, all of them professional exorcists, disappeared and was never seen again. The exorcists had come to relieve the village of the ghost of a miser, and we must presume had failed to quiet him. Near Bergum, at Buitenrust farm, is the scene of another tragedy by drowning, for there died Juffer Lysse. This maiden, disregarding too long her father's dying injunction to build a chapel, was naturally overturned in her carriage and drowned. Ever since has the wood been haunted, while the bind-weed, a haunting flower, is in these parts known as the Juffer Lysse blom.

From these scraps of old lore--all taken from the little Leeuwarden guide--it will be seen that Friesland is rich in romantic traditions and well worthy the attention of any maker of sagas.

# CHAPTER XVII

Groningen to Zutphen

Fresh tea--Dutch meals--The Doelens--Groningen--Roman Catholic priests--The boys'
penance--Luther and Erasmus--The peat country--Folk lore--Terburg--Thomas à Kempis--
Zwolle--The wild girl--Kampen--A hall of justice indeed--An ideal holiday-place--The wiseacres-
-Urk--Sir Philip Sidney--Zutphen--The scripture class--The wax works--Dutch public morality.

I remember the Doelen at Groningen for several reasons, all of them thoroughly
material. (Holland is, however, a material country.) First I would put the very sensible custom of
providing every guest who has ordered tea for breakfast with a little tea caddy. At the foot of the
table is a boiling urn from which one fills one's teapot, and is thus assured of tea that is fresh. So
simple and reasonable a habit ought to be the rule rather than the exception: but never have I
found it elsewhere. This surely is civilisation, I said.

The Doelen was also the only inn in Holland where an inclusive bottle of claret was
placed before me on the table; and it was the only inn where I had the opportunity of eating
ptarmigan with stewed apricots--a very happy alliance.

Good however as was the Groningen dinner, it was a Sunday dinner at the Leeuwarden
Doelen which remains in my memory. This also is a friendly unspoiled northern inn, where the
bill of fare is arranged with a nice thought to the requirements of the Free Frisian. I kept no note
of the meal, but I recollect the occurrence at one stage of plovers' eggs (which the Dutch eat hot,
dropping them into cold water for an instant to ensure the easy removal of the shell), and at
another, some time later, of duckling with prunes.

The popularity of the name Doelen as a Dutch sign might have a word of explanation.
Doelen means target, or shooting saloon; and shooting at the mark was a very common and
useful recreation with the Dutch in the sixteenth century. At first the shooting clubs met only to
shoot--as in the case of the arquebusiers in Rembrandt's "Night Watch," who are painted leaving
their Doelen; later they became more social and the accessories of sociability were added; and
after a while the accessories of sociability crowded out the shooting altogether, and nothing but
an inn with the name Doelen remained of what began as a rifle gallery.

At Groningen, which is a large prosperous town, and the birthplace both of Joseph
Israels and H.W. Mesdag, cheese and dairy produce are left behind. We are now in the grain
country. Groningen is larger than Leeuwarden--it has nearly seventy thousand inhabitants--and
its evening light seemed to me even more beautifully liquid. I sat for a long time in a cafe
overlooking the great square, feeding a very greedy and impertinent terrier, and alternately
watching an endless game of billiards and the changing hue of the sky as day turned to night and
the clean white stars came out. In Holland one can sit very long in cafes: I had dined and left a
table of forty Dutchmen just settling down to their wine, at six o'clock, with the whole evening
before me.

Groningen takes very good care of itself. It has trams, excellent shops and buildings, a
crowded inland harbour, and a spreading park where once were its fortifications. The mounds
in this park were the first hills I had seen since Laren. The church in the market square is

immense, with a high tower of bells that kept me awake, but had none of the soothing charm of Long John at Middelburg, whose praises it will soon be my privilege to sound.

The only rich thing in the whitewashed vastnesses of the church is the organ, built more than four hundred years ago by Rudolph Agricola of this province. I did not hear it.

At Groningen Roman Catholic priests become noticeable--so different in their stylish coats, square hats and canes, from the blue-chinned kindly slovens that one meets in the Latin countries. (In the train near Nymwegen, however, where the priests wear beavers, I travelled with a humorous old voluptuary who took snuff at every station and was as threadbare as one likes a priest to be.) Looking into the new Roman Catholic church at Groningen I found a little company of restless boys, all eyes, from whom at regular intervals were detached a reluctant and perfunctory couple to do the Stations of the Cross. I came as something like a godsend to those that remained, who had no one to supervise them; and feeling it as a mission I stayed resolutely in the church long after I was tired of it, writing a little and examining the pictures by Hendriex, a modern painter too much after the manner of the Christmas supplement--studied the while by this band of scrutinising penitents. I hope I was as interesting and beguiling as I tried to be. And all the time, exactly opposite the Roman Catholic church, was reposing in the library of the University no less a treasure than the New Testament of Erasmus, with marginal notes by Martin Luther. There it lay, that afternoon, within call, while the weary boys pattered from one Station of the Cross to another, little recking the part played by their country in sapping the power of the faith they themselves were fostering, and knowing nothing of the ironical contiguity of Luther's comments.

By leaving Groningen very early in the morning I gained another proof of the impossibility of rising before the Dutch. In England one can easily be the first down in any hotel--save for a sleepy boots or waiter. Not so in Holland. It was so early that I am able to say nothing of the country between Groningen and Meppel, the capital of the peat trade, save that it was peaty: heather and fir trees, shallow lakes and men cutting peat, as far as eye could reach on either side.

Here in the peat country I might quote a very pretty Dutch proverb: "There is no fuel more entertaining than wet wood and frozen peat: the wood sings and the peat listens". The Dutch have no lack of folk lore, but the casual visitor has not the opportunity of collecting very much. When there is too much salt in the dish they say that the cook is in love. When a three-cornered piece of peat is observed in the fire, a visitor is coming. When bread has large holes in it, the baker is said to have pursued his wife through the loaf. When a wedding morning is rainy, it is because the bride has forgotten to feed the cat.

I tarried awhile at Zwolle on the Yssel (a branch of the Rhine), because at Zwolle was born in 1617 Gerard Terburg, one of the greatest of Dutch painters, of whom I have spoken in the chapter on Amsterdam's pictures. Of his life we know very little; but he travelled to Spain (where he was knighted and where he learned not a little of use in his art), and also certainly to France, and possibly to England. At Haarlem, where he lived for a while, he worked in Frans Hals' studio, and then he settled down at Deventer, a few miles south of Zwolle, married, and became in time Burgomaster of the town. He died at Deventer in 1681. Zwolle has none of his pictures, and does not appear to value his memory. Nor does Deventer. How Terburg looked as Burgomaster of Deventer is seen in his portrait of himself in the Mauritshuis at The Hague. It was not often that the great Dutch painters rose to civic eminence. Rembrandt became a bankrupt, Frans Hals was on the rates, Jan Steen drank all his earnings. Of all Terburg's great contemporaries Gerard Dou seems to have had most sense of prosperity and position; but his interests were wholly in his art.

Terburg is not the only famous name at Zwolle. It was at the monastery on the Agneteberg, three miles away, that the author of The Imitation of Christ lived for more than sixty years and wrote his deathless book.

I roamed through Zwolle's streets for some time. It is a bright town, with a more European air than many in Holland, agreeable drives and gardens, where (as at Groningen) were once fortifications, and a very fine old gateway called the Saxenpoort, with four towers and five spires and very pretty window shutters in white and blue. The Groote Kerk is of unusual interest. It is five hundred years old and famous for its very elaborate pulpit--a little cathedral in itself-- and an organ. Zwolle also has an ancient church which retains its original religion--the church of Notre Dame, with a crucifix curiously protected by iron bars. I looked into the stadhuis to see a Gothic council room; and smoked meditatively among the stalls of a little flower market, wondering why some of the costumes of Holland are so charming and others so unpleasing. A few dear old women in lace caps were present, but there were also younger women who had made their pretty heads ugly with their decorations.

At Zwolle M. Havard was disappointed to find no wax figure of the famous wild girl found in the Cranenburg Forest in 1718. She roamed its recesses almost naked for some time, eluding all capture, but was at last taken with nets and conveyed to Zwolle. As she could not be understood, an account of her was circulated widely, and at length a woman in Antwerp who had lost a daughter in 1702 heard of her, and on reaching Zwolle immediately recognised her as her child. The magistrates, accepting the story, handed the girl to her affectionate parent, who at once set about exhibiting her throughout the country at a great profit. The story illustrates either the credulity of magistrates or the practical character of some varieties of maternal love.

Kampen, nearer the mouth of the Yssel, close to Zwolle, is exceedingly well worth visiting. The two towns are very different: Zwolle is patrician, Kampen plebeian; Zwolle suggests wealth and light-heartedness; at Kampen there is a large fishing population and no one seems to be wealthy. Indeed, being without municipal rates, it is, I am told, a refuge of the needy. Any old town that is on a river, and that river a mouth of the Rhine, is good enough for me; but when it is also a treasure house of mediæval architecture one's cup is full. And Kampen has many treasures: beautiful fourteenth-century gateways, narrow quaint streets, a cheerful isolated campanile, a fine church, and the greater portion of an odd but wholly delightful stadhuis in red brick and white stone, with a gay little crooked bell-tower and statues of great men and great qualities on its facade.

For one possession alone, among many, the stadhuis must be visited--its halls of justice, veritable paradises of old oak, with a very wonderful fireplace. The halls are really one, divided by a screen; in one half, the council room, sat the judges, in the other the advocates, and, I suppose, the public. The advocates addressed the screen, on the other side of which sat Fate, in the persons of the municipal fathers, enthroned in oak seats of unsurpassed gravity and dignity, amid all the sombre insignia of their office. The chimney-piece is an imposing monument of abstract Justice--no more elaborate one can exist. Solomon is there, directing the distribution of the baby; Faith and Truth, Law, Religion and Charity are there also. Never can a tribunal have had a more appropriate setting than at Kampen. The Rennes judiciaries should have sat there, to lend further ironical point to their decision. The stadhuis has other possessions interesting to anti-quaries: valuable documents, gold and silver work, the metal and leather squirts through which boiling oil was projected at the enemies of the town; while an iron cage for criminals, similar, I imagine, to that in which Jan of Leyden was exhibited, hangs outside.

Travellers visit Kampen pre-eminently to see the stadhuis chimney-piece and oak, but the whole town is a museum. I wish now that I had arranged to be longer there; but unaware of Kampen's charms I allowed but a short time both for Zwolle and itself. On my next visit to Holland Kampen shall be my headquarters for some days. Amid the restfulness of mediævalism, the friendliness of the fishing folk and the breezes of the Zuyder Zee, one should do well. A boat from Amsterdam to Kampen sails every morning.

Despite its Judgment Hall and its other merits Kampen is the Dutch Gotham. Any foolishly naive speech or action is attributed to Kampen's wise men. In one story the fathers of the town place the municipal sundial under cover to protect it from the rays of the sun. In another they meet together to deliberate on the failure of the water pipes and fire engines during a fire, and pass a rule that "on the evening preceding a fire" all hydrants and engines must be overhauled. M. Havard gives also the following instance of Kampen sagacity. A public functionary was explaining the financial state of the town. He asserted that one of the principal profits arose from the tolls exacted on the entrance of goods into the town. "Each gate," said the ingenious advocate, "has brought in ten million florins this year; that is to say, with seven gates we have gained seventy million florins. This is a most important fact. I therefore propose that the council double the number of gates, and in this way we shall in future considerably augment our funds." The Irishman who, when asked to buy a stove that would save half his fuel, replied that he would have two and save it all, was of the same school of logic.

From Kampen the island of Urk may be visited: but I have not been there. In 1787, I have read somewhere, the inhabitants of Urk decided to form a club in which to practise military exercises and the use of arms. When the club was formed it had but one member. Hence a Dutch saying--"It is the Urk club".

Nor did I stay at Deventer, but hastened on to Zutphen with my thoughts straying all the time to the grey walls of Penshurst castle in Kent and its long galleries filled with memories of Sir Philip Sidney--the gentle knight who was a boy there, and who died at Arnheim of a wound which he received in the siege of Zutphen three and a quarter centuries ago.

At Naarden we have seen how terrible was the destroying power of the Spaniards. It was at Zutphen that they had first given rein to their lust for blood. When Zutphen was taken by Don Frederic in 1572, at the beginning of the war, Motley tells us that "Alva sent orders to his son to leave not a single man alive in the city, and to burn every house to the ground. The Duke's command was almost literally obeyed. Don Frederic entered Zutphen, and without a moment's warning put the whole garrison to the sword. The citizens next fell a defenceless prey; some being stabbed in the streets, some hanged on the trees which decorated the city, some stripped stark naked, and turned out into the fields to freeze to death in the wintry night. As the work of death became too fatiguing for the butchers, five hundred innocent burghers were tied two and two, back to back, and drowned like dogs in the river Yssel. A few stragglers who had contrived to elude pursuit at first, were afterwards taken from their hiding-places, and hung upon the gallows by the feet, some of which victims suffered four days and nights of agony before death came to their relief."

On the day that I was in Zutphen it was the quietest town I had found in all Holland--not excepting Monnickendam between the arrival of the steam-trams. The clean bright streets were empty and still: another massacre almost might just have occurred. I had Zutphen to myself. I could not even find the koster to show me the church; and it was in trying door after door as I walked round it that I came upon the only sign of life in the place. For one handle at last yielding I found myself instantly in a small chapel filled with many young women engaged in a scripture class. The sudden irruption of an embarrassed and I imagine somewhat grotesque foreigner seems to have been exactly what every member of this little congregation was most desiring, and I never heard a merrier or more spontaneous burst of laughter. I stood not upon the order of my going.

The church is vast and very quiet and restful, with a large plain window of green glass that increases its cool freshness; while the young leaves of a chestnut close to another window add to this effect. The koster coming at last, I was shown the ancient chained library in the chapter house, and he enlarged upon the beauties of a metal font. Wandering out again into this city of silence I found in the square by the church an exhibition of wax works which was to be opened at four o'clock. Making a note to return to it at that hour, I sought the river, where the timber is floated down from the German forests, and lost myself among peat barges and other craft, and walked some miles in and about Zutphen, and a little way down a trickling stream whence the view of the city is very beautiful; and by-and-by found myself by the church and the wax works again, in a town that since my absence had quite filled with bustling people--four o'clock having struck and the Princess of the Day Dream having (I suppose) been kissed. The change was astonishing.

Wax works always make me uncomfortable, and these were no exception; but the good folk of Zutphen found them absorbing. The murderers stood alone, staring with that fixity which only a wax assassin can compass; but for the most part the figures were arranged in groups with dramatic intent. Here was a confessional; there a farewell between lovers; here a wounded Boer meeting his death at the bayonet of an English dastard; there a Queen Eleanor sucking poison from her husband's arm. A series of illuminated scenes of rapine and disaster might be studied through magnifying glasses. The presence of a wax bust of Zola was due, I imagine, less to his illustrious career than to the untoward circumstances of his death. The usual Sleeping Beauty heaved her breast punctually in the centre of the tent.

In one point only did the exhibition differ from the wax works of the French and Italian fairs--it was undeviatingly decent. There were no jokes, and no physiological models. But the Dutch, I should conjecture, are not morbid. They have their coarse fun, laugh, and get back to business again. Judged by that new short-cut to a nation's moral tone, the picture postcard, the Dutch are quite sound. There is a shop in the high-spirited Nes Straat at Amsterdam where a certain pictorial ebullience has play, but I saw none other of the countless be-postcarded windows in all Holland that should cause a serious blush on any cheek; while the Nes Straat specimens were fundamentally sound, Rabelaisian rather than Armand-Sylvestrian, not vicious but merely vulgar.

# CHAPTER XVIII

Arnheim to Bergen-op-Zoom

Arnheim the Joyous--A wood walk--Tesselschade Visscher and the Chambers of Rhetoric--Epigrams--Poet friends--The nightingale--An Arnheim adventure--Ten years at one book--Dutch and Latin--Dutch and French--A French story--Dutch and English--The English

Schole-Master--Master and scholar--A nervous catechism--Avoiding the birch--A riot of courtesy--A bill of lading--Dutch proverbs--The Rhine and its mouths--Nymwegen--Lady Mary Wortley Montagu again--Painted shutters--The Valkhof--Hertogenbosch--Brothers at Bommel--The hero of Breda--Two beautiful tombs--Bergen-op-Zoom--Messrs. Grimston and Red-head--Tholen--The Dutch feminine countenance.

At Arnheim we come to a totally new Holland. The Maliebaan and the park at Utrecht, with their spacious residences, had prepared us a little for Arnheim's wooded retirement; but not completely. Rotterdam is given to shipping; The Hague makes laws and fashions; Leyden and Utrecht teach; Amsterdam makes money. It is at Arnheim that the retired merchant and the returned colonist set up their home. It is the richest residential city in the country. Arnheim the Joyous was its old name. Arnheim the Comfortable it might now be styled.

It is the least Dutch of Dutch towns: the Rhine brings a bosky beauty to it, German in character and untamed by Dutch restraining hands. The Dutch Switzerland the country hereabout is called. Arnheim recalls Richmond too, for it has a Richmond Hill--a terrace-road above a shaggy precipice overlooking the river.

I walked in the early morning to Klarenbeck, up and down in a vast wood, and at a point of vantage called the Steenen Tafel looked down on the Rhine valley. Nothing could be less like the Holland of the earlier days of my wanderings--nothing, that is, that was around me, but with the farther bank of the river the flatness instantly begins and continues as far as one can see in the north. It was a very beautiful morning in May, and as I rested now and then among the resinous pines I was conscious of being traitorous to England in wandering here at all. No one ought to be out of England in April and May. At one point I met a squirrel--just such a nimble short-tempered squirrel as those which scold and hide in the top branches of the fir trees near my own home in Kent--and my sense of guilt increased; but when, on my way back, in a garden near Arnheim I heard a nightingale, the treachery was complete.

And this reminds me that the best poem of the most charming figure in Dutch literature--Tesselschade Visscher--is about the nightingale. The story of this poetess and her friends belongs more properly to Amsterdam, or to Alkmaar, but it may as well be told here while the Arnheim nightingale--the only nightingale that I heard in Holland--is plaining and exulting.

Tesselschade was the daughter of the poet and rhetorician Roemer Visscher. She was born on 25th March, 1594, and earned her curious name from the circumstance that on the same day her father was wrecked off Texel. In honour of his rescue he named his daughter Tesselschade, or Texel wreck, thereby, I think, eternally impairing his right to be considered a true poet. As a matter of fact he was rather an epigrammatist than a poet, his ambition being to be known as the Dutch Martial. Here is a taste of his Martial manner:--

Jan sorrows--sorrows far too much: 'tis true A sad affliction hath distressed his life;-- Mourns he that death hath ta'en his children two? O no! he mourns that death hath left his wife.

I have said that Visscher was a rhetorician. The word perhaps needs a little explanation, for it means more than would appear. In those days rhetoric was a living cult in the Netherlands: Dutchmen and Flemings played at rhetoric with some of the enthusiasm that we keep for cricket and sport.

Every town of any importance had its Chamber of Rhetoric. "These Chambers," says Longfellow in his Poets and Poetry of Europe, "were to Holland, in the fifteenth century, what the Guilds of the Meistersingers were to Germany, and were numerous throughout the Netherlands. Brussels could boast of five; Antwerp of four; Louvain of three; and Ghent, Bruges, Malines, Middelburg, Gouda, Haarlem, and Amsterdam of at least one.

Each Chamber had its coat of arms and its standard, and the directors bore the title of Princes and Deans. At times they gave public representations of poetic dialogues and stage-plays, called Spelen van Sinne, or Moralities.

Like the Meistersingers, they gave singular titles to their songs and metres. A verse was called a Regel; a strophe, a Clause; and a burden or refrain, a Stockregel. If a half-verse closed as a strophe, it was a Steert, or tail.

Tafel-spelen, and Spelen van Sinne, were the titles of the dramatic exhibitions; and the rhymed invitation to these was called a Charte, or Uitroep (outcry). Ketendichten (chain-poems) are short poems in which the last word of each line rhymes with the first of the line following; Scaekberd (checkerbourd), a poem of sixty-four lines, so rhymed, that in every direction it forms a strophe of eight lines; and Dobbel-steert (double-tail), a poem in which a double rhyme closes each line. [5]

"The example of Flanders was speedily followed by Zeeland and Holland. In 1430, there was a Chamber at Middelburg; in 1433, at Vlaardingen; in 1434, at Nieuwkerk; and in 1437, at Gouda. Even insignificant Dutch villages had their Chambers. Among others, one was founded in the Lier, in the year 1480. In the remaining provinces they met with less encouragement. They existed, however, at Utrecht, Amersfoort, Leeuwarden, and Hasselt. The purity of the language was completely undermined by the rhyming self-called Rhetoricians, and their abandoned courses brought poetry itself into disrepute. All distinction of genders was nearly abandoned; the original abundance of words ran waste; and that which was left became completely overwhelmed by a torrent of barbarous terms."

Wagenaer, in his "Description of Amsterdam," gives a copy of a painter's bill for work done for a rhetorician's performance at the play-house in the town of Alkmaar, of which the following is a translation:--

"Imprimis, made for the Clerks a Hell; Item, the Pavilion of Satan; Item, two pairs of Devil's-breeches; Item, a Shield for the Christian Knight; Item, have painted the Devils whenever they played; Item, some Arrows and other small matters. Sum total; worth in all xii. guilders. "Jaques Mol.

"Paid, October viii., 95 [1495]."

Among the Dutch pictures at the Louvre is an anonymous work representing the Committee of a Chamber of Rhetoric.

Roemer Visscher, the father of the poetess, was a leading rhetorician at Amsterdam, and the president of the Eglantine Chamber of the Brother's Blossoming in Love (as he and his fellow-rhetoricians called themselves). None the less, he was a sensible and clever man, and he brought up his three daughters very wisely. He did not make them blue stockings, but saw that they acquired comely and useful arts and crafts, and he rendered them unique by teaching them to swim in the canal that ran through his garden. He also was enabled to ensure for them the company of the best poetical intellects of the time--Vondel and Brederoo, Spiegel, Hooft and Huyghens.

Of these the greatest was Joost van den Vondel, a neighbour of Visscher's in Amsterdam, the author of "Lucifer," a poem from which it has been suggested that Milton borrowed. Like Izaak Walton Vondel combined haberdashery with literature. Spiegel was a wealthy patron of the arts, and a president, with Visscher, of the Eglantine Chamber with the painfully sentimental name. Constantin Huyghens wrote light verse with intricate metres, and an occasional epigram. Here is one:--

On Peter's Poetry.

When Peter condescends to write, His verse deserves to see the light. If any further you inquire, I mean--the candle or the fire.

Also a practical statesman, it was to Huyghens that Holland owes the beautiful old road from The Hague to Scheveningen in which Jacob Cats built his house. Among these friends Anna and Tesselschade grew into cultured women of quick and sympathetic intellect. Both wrote poetry, but Tesselschade's is superior to her sister's. Among Anna's early work were some additions to a new edition of her father's Zinne-Poppen, one of her poems running thus in the translation by Mr, Edmund Gosse in the very pleasant essay on Tesselschade in his Studies in the Literature of Northern Europe:--

A wife that sings and pipes all day, And never puts her lute away, No service to her hand finds she; Fie, fie! for this is vanity!

But is it not a heavenly sight To see a woman take delight With song or string her husband dear, When daily work is done, to cheer?

Misuse may turn the sweetest sweet To loathsome wormwood, I repeat; Yea, wholesome medicine, full of grace, May prove a poison--out of place.

They who on thoughts eternal rest, With earthly pleasures may be blest; Since they know well these shadows gay, Like wind and smoke, will pass away.

Tesselschade, who was much loved by her poet friends, disappointed them all by marrying a dull sailor of Alkmaar named Albert Krombalgh. Settling down at Alkmaar, she continued her intercourse with her old companions, and some new ones, by letter. Among her new friends were Barlaeus, or Van Baerle, the first Latinist of the day, and Jacob Cats. When her married life was cut short some few years later, Barlaeus proposed to the young widow; but it was in vain, as she informed him by quoting from Cats these lines:--

135

When a valvèd shell of ocean Breaks one side or loses one, Though you seek with all devotion You can ne'er the loss atone, Never make again the edges Bite together, tooth for tooth, And, just so, old love alleges Nought is like the heart's first troth.

These are Tesselschade's lines upon the nightingale in Mr. Gosse's happy translation:-- THE WILD SONGSTER.

Praise thou the nightingale, Who with her joyous tale Doth make thy heart rejoice, Whether a singing plume she be, or viewless wingèd voice;

Whose warblings, sweet and clear, Ravish the listening ear With joy, as upward float The throbbing liquid trills of her enchanted throat;

Whose accents pure and ripe Sound like an organ pipe, That holdeth divers songs, And with one tongue alone sings like a score of tongues.

The rise and fall again In clear and lovely strain Of her sweet voice and shrill, Outclamours with its songs the singing springing rill.

A creature whose great praise Her rarity displays, Seeing she only lives A month in all the year to which her song she gives.

But this thing sets the crown Upon her high renown, That such a little bird as she Can harbour such a strength of clamorous harmony.

Arnheim presents after dinner the usual scene of contented movement. The people throng the principal streets, and every one seems happy and placid. The great concert hall, Musis Sacrum, had not yet begun its season when I was there, and the only spectacle which the town could muster was an exhibition of strength by two oversized boys, which I avoided.

At Arnheim, I should relate, an odd thing happened to my companion. When she was there last, in 1894, she had need to obtain linseed for a poultice, and visited a chemist for the purpose. He was an old man, and she found him sitting in the window studying his English grammar. How long his study had lasted I have no notion, but he knew less of our tongue than she of his, and to get the linseed was no easy matter. Ten years passed and recollection of the Arnheim chemist had clean evaporated; but chancing to look up as we walked through the town, the sight of the old chemist seated in his shop-window poring over a book brought the whole incident back to her. We stepped to the window and stole a glance at the volume: it was an English Grammar. He had been studying it ever since the night of the linseed poultice.

It was, we felt, an object-lesson to us, who during the same interval had taken advantage of every opportunity of neglecting the Dutch tongue.

That tongue, however, is not attractive. Even those who have spoken it to most purpose do not always admire it. I find that Kasper van Baerle wrote: "What then do we Netherlanders speak? Words from a foreign tongue: we are but a collected crowd, of feline origin, driven by a strange fatality to these mouths of the Rhine. Why, since the mighty descendants of Romulus here pitched their tents, choose we not rather the holy language of the Romans!"

We may consider Dutch a harsh tongue, and prefer that all foreigners should learn English; but our dislike of Dutch is as nothing compared with Dutch dislike of French as expressed in some verses by Bilderdyk when the tyranny of Napoleon threatened them:--

Begone, thou bastard-tongue! so base--so broken-- By human jackals and hyenas spoken; Formed of a race of infidels, and fit To laugh at truth--and scepticise in wit; What stammering, snivelling sounds, which scarcely dare, Bravely through nasal channel meet the ear-- Yet helped by apes' grimaces--and the devil, Have ruled the world, and ruled the world for evil!

But French is now the second language that is taught in Dutch schools. German comes first and English third.

The Dutch language often resembles English very closely; sometimes so closely as to be ridiculous. For example, to an English traveller who has been manoeuvring in vain for some time in the effort to get at the value of an article, it comes as a shock comparable only to being run over by a donkey cart to discover that the Dutch for "What is the price?" is "Wat is de prijs?" The best old Dutch phrase-book is The English Schole-Master, the copy of which that lies before me was printed at Amsterdam by John Houman in the year 1658. I have already quoted a short passage from it, in Chapter II. This is the full title:--

The English Schole-Master; or Certaine rules and helpes, whereby the natives of the Netherlandes, may bee, in a short time, taught to read, understand, and speake the English tongue. By the helpe whereof the English also may be better instructed in the knowledge of the Dutch tongue, than by any vocabulars, or other Dutch and English books, which hitherto they have had, for that purpose.

There is internal evidence that the book was the work of a Dutchman rather than an Englishman; for the Dutch is better than the English. I quote (omitting the Dutch) part of one of the long dialogues between a master and scholar of which the manual is largely composed. Much of its interest lies in the continual imminence of the rod and the skill of the child in saving the situation:--

M. In the meane time let me aske you one thing more. Have you not in to-day at the holy sermon?

S. I was there.

M. Who are your witnesses?

S. Many of the schoole-fellowes who saw me can witnes it.

M. But some must be produced.

S. I shall produce them when you commaund it.

M. Who did preach?

S. Master N. M. At what time began he?

S. At seven a clock.

M. Whence did he take his text?

S. Out of the epistle of Paul to the Romanes.

M. In what chapter?

S. In the eighth.

M. Hitherto you have answered well: let us now see what follows. Have you remembred anything?

S. Nothing that I can repeat.

M. Nothing at al? Bethink (your self) a little, and take heed that you bee not disturbed, but bee of good courage.

S. Truly master I can remember nothing.

M. What, not one word?

S. None at all.

M. I am ready to strike you: what profit have you then gotten?

S. I know not, otherwise than that perhaps I have in the mean time abstained from evill.

M. That is some what indeed, if it could but so be that you have kept your self wholy from evill.

S. I have abstained so much as I was able. M. Graunt that it bee so, yet you have not pleased God, seeing it is written, depart from evill and doe good, but tell mee (I pray thee) for what cause principally did you goe thither?

S. That I might learne something.

M. Why have you not done so?

S. I could not.

M. Could you not, knave? yea you would not, or truly you have not addicted your self to it.

S. I am compelled to confesse it.

M. What compelleth you?

S. My Conscience, which accuseth me before God.

M. You say well: oh that it were from the heart.

S. Truly I speak it from myne heart.

M. It may bee so: but goe to, what was the cause that you have remembred nothing?

138

S. My negligence: for I attended not diligently.

M. What did you then?

S. Sometimes I slept.

M. So you used to doe: but what did you the rest of the time?

S. I thought on a thousand fooleries, as children are wont to doe. M. Are you so very a child, that you ought not to be attentive to heare the word of God?

S. If I had bin attentive, I should have profitted something.

M. What have you then meritted?

S. Stripes.

M. You have truly meritted them, and that very many.

S. I ingenuously confess it.

M. But in word only I think.

S. Yea truly from myne heart.

M. Possibly, but in the meane time prepare to receive stripes.

S. O master forgive it, I beseech you, I confes I have sinned, but not of malice.

M. But such an evill negligence comes very neare wickedness (malice).

S. Truly I strive not against that: but nevertheles I implore your clemencie through Jesus Christ.

M. What will you then doe, if I shall forgive you?

S. I will doe my dutie henceforth, as I hope.

M. You should have added thereto, by God's helpe: but you care little for that.

S. Yea master, by God's help, I will hereafter doe my duty. M. Goe to, I pardon you the fault for your teares: and I forgive it you on this condition, that you bee myndful of your promise.

S. I thank you most Courteous master.

M. You shall bee in very great favour with mee, if you remember your promise.

S. The most good and great God graunt that I may.

M. That is my desire, that hee would graunt it.

Here is another dialogue. Whether the riot of courtesy displayed in it was typical of either England or Holland at that time I cannot say; but in neither country are we now so solicitous:--

139

Salutations at meeting and parting.

Clemens. David.

C. God save you David.

D. And you also Clemens.

C. God save you heartily.

D. And you also, as heartily.

C. How do you?

D. I am well I thank God; at your service: and you Clemens, how is it with you? well?

C. I am also in health: how doth your father and mother?

D. They are in good health praised be God. C. How goes it with you my good friend?

D. It goeth well with mee, goes it but so well with you.

C. I wish you good health.

D. I wish the same to you also.

C. I salute you.

D. And I you also.

C. Are you well? are you in good health?

D. I am well, indeed I am in good health, I am healthful, and in prosperity.

C. That is good. That is well. That is pleasing to me. That maketh mee glad. I love to hear that. I beseech you to take care of your health. Preserve your health.

D. I can tarry no longer now. I am in haste to be gone. I must go. I have need of my time. I cannot abide standing here. Fare you well God be with you. God keep you still. I wish your health may continue.

C. And you also my loving friend, God protect you. God guide you. God bee with you. May it please you in my behalf, heartily to salute your wife and children.

D. I will do your message. But I pray, commend mee also to your father and mother.

At the end of the book are some forms, in Dutch and English, of mercantile letters, among them a specimen bill of lading of which I quote a portion as an example of the gracious way in which business was done in old and simpler days:-- I, J.P. of Amsterdam, master under God of my ship called the Saint Peter at this present lying ready in the river of Amsterdam to saile with the first goode winde which God shall give toward London, where my right unlading shal be, acknowledge and confes that I have receaved under the hatches of my foresaid ship of

140

you S.J., merchaunt, to wit: four pipes of oile, two chests of linnen, sixteen buts of currents, one bale of canvase, five bals of pepper, thirteen rings of brasse wyer, fiftie bars of iron, al dry and wel conditioned, marked with this marke standing before, all which I promise to deliver (if God give me a prosperous voyage with my said ship) at London aforesaid, to the worshipful Mr. A.J. to his factour or assignes, paying for the freight of the foresaid goods 20 fs. by the tun.

Quaintness and humour are not confined to the ancient phrase-books. An English-Dutch conversational manual from which the languages are still learned has a specimen "dialogue" in a coach, which is opened by the gentleman remarking genially and politely to his fellow-passenger, a lady, "Madame, shall we arrange our legs".

It occurs to me that very little Dutch has found its way into these pages. Let me therefore give the first stanza of the national song, "Voor Vaderland en Vorst":--

Wien Neêrlandsch bloed in de aderen vloeit, Van vreemde smetten vrij, Wiens hart voor land en Koning gloeit, Verhef den sang als wij: Hij stel met ons, vereend van zin, Met onbeklemde borst, Het godgevallig feestlied in Voor Vaderland en Vorst.

These are brave words. A very pedestrian translation runs thus:--

Who Ne'erland's blood feel nobly flow, From foreign tainture free, Whose hearts for king and country glow, Come, raise the song as we: With breasts serene, and spirits gay, In holy union sing The soul-inspiring festal lay, For Fatherland and King.

And now a specimen of really mellifluous Dutch. "How would you like," is the timely question of a daily paper this morning, as I finish this chapter, "to be hit by a 'snellpaardelooszoondeerspoorwegpitroolrijtung?' That is what would happen to you if you were run down by a motor-car in Holland. The name comes from 'snell,' rapid; 'paardeloos,' horseless; 'zoondeerspoorweg,' without rails; 'pitroolrijtung,' driven by petroleum.

Only a Dutchman can pronounce it."

Let me spice this chapter by selecting from the pages of proverbs in Dutch and English a few which seem to me most excellent. No nation has bad proverbs; the Dutch have some very good ones.

Many cows, much trouble.

Even hares pull a lion by the beard when he is old. Men can bear all things, except good days.

The best pilots are ashore.

Velvet and silk are strange herbs: they blow the fire out of the kitchen. It is easy to make a good fire of another's turf.

It is good cutting large girths of another man's leather. High trees give more shadow than fruit.

An old hunter delighteth to hear of hunting. It hath soon rained enough in a wet pool.

God giveth the fowls meat, but they must fly for it. An idle person is the devil's pillow.

No hen so witty but she layeth one egg lost in the nettles. It happeneth sometimes that a good seaman falls overboard. He is wise that is always wise.

When every one sweeps before his own house, then are the streets clean. It is profitable for a man to end his life, before he die.

Before thou trust a friend eat a peck of salt with him. It's bad catching hares with drums.

The pastor and sexton seldom agree. No crown cureth headache.

There is nothing that sooner dryeth up than a tear.

Land purchase and good marriage happen not every day. When old dogs bark it is time to look out.

Of early breakfast and late marriage men get not lightly the headache. Ride on, but look about.

Nothing in haste, but to catch fleas.

To return to Arnheim: of the Groote Kerk I remember only the very delicate colouring of the ceiling, and the monument of Charles van Egmont, Duke of Guelders. I had grown tired of architecture: it seemed goodlier to watch the shipping on the river, which at Arnheim may be called the Rhine without hesitation. All the traffic to Cologne must pass the town. Hitherto one had had qualms about the use of the word, having seen the Rhine under various aliases in so many places. The Maas at Rotterdam is a mouth of the Rhine; but before it can become the Rhine proper it becomes the Lek, What is called the true mouth of the Rhine is at Katwyk. At Dordrecht again is another of the Rhine's mouths, the Waal, which runs into the old Maas and then into the sea. The Yssel, still another mouth of the Rhine, which I saw at Kampen on its way into the Zuyder Zee, breaks away from the parent river just below Arnheim. As a matter of fact all Holland is on the Rhine, but the word must be used with care.

If one would study Dutch romantic scenery I think Nymwegen on the whole a better town to stay in than Arnheim. It is simpler in itself, richer in historic associations, and the country in the immediate east is very well worth exploring--hill and valley and pine woods, with quaint villages here and there; and, for the comfortable, a favourite hotel at Berg en Daal from which great stretches of the Rhine may be seen.

To see Nymwegen itself to greater advantage, with its massed houses and towers presenting a solid front, one must go over the iron bridge to Lent and then look back across the river. At all times the old town wears from this point of view an interesting and romantic air, but never so much as at evening.

Some versions of "Lohengrin" set the story at Nymwegen; but the Lohengrin monument is at Kleef, a few miles above the confluence of the Rhine and the Waal, the river on which Nymwegen stands.

Lady Mary Wortley Montagu, who was at Nymwegen in 1716, drew an odd comparison between that town and the English town of Nottingham. If Edinburgh is the modern Athens there is no reason why Nottingham should not be the English Nymwegen. Lady Mary writes to her friend Sarah Chiswell: "If you were with me in this town, you would be ready to expect to receive visits from your Nottingham friends. No two places were ever more resembling; one has but to give the Maese the name of the Trent, and there is no distinguishing the prospects--the houses, like those of Nottingham, built one above another, and are intermixed in the same manner with trees and gardens. The tower they call Julius Cæsar's has the same situation with Nottingham Castle; and I cannot help fancying I see from it the Trent-field, Adboulton, &c., places so well known to us. 'Tis true, the fortifications make a considerable difference...."

Nymwegen reminded me of nothing but itself. It is in reality two towns: a spacious residential town near the station, with green squares, and statues, and modern houses (one of them so modern as to be employing a vacuum cleaner, which throbbed and panted in the garden as I passed); and the old mediæval Nymwegen, gathered about one of the most charming market places in all Holland--a scene for comic opera. The Dutch way of chequering the shutters in blue and yellow (as at Middelburg) or in red and black, or red and white, is here practised to perfection. The very beautiful weigh-house has red and black shutters; the gateway which leads to the church has them too.

Never have I seen a church so hemmed in by surrounding buildings. The little houses beset it as the pigmies beset Antæus. After some difficulty I found my way in, and wandered for a while among its white immensities. It is practically a church within a church, the region of services being isolated in the midst, in the unlovely Dutch way, within hideous wooden walls. It is very well worth while to climb the tower and see the great waterways of this country beneath you. The prospect is mingled wood and polder: to the east and south-east, shaggy hills; to the west, the moors of Brabant; to the north, Arnheim's dark heights.

Nymwegen has many lions, chief of which perhaps is the Valkhof, in the grounds above the river--the remains of a palace of the Carlovingians. It is of immense age, being at once the oldest building in Holland and the richest in historic memories. For here lived Charlemagne and Charles the Bald, Charles the Bold and Maximilian of Austria. The palace might still be standing were it not for the destructiveness of the French at the end of the eighteenth century. A picture by Jan van Goyen in the stadhuis gives an idea of the Valkhof in his day, before vandalism had set in.

As some evidence of the town's pride in her association with these great names the curfew, which is tolled every evening at eight o'clock, but which I did not hear, is called Charlemagne's Prayer. The façade of the stadhuis is further evidence, for it carries the statues of some of the ancient monarchs who made Nymwegen their home.

Within the stadhuis is another of the beautiful justice halls which Holland possesses in such profusion, the most interesting of which we saw at Kampen. Kampen's oak seats are not, however, more beautiful than those of Nymwegen; and Kampen has no such clock as stands here, distilling information, tick by tick, of days, and years, and sun, and moon, and stars. The stadhuis has also treasures of tapestry and Spanish leather, and a museum containing a very fine collection of antiquities, including one of the famous wooden petticoats of Nymwegen--a painted barrel worn as a penance by peccant dames.

From Nymwegen the train took me to Hertzogenbosch, or Bois le Duc, the capital of Brabant. It is from Brabant, we were told by a proverb which I quoted in my first chapter on Friesland, that one should take a sheep. Great flocks of sheep may be seen on the Brabant moors, exactly as in Mauve's pictures. They are kept not for food, for the Dutch dislike mutton, but for wool.

Bois le Duc has the richest example of mediæval architecture in Holland--the cathedral of St. John, a wonderful fantasy in stone, rich not only without, but, contrary to all Dutch precedent, within too; for we are at last again among a people who for the most part retain the religion of Rome. The glass of the cathedral is poor, but there is a delicate green pattern on the vaulting which is very charming. The koster is proudest of the pulpit, and of a figure of the Virgin "which is carried in procession through the town every evening between July 7th and 16th".

But I was not interested so much in particular things as in the cathedral as a whole. To be in the midst of this grey Gothic environment was what I desired, and after a little difficulty I induced the koster to leave me to wander alone. It was the first church in Holland with the old authentic thrill.

Bois le Duc (as it is more simple to call it) is a gay town with perhaps the most spirited market place in the country. The stalls have each an awning, as in the south of Europe, and the women's heads are garlanded with flowers. I like this method of decoration as little as any, but it carries with it a pleasant sense of festivity.

From Bois le Duc one may go due north to Utrecht and Amsterdam, passing on the way Bommel, with its tall and impressive tower rising from its midst. Or one may keep to the western route and reach Walcheren. That is my present course, and Bommel may be left with a curious story of the Spaniards in 1599. "Two brothers who had never seen, and had always been inquiring for, each other, met at last by chance at the siege, where they served in two different companies. The elder, who was called Hernando Diaz, having heard the other mentioned by the name of Encisso, which was his mother's surname, and which he had taken through affection, a thing common in Spain, put several questions to him concerning a number of family particulars, and knew at last by the exactness of his answers that he was the brother he had been so long seeking after; upon which both proceeding to a close embrace, a cannon ball struck off both their heads, without separating their bodies, which fell clinging together."

Helvoet, on the way to Tilburg, is the scene of an old but honourable story. Ireland tells us that George the Second, being detained by contrary winds on his return from Hanover, reposed at Helvoet until the sea should subside. While there he one day stopped a pretty Dutch girl to ask her what she had in her basket. "Eggs, mynheer." "And what is the price?" "A ducat a piece, mynheer." "Are eggs so scarce then in Holland?" "No. mynheer, but kings are."

At Tilburg I did not tarry, but rode on to Breda (which is pronounced with all the accent on the second syllable) and which is famous for a castle (now a military school) and a tomb. The castle, a very beautiful building, was built by Count Henry of Nassau. On becoming in due course the property of William the Silent, it was confiscated by the Duke of Alva. How it was won back again is a story worth telling.

The great achievement belonged to a simple boatman named Adrian. Whether or not he had read or heard of the Trojan horse is not known, but his scheme was not wholly different. Briefly he recommended Prince Maurice to conceal soldiers in his peat boat, under the peats, to be conveyed as peat into the Spanish garrison. The plan was approved and Captain Heranguière was placed in charge of it.

144

The boat was laden and Adrian poled it into the fortress; and all was going well until the coldness of the night set the soldiers coughing. All were affected, but chiefly Lieutenant Hells, who, vainly attempting to be silent, at last implored his comrades to kill him lest he ruin the enterprise. Adrian, however, prevented this grim necessity by pumping very hard and thus covering the sound.

It had been arranged that the Prince should be outside the city at a certain hour. Just before the time Heranguière and his men sprang out of their hiding, killed the garrison, opened the gates, and the castle was won again, Heranguière was rewarded by being made governor of Breda; Adrian was pensioned, and the boat was taken from its native elements and exalted into an honoured position in the castle. When, however, the Spanish general Spinola recaptured Breda, one of his first duties was to burn this worthy vessel.

The jewel of Breda, which is a spreading fortified town, is the tomb of Count Engelbert I. of Nassau, in one of the chapels of the great church. The count and his lady, both sculptured in alabaster, lie side by side beneath a canopy of black marble, which is borne by four warriors also of alabaster.

On the canopy are the arms and accoutrements of the dead Count. The tomb, which was the work of Vincenz of Bologna in the sixteenth century, is wholly satisfying in its dignity, austerity and grace.

To the font in Breda cathedral William III. attached the privilege of London citizenship. Any child christened there could claim the rights of a Londoner, the origin of the sanction being the presence of English soldiers at Breda and their wish that their children should be English too. Whether or not the Dutch guards who were helping the English at the end of the seventeenth century had a similar privilege in London I do not know. Late one Saturday evening I watched in a milk shop at Breda a conscientious Dutch woman at work. She had just finished scrubbing the floor and polishing the brass, and was now engaged in laying little paths of paper in case any chance customer should come in over night and soil the boards before Sunday. I thought as I stood there how impossible it would be for an English woman tired with the week to sit up like this to clean a shop against the next day. Sir William Temple has a pleasant story illustrating at once the inherent passion for cleanliness in the Dutch women and also their old masterfulness. It tells how a magistrate, paying an afternoon call, was received at the door by a stout North Holland lass who, lest he should soil the floor, took him bodily in her arms and carried him to a chair; sat him in it; removed his boots; put a pair of slippers on his feet; and then led him to her mistress's presence.

Bergen-op-Zoom has its place in history; but it is a dull town in fact. Nor has it beautiful streets, with the exception of that which leads to the old Gevangenpoort with its little painted towers. I must confess that I did not like Bergen-op-Zoom. It seemed to me curiously inhospitable and critical; which was of course a wrong attitude to take up towards a countryman of Grimston and Redhead; Who are Grimston and Redhead? I seem to hear the reader asking. Grimston and Redhead were two members of the English garrison when the Prince of Parma besieged Bergen-op-Zoom in 1588, and it was their cunning which saved the town. Falling intentionally into the Prince's hands they affected to inform him of the vulnerability of the defences, and outlined a scheme by which his capture of a decisive position was practically certain. Having been entrusted with the conduct of the attack, they led his men, by preconcerted design, into an ambush, with the result that the siege was raised.

145

All being fair in love and war one should, I suppose, be at the feet of these brave fellows; but I have no enthusiasm for that kind of thing. At the same time there is no doubt that the Dutch ought to, and therefore I am the more distressed by Bergen-op-Zoom's rudeness to our foreign garb.

Bergen had seen battle before the siege, for when it was held by the Spanish, at the beginning of the war, a naval engagement was held off it in the Scheldt, between the Spanish fleet and the Beggars of the Sea, whom we are about to meet. The victory was to the Beggars. Later, in 1747, Bergen was besieged again, this time by the French and much more fiercely than by the Spaniards.

From Bergen-op-Zoom we went to Tholen, passing the whitest of windmills on the way. Tholen is an odd little ancient town gained by a tramway and a ferry. Head-dresses here, as at Bois le Duc, are very much over-decorated with false flowers; but in a little shop in one of the narrow and deserted streets we found some very pretty lace. We found, also on the edge of the town, a very merry windmill; and we had lunch at an inn window which commanded the harnessing of the many market carts, into every one of which climbed a stolid farmer and a wife brimming with gossip.

In the returning steam-tram from Tholen to Bergen-op-Zoom was a Dutch maiden. So typical was she that she might have been a composite portrait of all Dutch girls of eighteen--smooth fair features, a very clear complexion, prim clothes. A friend getting in too, she talked; or rather he talked, and she listened, and agreed or dissented very quietly, and I had the pleasure of watching how admirably adapted is the Dutch feminine countenance for the display of the nuances of emotion, the enregistering of every thought.

Expression after expression flitted across her face and mouth like the alternate shadow and sun in the Weald on a breezy April day. A French woman's many vivacious and eloquent expressions seem to come from within; but the Dutch present a placid sensitised surface on which their companions' conversation records the most delicate tracery. This girl's little reluctant smiles were very charming, and we were at Bergen-op-Zoom again before I knew it. Chapter XIX

Middelburg

The friendly Zeelanders--A Spanish heritage--Deceptive Dutch towns--The Abbey Hotel--The Abbey of St. Nicholas--Middelburg's art--Sentimental songs--The great Tacius--The siege of Middelburg--A round-faced

city--When disfigurement is beauty--Green paint--Long John--Music in the night--Foolish Betsy--The Stadhuis--An Admiral and stuffed birds--The law of the paving-stones--Veere--The prey of the sea--A mammoth church--Maximilian's cup.

With Middelburg I have associated, for charm, Hoorn; but Middelburg stands first. It is serener, happier, more human; while the nature of the Zeelander is to the stranger so much more ingratiating than that of the North Hollander. The Zeelander--and particularly the Walcheren islander--has the eccentricity to view the stranger as a natural object rather than a phenomenon. Flushing being avowedly cosmopolitan does not count, but at Middelburg, the capital of Zeeland, you may, although the only foreigner there, walk about in the oddest clothes and receive no embarrassing attentions.

It is not that the good people of Walcheren are quicker to see where their worldly advantage lies. They are not schemers or financiers. The reason resides in a native politeness, a heritage, some have conjectured, from their Spanish forefathers. One sees hints of Spanish blood also in the exceptional flexibility and good carriage of the Walcheren women. Whatever the cause of Zeeland's friendliness, there it is; and in Middelburg the foreigner wanders at ease, almost as comfortable and self-possessed as if he were in France.

And it is the pleasantest town to wander in, and an astonishingly large one. A surprising expansiveness, when one begins to explore them, is an idiosyncrasy of Dutch towns. From the railway, seeing a church spire and a few roofs, one had expected only a village; and behold street runs into street until one's legs ache. This is peculiarly the case with Gorinchem, which is almost invisible from the line; and it is the case with Middelburg, and Hoorn, and many other towns that I do not recall at this moment.

My advice to travellers in Walcheren is to stay at Middelburg rather than at Flushing (they are very nigh each other) and to stay, moreover, at the Hotel of the Abbey. It is not the best hotel in Holland as regards appointment and cuisine; but it is certainly one of the pleasantest in character, and I found none other in so fascinating a situation. For it occupies one side of the quiet square enclosed by the walls of the Abbey of St. Nicholas (or Abdij, as the Dutch oddly call it), and you look from your windows through a grove of trees to the delicate spires and long low facade of this ancient House of God, which is now given over to the Governor of Zeeland, to the library of the Province, and to the Provincial Council, who meet in fifteenth century chambers and transact their business on nouveau art furniture.

What the Abbey must have been before it was destroyed by fire we can only guess; but one thing we know, and that is that among its treasures were paintings by the great Mabuse (Jan Gossaert), who once roystered through Middelburg's quiet streets. Another artist of Middelburg was Adrian van der Venne, who made the quaint drawings for Jacob Cats' symbols, of which we have seen something in an earlier chapter. But the city has never been a home of the arts. Beyond a little tapestry, some of which may be seen in the stadhuis, and some at the Abbey, it made nothing beautiful. From earliest times the Middelburgers were merchants--wool merchants and wine merchants principally, but always tradespeople and always prosperous and contented.

A tentoonstelling (or exhibition) of copper work was in progress when I was there last summer; but it was not interesting, and I had better have taken the advice of the Music Hall manager, in whose grounds it was held, and have saved my money. His attitude to repoussé work was wholly pessimistic, part prejudice against the craft of the metal-worker in itself, but more resentment that florins should be diverted into such a channel away from comic singers and acrobats. Seated at one of the garden tables we discussed Dutch taste in varieties. The sentimental song, he told me, is a drug in Holland. Anything rather than that. No matter how pretty the girl may be, she must not sing a sentimental song. But if I wished to witness the only way in which a sentimental song would "go down," I must visit his performance that evening--reserved seats one, fifty,--and hear the great Tacius. He drew from his pocket a handbill which was at that moment being scattered broadcast over Middelburg. It bore the name of this marvel, this solver of the sentimental riddle, and beneath it three interrogation marks. The manager winked. "That," he said, "will excite interest."

We went that evening and heard Tacius--a portly gentleman in a ball dress and a yellow wig, who after squeaking five-sixths of a love song in a timid falsetto which might pass for a woman's voice, roared out the balance like a bull. He brought down the house.

Like most other Dutch towns Middelburg had its period of siege. But there was this difference, that Middelburg was held by the Spanish and besieged by the Dutch, whereas the custom was for the besiegers to be Spanish and the besieged Dutch. Middelburg suffered every privation common to invested cities, even to the trite consumption of rats and dogs, cats and mice, Just as destruction seemed inevitable--for the Spanish commander Mondragon swore to fire it and perish with it rather than submit--a compromise was arranged, and he surrendered without dishonour, the terms of the capitulation (which, however, Spain would not allow him to carry out) being another illustration of the wisdom and humanity of William the Silent.

Middelburg has never known a day's suffering since her siege. A local proverb says, "Goed rond, goed Zeeuwsch"--very round, very

Zeelandish--and an old writer--so M. Havard tells us--describes Middelburg as a "round faced city". If by round we mean not only circular but also plump and comfortable, we have Middelburg and its sons and daughters very happily hit off. Structurally the town is round: the streets curve, the Abbey curves; seen from a balloon or the summit of the church tower, the plan of the city would reveal itself a circle. And there is a roundness also in the people. They smile roundly, they laugh roundly, they live roundly. The women and girls of Middelburg are more comely and winsome than any in Holland. Their lace caps are like driven snow, their cheeks shine like apples. But their way with their arms I cannot commend. The sleeve of their bodices ends far above the elbow, and is made so tight that the naked arm below expands on attaining its liberty, and by constant and intentional friction takes the hue of the tomato. What, however, is to our eyes only a suggestion of inflammation, is to the Zeelander a beauty. While our impulse is to recommend cold cream, the young bloods of Middelburg (I must suppose) are holding their beating hearts. These are the differences of nations--beyond anything dreamed of in Babel.

The principal work of these ruddy-armed and wide-hipped damsels seems to be to carry green pails on a blue yoke--and their perfect fitness in Middelburg's cheerful and serene streets is another instance of the Dutch cleverness in the use of green paint. These people paint their houses every year--not in conformity with any written law, but upon a universal feeling that that is what should be done. To this very pretty habit is largely due the air of fresh gaiety that their towns possess. Middelburg is of the gayest.

Greenest of all, as I have said, is perhaps Zaandam. Sometimes they paint too freely, even the trunks of trees and good honest statuary coming under the brush. But for the most part they paint well.

It is not alone the cloistral Gothic seclusion in which the Abbey hotel reposes that commends it to the wise: there is the further allurement of Long John. Long John, or De Lange Jan, is the soaring tower of the Abbey church, now the Nieuwe Kerk. So long have his nearly 300 feet dominated Middelburg--he was first built in the thirteenth century, and rebuilt in the sixteenth--that he has become more than a structure of bricks and copper: a thinking entity, a tutelary spirit at once the pride and the protector of the town. His voice is heard more often than any belfry beneath whose shadow I have lain. Holland, as we have seen, is a land of bells and carillons; nowhere in the world are the feet of Time so dogged; but Long John is the most faithful sleuth of all. He is almost ahead of his quarry. He seems to know no law; he set out, I believe, with a commission entitling him to ring his one and forty bells every seven and a half minutes, or eight times in the hour; but long since he must have torn up that warranty, for he is now his own master, breaking out into little sighs of melancholy or wistful music whenever the mood takes him. I have never heard such profoundly plaintive airs as his--very beautiful, very grave, very deliberate. One cannot say more for persistent chimes than this--that at the Abbey hotel it is no misfortune to wake in the night.

Long John has a companion in Foolish Betsy. Foolish Betsy is the stadhuis clock, so called (Gekke Betje) from her refusal to keep time with the giant: another instance of the power which John exerts over the town, even to the wounding of chivalry. The Nieuwe Kerk would be nothing without its tower--it is one of the barest and least interesting churches in a country which has reduced to the finest point the art of denuding religion of mystery--but the stadhuis would still be wonderful even without its Betsy, There is nothing else like it in Holland, nothing anywhere quite so charming in its shameless happy floridity. I cannot describe it: the building is too complicated, too ornate; I can only say that it is wholly captivating and thoroughly out of keeping with the Dutch genius--Spanish influence again apparent. Beneath the eaves are four and twenty statues of the Counts of Holland and Zeeland, and the roof is like a mass-meeting of dormer windows.

In addition to the stadhuis museum, which is dedicated to the history of Middelburg and Zeeland, the town has also a municipal museum, too largely given over to shells and stuffed birds, but containing also such human relics as the wheel on which Admiral de Ruyter as a boy helped his father to make rope, and also the first microscope and the first telescope, both the work of Zacharias Jansen, a Zeeland mathematician. More interesting perhaps are the rooms in the old Zeeland manner, corresponding to the Hindeloopen rooms which we have seen at Leeuwarden, but lacking their cheerful richness of ornamentation. It is certainly a museum that should be visited, albeit the stuffed birds weigh heavily on the brow.

After all, Middelburg's best museum is itself. Its streets and houses are a never-ending pleasure. Something gladdens the eye at every turn--a blue and yellow shutter, a red and black shutter, a turret, a daring gable, a knot of country people, a fat Zeeland baby, a milk-can rivalling the sun, an old woman's lace cap, a young woman's merry mouth. Only in two respects is the town unsatisfactory, and both are connected with its streets. The liberty given to each householder to erect an iron fence across the pavement at each limit of his property makes it necessary to walk in the road, and the pavé of the road is so rough as to cause no slight suffering to any one in thin boots. M. Havard has an amusing passage on this topic, in which he says that the ancient fifteenth-century punishment for marital infidelity, a sin forbidden by the municipal laws no less than by Heaven, was the supply by the offending man of a certain number of paving stones. After such an explanation, the genial Frenchman adds, we must not complain:--

Nos pères ont péchés, nos pères ne sont plus, Et c'est nous qui portons la peine de leurs crimes.

The island of Walcheren is quickly learned. From Middelburg one can drive in a day to the chief points of interest--Westcapelle and Domburg, Veere and Arnemuiden. Of these Veere is the jewel--Veere, once Middelburg's dreaded rival, and in its possession of a clear sea-way and harbour her superior, but now forlorn. For in the seventeenth century Holland's ancient enemy overflowed its barriers, and the greater part of Veere was blotted out in a night. What remains is a mere symbol of the past; but there is enough to loiter in with perfect content, for Veere is unique. Certainly no little town is so good to approach--with the friendliness of its red roofs before one all the way, the unearthly hugeness of its church and the magic of its stadhuis tower against the blue.

The church, which is visible from all parts of the island, is immense, in itself an indication of what a city Veere must have been. It rises like a mammoth from the flat. Only the east end is now used for services; the vast remainder, white and naked, is given up to bats and the handful of workmen that the slender restoration funds make it possible to employ. For there is some idea of Veere's church being one day again in perfect repair; but that day will not be in our time. The ravages of the sea only emptied it: the sea does not desecrate. It was Napoleon who disgraced the church by converting it into barracks. Other relics of Veere's past are the tower at the harbour mouth (its

fellow-tower is beneath the sea) and the beautifully grave Scotch house on the quay, once the centre of the Scottish wool trade of these parts.

The stadhuis also remains, a dainty distinguished structure which might be the infant daughter of the stadhuis at Middelburg. Its spire has a slender aerial grace; on its façade are statues of the Lords of Veere and their Ladies, Within is a little museum of antiquities, one of whose most interesting possessions is the entry in the Veere register, under the date July 2nd, 1608, of the marriage of Hugo Grotius with Maria Reygersbergh of Veere, whom we have seen at Loevenstein assisting in her husband's escape from prison. The museum is in the charge of a blond custodian, a descendant of sea kings, whose pride in the golden goblet which Maximilian of Burgundy, Veere's first Marquis, gave to the town in 1551, is almost paternal. He displays it as though it were a sacred relic, and narrates the story of Veere's indignation when a millionaire attempted to buy it, so feelingly as to fortify and complete one's suspicions that money after all is but dross and the love of it the root of evil.

# CHAPTER XX

Flushing

Middelburg once more--The Flushing baths--Shrimps and chivalry--A Dutch boy--Charles V. at Souburg--Flushing and the Spanish yoke--Philip and William the Silent--The capture of Brill--A far-reaching drunken impulse--Flushing's independence--Admiral de Ruyter--England's Revenge--The Middelburg kermis--The aristocracy of avoirdupois--The end.

It is wiser I think to stay at Middelburg and visit Flushing from there than to stay at Flushing. One may go by train or tram. In hot weather the steam-tram is the better way, for then one can go direct to the baths and bathe in the stillest arm of the sea that I know. Here I bathed on the hottest day of last year, 1904, among merry albeit considerable water nymphs and vivacious men. These I found afterwards should have dwelt in the water for ever, for they emerged, dried and dressed, from the machines, something less than ordinary Batavians. I perhaps carried disillusionment also.

For safe bathing the Flushing baths could not well be excelled, but I never knew shore so sandy. To rid one's self of sand is almost an impossibility. With each step it over-tops one's boots.

Returning to Middelburg from Flushing one evening, in the steam-tram, we found ourselves in a compartment filled with happy country people, most of them making for the kermis, then in full swing in the Middelburg market place. A pedlar of shrimps stood by the door retailing little pennyworths, and nothing would do but the countryman opposite me must buy some for his sweetheart. When he had bought them he was for emptying them in her lap, but I tendered the wrapper of my book just in time: an act of civility which brought out all his native friendliness. He offered us shrimps, one by one, first peeling them with kindly fingers of extraordinary blackness, and we ate enough to satisfy him that we meant well: and then just as we reached Middelburg, he gave me a cigar and walked all the way to the Abbey with me, watching me smoke it. It was an ordeal; but I hope, for the honour of England, that I carried it through successfully and convinced him that an Englishman knows what to do with courtesy when he finds it.

In the same tram and on the very next seat to us was the pleasantest little boy that I think I ever saw: a perfect miniature Dutchman, with wide black trousers terminating in a point, pearl buttons, a tight black coat, a black hat, and golden neck links after the Zeeland habit. He was perhaps four, plump and red and merry, and his mother, who nursed his baby sister, was immensely proud of him. Some one pressed a twopenny bit into his hand as he left the car, and I watched him telling the great news to half a dozen of the women who were waiting by the side of the road, while his face shone like the setting sun.

They got off at Souburg, the little village between Flushing and Middelburg where Charles V. was living in 1556, after his abdication, before he sailed for his last home. It is odd to have two such associations with Souburg--the weary emperor putting off the purple, and the little Dutch boer bursting jollily through black velvet.

Flushing played a great part in the great war. It was from Flushing that Charles V. sailed in 1556; from Flushing that Philip II. sailed in 1559; neither to return. It was Flushing that heard

Philip's farewell to William of Orange, which in the light of after events may be called the declaration of war that was to release the Netherlands from the tyranny of Spain and Rome. "As Philip was proceeding on board the ship which was to bear him for ever from the Netherlands, his eyes lighted upon the Prince. His displeasure could no longer be restrained. With angry face he turned upon him, and bitterly reproached him for having thwarted all his plans by means of his secret intrigues. William replied with humility that everything which had taken place had been done through the regular and natural movements of the states. Upon this the King, boiling with rage, seized the Prince by the wrist, and, shaking it violently, exclaimed in Spanish, 'No los estados, ma vos, vos, vos!'--Not the estates, but you, you, you!--repeating thrice the word 'vos,' which is as disrespectful and uncourteous in Spain as 'toi' in French." That was 26th August, 1559. Philip's fleet consisted of ninety ships, victualled, among other articles, with fifteen thousand capons, and laden with such spoil as tapestry and silks, much of which had to be thrown overboard in a storm to lighten the labouring vessels. It seemed at one time as if the fleet must founder, but Philip reached Spain in safety, and hastened to celebrate his escape, and emphasise his policy of a universal religion, by an extensive auto da fé.

Flushing did not actually begin the war, in 1572, after the capture of Brill at the mouth of the Maas, by the Water Beggars under De la Marck, but it was the first town to respond to that invitation of revolt against Alva and Spain. The foundations of the Dutch Republic may have been laid at Brill, but it was the moral support of Flushing that established them.

The date of the capture of Brill was April 1st, and Alva, who was then at Brussels, suffered tortures from the Belgian wits. The word Brill, by a happy chance, signifies spectacles, and a couplet was sung to the effect that

On April Fool's Day Duke Alva's spectacles were stolen away;

while, says Motley, a caricature was circulated depicting Alva's spectacles being removed from his nose by De la Marck, while the Duke uttered his habitual comment "'Tis nothing. 'Tis nothing."

What, however, began as little more than the desperate deed of some hungry pirates, to satisfy their immediate needs, was soon turned into a very far-reaching "something," by the action of Flushing, whose burghers, under the Seigneur de Herpt, on hearing the news of the rebellion of Brill, drove the Spanish garrison from the town. A number of Spanish ships chancing to arrive on the same day, bringing reinforcements, were just in time to find the town in arms. Had they landed, the whole revolt might have been quelled, but a drunken loafer of the town, in return for a pot of beer, offered to fire a gun at the fleet from the ramparts. He was allowed to do so, and without a word the fleet fell into a panic and sailed away. The day was won. It might almost be said that that shot--that pot of beer--secured the freedom of the Netherlands. Let this be remembered when John Barleycorn is before his many judges.

A little later Brill sent help, and Flushing's independence was secure. Motley describes this band of assistants in a picturesque passage:--

"The expedition seemed a fierce but whimsical masquerade. Every man in the little fleet was attired in the gorgeous vestments of the plundered churches, in gold-embroidered cassocks, glittering mass-garments, or the more sombre cowls and robes of Capuchin friars. So sped the early standard bearers of that ferocious liberty which had sprung from the fires in which all else for which men cherish their fatherland had been consumed.

So swept that resolute but fantastic band along the placid estuaries of Zeeland, waking the stagnant waters with their wild beggar songs and cries of vengeance.

"That vengeance found soon a distinguished object. Pacheco, the chief engineer of Alva, who had accompanied the Duke in his march from Italy, who had since earned a world-wide reputation as the architect of the Antwerp citadel, had been just despatched in haste to Flushing to complete the fortress whose construction had been so long delayed. Too late for his work, too soon for his safety, the ill-fated engineer had arrived almost at the same moment with Treslong and his crew. He had stepped on shore, entirely ignorant of all which had transpired, expecting to be treated with the respect due to the chief commandant of the place, and to an officer high in the confidence of the Governor-general. He found himself surrounded by an indignant and threatening mob. The unfortunate Italian understood not a word of the opprobrious language addressed to him, but he easily comprehended that the authority of the Duke was overthrown.

"Observing De Ryk, a distinguished partisan officer and privateersman of Amsterdam, whose reputation for bravery and generosity was known to him, he approached him, and drawing a seal ring from his finger kissed it, and handed it to the rebel chieftain. By this dumb-show he gave him to understand that he relied upon his honor for the treatment due to a gentleman. De Ryk understood the appeal, and would willingly have assured him, at least, a soldier's death, but he was powerless to do so. He arrested him, that he might be protected from the fury of the rabble; but Treslong, who now commanded in Flushing, was especially incensed against the founder of the Antwerp citadel, and felt a ferocious desire to avenge his brother's murder upon the body of his destroyer's favourite.

"Pacheco was condemned to be hanged upon the very day of his arrival. Having been brought forth from his prison, he begged hard but not abjectly for his life. He offered a heavy ransom, but his enemies were greedy for blood, not for money. It was, however, difficult to find an executioner. The city hangman was absent, and the prejudice of the country and the age against the vile profession had assuredly not been diminished during the five horrible years of Alva's administration. Even a condemned murderer, who lay in the town gaol, refused to accept his life in recompence for performing the office. It should never be said, he observed, that his mother had given birth to a hangman. When told, however, that the intended victim was a Spanish officer, the malefactor consented to the task with alacrity, on condition that he might afterwards kill any man who taunted him with the deed.

"Arrived at the foot of the gallows, Pacheco complained bitterly of the disgraceful death designed for him. He protested loudly that he came of a house as noble as that of Egmont or Hoorn, and was entitled to as honourable an execution as theirs had been. 'The sword! the sword!' he frantically exclaimed, as he struggled with those who guarded him. His language was not understood, but the name of Egmont and Hoorn inflamed still more highly the rage of the rabble, while his cry for the sword was falsely interpreted by a rude fellow who had happened to possess himself of Pacheco's rapier, at his capture, and who now paraded himself with it at the gallows foot. 'Never fear for your sword, Señor,' cried this ruffian; 'your sword is safe enough, and in good hands. Up the ladder with you, Señor; you have no further use for your sword.' Pacheco, thus outraged, submitted to his fate. He mounted the ladder with a steady step, and was hanged between two other Spanish officers.

"So perished miserably a brave soldier, and one of the most distinguished engineers of his time; a man whose character and accomplishments had certainly merited for him a better fate. But while we stigmatize as it deserves the atrocious conduct of a few Netherland partisans, we should remember who first unchained the demon of international hatred in this unhappy land, nor should it ever be forgotten that the great leader of the revolt, by word, proclamation, example, by entreaties, threats, and condign punishment, constantly rebuked and, to a certain extent, restrained the sanguinary spirit by which some of his followers disgraced the noble cause which they had espoused."

Flushing's hero is De Ruyter, whose rope-walk wheel we saw at Middelburg, and whose truculent lineaments have so often frowned at us from the walls of picture gallery and stadhuis throughout the country--almost without exception from the hand of Ferdinand Bol, or a copyist.

Scratch a sea-dog and you find a pirate; De Ruyter, who stands in stone for all time by Flushing harbour, lacking the warranty of war would have been a Paul Jones beyond eulogy. You can see it in his strong brows, his determined mouth, his every line. It is only two hundred and thirty-seven years, only seven generations, since he was in the Thames with his fleet, and London was panic-stricken. No enemy has been there since. The English had their revenge in 1809, when they bombarded Flushing and reduced it to only a semblance of what it had been. Among the beautiful buildings which our cannon balls destroyed was the ancient stadhuis. Hence it is that Flushing's stadhuis to-day is a mere recent upstart.

Flushing does little to amuse its visitors after the sun has left the sea; and we were very glad of the excuse offered by the Middelburg kermis to return to our inland city each afternoon. The Middelburg kermis is a particularly merry one. The stalls and roundabouts fill the market square before the stadhuis, packed so closely that the revolving horses nearly carry the poffertje restaurants round with them. The Dutch roundabouts, by the way, still, like the English, retain horses: they have not, like the French, as I noticed at three fairs in and about Paris last autumn, taken to pigs and rabbits. I examined the Middelburg kermis very thoroughly. Few though the exhibits were, they included two fat women. Their booths stood on opposite sides of the square, all the fun of the fair between them. In the west was Mlle. Jeanne; in the east the Princess Sexiena. Jeanne was French, Sexiena came from the Fatherland. Both, though rivals, used the same poster: a picture of a lady, enormous, décolletée, highly-coloured, stepping into a fiacre, to the cocher's intense alarm. Before one inspected the rival giantesses this community of advertisement had seemed to be a mistake; after, its absurdity was only too apparent, for although the Princess was colossal, Mlle. Jeanae was more so. Mlle. Jeanne should therefore have employed an artist to make an independent allurement.

Both also displayed outside the booths a pair of corsets, but here, I fancy, the advantage was with Mlle. Jeanne, although such were the distractions of the square that it was difficult to keep relative sizes in mind as one crossed it.

We visited the Princess first and found her large enough. She gasped on a dais--it was the hottest week of the year. She was happy, she said, except in such warmth. She was not married: Princes had sighed for her in vain. She rode a bicycle, she assured us, and enjoyment in the incredulity of her hearers was evidently one of her pleasures. Her manager listened impatiently, for our conversation interrupted his routine; he then took his oath that she was not padded, and bade her exhibit her leg. She did so, and it was like the mast of a ship.

I dropped five cents into her plate and passed on to Mlle. Jeanne. The Princess had been large enough; Mlle. Jeanne was larger. She wore her panoply of flesh less like a flower than did her rival. Her expression was less placid; she panted distressfully as she fanned her bulk. But in conversation she relaxed. She too was happy, except in such heat. She neither rode a bicycle nor walked--save two or three steps. As her name indicated, she too was unmarried, although, her manager interjected, few wives could make a better omelette. But men are cowards, and such fortresses very formidable. As we talked, the manager, who had entered the booth as blasé an entrepreneur as the Continent holds, showed signs of animation. In time he grew almost enthusiastic and patted Mlle.'s arms with pride. He assisted her to exhibit her leg quite as though its glories were also his. The Princess's leg had been like the mast of a ship; this was like the trunk of a Burnham beech.

And here, at Flushing, we leave the country. I should have liked to have steamed down the Scheldt to Antwerp on one of the ships that continually pass, if only to be once more among the friendly francs with their noticeable purchasing power, and to saunter again through the Plantin Museum among the ghosts of old printers, and to stand for a while in the Museum before Van Eyck's delicious drawing of Saint Barbara. But it must not be. This is not a Belgian book, but a Dutch book; and here it ends.

# CONTENTS